THE
MESSAGE
IN YOUR
EMOTIONS

THE
MESSAGE
IN YOUR
EMOTIONS

WAYNE McDILL

BROADMAN
& HOLMAN
PUBLISHERS

Nashville, Tennessee

Printed in the United States of America

4262-75
0-8054-6275-9

Published by
Broadman & Holman Publishers
Nashville, Tennessee

Design: Steven Boyd

Dewey Decimal Classification: 152.4
Subject Heading: EMOTIONS
Library of Congress Card Catalog Number: 95-40565

Unless otherwise noted, all Scripture quotations are from the Holy
Bible, New International Version,copyright© 1973, 1978, 1984 by
International Bible Society. Other versions are NRSV, New Revised
Standard Version of the Bible, copyright © 1989 by the Division of
Christian Education of the National Council of Churches of Christ
in the United States of America, used by permission, all rights re-
served; and NKJV, New King James Version, copyright © 1979,
1980, 1982, Thomas Nelson, Inc., Publishers.

Library of Congress Cataloging-in-Publication Data

McDill, Wayne
    The message in your emotions / Wayne McDill.
        p.   cm.
    Includes bibliographical references
    ISBN 0-8054-6275-9
    1. Emotions—Religious aspects—Christianity. 2.Conduct of
life. 3. Responsibility.
    I. Title.
BV4597.3.M39 1996
248.4—dc20

        95-40565
        CIP

96 97 98 99 00 5 4 3 2 1

To those who are hurting
With a hope for healing

▼

Contents

▼

Preface

▼

My first formal experience in training for counseling came as a graduate student at Southwestern Seminary. John Drakeford, a psychology professor at the seminary, operated a counseling center in which graduate students played a major role. The approach employed, called Integrity Therapy, followed the pioneering work of O. Hobart Mowrer in its emphasis on responsibility and oral confession in a small group context.

Sharon and I had been in a process of sorting out our own psychological journeys for several years. We had both come from what are now called dysfunctional families. Our fathers were alcoholics. We were both firstborn. These factors and others contributed toward an interesting mixture of hang-ups we shared.

I was fascinated with Drakeford's work and the opportunity to be involved. Of course I was interested in understanding my own emotional makeup. Furthermore, my work in the pastorate brought a steady stream of troubled people to me. I was even counseling with two ministers who struggled with homosexuality. I was not at all sure I knew how to help any of them. I was determined, however, to find some workable system for sorting out the complex and mysterious workings of the human psyche.

My efforts to find a workable counseling method were based on two assumptions. First, I believed that the nature of man, like the rest of creation, was sensible and understandable. There were patterns to God's creative work—a design. So I made notes, recording observations on the wonderful variety of emotions we experience, particularly the painful ones. Somewhere here was a clear trail back to the source of trouble.

My second assumption was that the wisdom of biblical principles holds answers for emotional distress. I accepted the Bible as authoritative and completely trustworthy. I believed that there were timeless truths revealed in its laws, history, letters, sermons, and stories. If we could get past legalism on the one hand and liberalism on the other, we could identify universal principles to guide every aspect of life.

So out of this pilgrimage came the ideas in this book. I have no pretensions that this model for self-understanding will end the search. What follows on these pages is a method for taking the mystery out of our emotions and letting them speak to us. It has been helpful to me. My hope is that it will be helpful to others as well.

I have received invaluable help with the manuscript from Bill Curtis, from sons Michael and Matthew, and from friend and colleague Julian Motley. The reference staff at the Southeastern Seminary library has been of great help with research. I am grateful to Bill Clarke and his crew for many hours of work and some amazing discoveries.

Most of all, I am grateful to my wife, Sharon, who has put up with me during this sometimes stressful project. She has read, edited, and improved every chapter. It is as much hers as mine.

My hope and prayer is that the reader may find help here for decoding the message in emotions and moving from emotional pain to victorious life in Jesus Christ.

▼

—

O N E

Tell me how you feel

▼

"I am not capable of emotion," he says with an unfeeling sense of loss. Commander Data of "Star Trek: The Next Generation" makes us feel just a little bit sorry for him because he can't feel anything. He is an android, a sophisticated robot designed to look and function like a human being. Even though he has mental and physical abilities far surpassing men, his creator did not program emotion into his "neuroprocessor." Data's life goal is to become as human as possible, which means, of course, experiencing emotion.

This subplot of the "Star Trek" series is especially interesting because it gives us an imaginative glimpse of what it might be like to be without emotion. Data does not fall in love. He does not become angry. He is never lonely or discouraged. He cannot experience the difference between happiness and sadness. He is never enthusiastic. Neither is he ever apathetic. He is highly intelligent, rational, and predictable. But he is also incomplete. He is not human. He has no emotion.

Emotion is so much a part of being human that we cannot think of "human" without it. Our emotions motivate us, harass us, provoke us. Someone without emotion must be an android like Data or some other alien creature. Every experience of life is colored and shaped by emotion. Birth and death, work and play, victory and defeat, gain and loss—they all are interpreted by emotion.

The Bible is amazingly candid in its portrayal of the emotional ups and downs of the heroes of faith. We see biblical characters at their best and their worst, affected by their emotions just as we are today. They often struggle with the depth of their feelings. David wrote, "Why are you downcast, O my soul? Why so disturbed within me? Put your hope in God" (Ps. 43:5). As He faced the cross, Jesus told His closest disciples, "My soul is overwhelmed with sorrow" (Matt. 26:38). Paul wrote to the troublesome Corinthians "out of great distress and anguish of heart and with many tears" (2 Cor. 2:4).

Anger is described vividly, as when Saul's anger "flared up at Jonathan" in his jealousy of David. Jonathan responded in kind, getting up from the table "in fierce anger" (1 Sam. 20:30, 34). Another angry exchange is described between Rachel and Jacob. She was jealous of her fruitful sister and demanded children of Jacob, who became angry with her (Gen. 30:1–2). But Paul wrote that believers must rid themselves of anger and warned fathers, "Do not embitter your children, or they will become discouraged" (Col. 3:21).

The Bible describes a variety of emotions in picturesque ways. Poor self-worth seems to be David's feeling as he says, "I am a worm and not a man, scorned by men and despised by the people" (Ps. 22:6). One psalmist says in his loneliness, "I am like a desert owl, like an owl among the ruins . . . like a bird alone on a roof" (Ps. 102:6–7). As his conscience testifies of his guilt, David writes, "When I kept silent, my bones wasted away through my groaning all day long. . . . my strength was sapped as in the heat of summer" (Ps. 32:3–4).

The word *joy* appears in the Bible almost too often to count. Through all their emotional trouble, men of faith looked to God, saying, "You turned my wailing into dancing; you removed my sackcloth and clothed me with joy" (Ps. 30:11). The psalmist describes those who are looking for better days after they are restored to their homeland, predicting, "Those who sow in tears will reap with songs of joy" (Ps. 126:5). The angel promises Zechariah about the birth of John, "He will be a joy and delight to you, and many will rejoice because of his birth" (Luke 1:14).

Emotion and Life

We think of man's inner person as made up of *mind, will,* and *emotion.* By "mind" we refer to his intellectual abilities: he can think, reason, grasp an idea. By "will" we mean he can choose from among alternatives; he can decide. By "emotion" we mean that he experiences occasional surges of feeling along with deep undercurrents of passion and desire in reaction to his circumstances. Interwoven with these aspects of the inner man is the moral intuition we call *conscience.*

Though this study will touch on mind, will, and conscience as well, the focus is on *emotion.* Consider the place of emotion in human life.

Emotion is natural. Certain expressions of emotion are obvious in all animal life. In man they are far more complex and varied. Almost from birth, infants express themselves in emotion. Children tend to be much more expressive with emotions than adults. They cry easily when disappointed. They dance and squeal when delighted. They show surprise and disgust with faces that send you running for the camera. Emotions are as natural to them as breathing.

Emotion is universal. Though customs vary from culture to culture, emotion is universal. Paul Ekman, an American researcher, showed people in the United States, Brazil, Chile, Argentina, and Japan photographs of facial expressions. All were able to identify the expressions of six basic emotions: happiness, sadness, anger, disgust, surprise, and fear.[1] With the amazing variety in temperament, culture, and intelligence across this world, emotion is still common to man.

Emotion is mysterious. As universal as emotion is, we still have difficulty understanding it. We don't know why we lose our tempers over trifles. We can't understand why we cry at movies like *The Lion King,* an animated cartoon. Men have trouble understanding the emotional responses of women, as

3

women do with men. Psychologists still differ as to where emotions come from, how they work, and what they mean.

Emotion is autonomous. One of the mysteries of emotion is the independent control it has. Our feelings seem to have a will of their own. "Falling in love," for example, can hit you like a flu virus before you even realize it. When I was fourteen I went crazy like that over a girl my age who was visiting for the summer. I moped around, couldn't eat, sighed a lot, and generally incurred the disgust of my family. But what could I do about it? I was in looove!

Emotion is troublesome. Plato wrote that "the passionate are like men standing on their heads; they see all things the wrong way." Emotions cloud our normal thinking processes and often cause us to react in ways we shouldn't. We say things in anger that hurt the ones we love most. We buy a new car in the excitement of its appeal. We cry and lose our composure, adding embarrassment to insecurity. We laugh when it really isn't funny because we are uncomfortable.

Emotion is wonderful. Imagine a football game without the cheers, the high fives, and the end-zone dance. Imagine a relationship without the warmth, affection, and trust. Imagine Christmas without the anticipation, the delight, and the excitement. Emotion adds the spicy flavor to life. It provides the color and zest that mere rational and volitional responses can never deliver. It is the adventure of life played out in your passions. Emotion is a wonderful wind that can fill your sails or sink your ship.

The premise of this book is that *there is a message in your emotions.* What is the message? Why do we need such a message? How do we decipher it? All of these questions will be answered in the pages to come. For now let's consider where emotions come from and how they work.

Nature's Warning System

"Let me take a look at that throat," he said. "Mmm hmmm. OK, let's see about the ears." He peered through a lighted instrument into both my ears. Next came the nose.

"Been coughing any?" he asked. "Any soreness here?" He felt knowingly along the sides of my neck. From that brief examination and my complaint of a sore throat, my doctor came up with a cause, upper respiratory infection, and prescribed some antibiotics.

We've all been through a similar experience. The doctor looks you over, asks a few questions, and offers a pretty accurate guess as to your problem. How does he do that? Simple. There's a direct link between disease and symptoms. When you know the symptoms of a particular ailment, nature's dependability allows you to reason back to the disease.

One of the primary clues physicians use to discover what is ailing you is to ask, "Where does it hurt?" God has built a marvelous warning system into our physical makeup. When we feel pain we know something is wrong. Like a siren going off in our minds, pain directs our immediate attention to a hurt finger, sick stomach, or throbbing tooth. We don't ignore these persistent signals.

Emotional pain is also normal. It is a warning that something is out of order, that some nonphysical injury or disease threatens you. You may feel just a little loneliness, a bit of anger, a mild frustration, or you could experience more serious and ongoing suffering. Either way, the alarm is designed to get your attention, to send you a message about a threat in some area of your life. There is a message in your emotions.

Like your body, your psychological and spiritual system is designed for health and happiness. Just as the Creator has established laws that govern your physical nature, so He has set laws by which your inner nature operates. Principles for good nutrition, exercise, and a disciplined lifestyle were not *invented* by medical science. They were *discovered* because they are inherent in the way the physical world works. So it is with the psychological and spiritual dimension. You must operate according to the principles that God intended in His design of humanity.

The Roots of Stress

When a wild animal is threatened, his body immediately gears up for action. Born with a marvelous mechanism for survival, his nervous system flashes an instant warning to all points. Special glands send a "supercharge" of energy to his muscles. His heart beats faster, his strength is enhanced, and his senses are sharpened. He is ready for "fight" or "flight."

You are equipped with a similar mechanism. When you are threatened in any way, the same process instantly prepares you for fight or flight. Notice how charged up you get when you almost fall from a height, are threatened by a snarling dog, or nearly have a serious auto accident. You can actually feel your whole body surging with adrenaline in response to the threat.

But you also face threats that are not so tangible. Layoffs are rumored at work. The doctor calls you in to go over test results. Your husband forgets your birthday. You can feel angry, frustrated, and unloved. When these threatening circumstances are serious enough to you, your fight or flight mechanism goes into action to get you ready to protect yourself. You feel the tenseness, the irritability, the nervous energy, the uneasy stomach.

Now you have a real problem. You are all geared up but have no place to go. You are ready for fight or flight, but who do you fight? Where do you run? The threats are real enough to set off the internal alarm but not tangible enough to get your hands on. How do you defend yourself when you are worried or lonely? How do you run away from your anger or guilt?

Stress is a major complaint in our high-intensity lifestyle. Most of us sense that undercurrent of a nameless, faceless threat. Medical researchers are gathering more and more evidence that stress sets the stage for many diseases. In fact, stress may actually cause the disease to take hold in your body. Some estimates indicate that as many as 80 percent of patients in hospitals are there because of the way they live— bad habits, foolish lifestyles, or the inability to deal with stress.

In the natural order of creation, stress was never intended to be so destructive. It is an expression of normal survival mechanisms. Stress can be a good thing. It can stimulate creativity and motivate us to give our best to the challenges life throws at us. Only as muscles are stressed do they grow in strength. Stressful circumstances can help build character if we respond to them wisely. As we understand the message in our emotions, we can plan that wise response.

Sorting Out Negative Emotions

Years ago, as a pastoral counselor, I had learned that our emotions offered a key to our psychological and spiritual problems. But I couldn't make the direct connection often enough to identify the trouble. Emotions are often complex and overlapping. Though we may be able to identify the event or circumstance that causes the emotion, we often cannot tell why it affects us the way it does.

So I began to list every negative emotion I could think of. I had others look at the list and add to it. After making as complete a list as I could, I tried to sort into groups all the feelings we had named. Loneliness seemed to go with alienation. Guilt and shame went together. Anger, irritation, and resentment were related. Most of the feelings came together naturally into seven groups with similar qualities.

I noticed some more generalized expressions of emotional pain that I could not connect to any of the seven areas. These were *anxiety* (the sense of dread or panic) and *depression* (anything from the "blues" to outright despair). These two words seemed to describe a more diffuse and faceless discomfort that did not belong to any of the clusters. They were more serious, more painful. They seemed to represent a deeper level of floating distress that had somehow lost contact with its cause.

The diagram on the following page indicates seven basic groups of emotional pain, organized in clusters of related feelings. Each cluster is gathered around a central emotion that expresses the main thrust of that distress. There is a basic kinship among all the emotions grouped together in each cluster. In the center of the diagram are the general expressions of emotional pain—anxiety and depression.

There are technical definitions for many of the words I have used to identify emotional pain. In many cases these definitions differ from one writer or counselor to another, and the definitions are often different from common usage.

In this study I will simply talk about how we feel and use the best word I can to identify that emotion. My definitions are descriptive and functional; they are not intended as technical medical explanations.

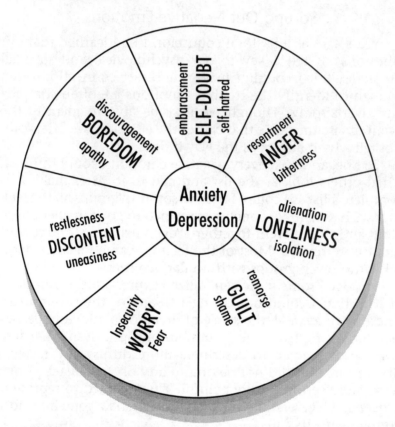

One interesting factor not illustrated in the diagram is that emotions sustained over a period of time create attitudes that can continue beyond the experience of the emotion. While an emotion is generally a reaction to some circumstance, an attitude is a basic disposition in a particular area. While embarrassment is an emotional response, low self-esteem is an attitude. Anger is an emotion, while hostility is an attitude. Boredom is an emotion, but indifference is an attitude. When negative feelings cause negative attitudes to develop, these attitudes only invite more threatening occasions for emotional pain.

Seven Kinds of Trouble

The major part of the book will deal with the seven clusters of emotional pain and how to respond to each one. At this point I want to introduce briefly the seven clusters and show the connection with seven areas of responsibility.

The first cluster of emotional pain relates to *self-doubt*. It means that you feel inferior or unworthy instead of confident and positive. These feelings can range all the way from a minor embarrassment to real humiliation, and they signal that your own self-worth is threatened. You are afraid of failing, afraid you can't handle the job, second-guessing what you said, maybe even suspicious that those around you are laughing at you behind your back.

The second cluster centers on the emotion of *anger*. Anger is the heated passion that surges in the face of mistreatment or injustice or when you do not get your way. It is a feeling of aggression and hostility, of animosity and fury at a person or condition that enrages you. It can be provoked by the sight of a child being mistreated, an insulting comment, or someone getting your parking place. Associated with anger are feelings of irritation, contempt, bitterness, and resentment.

Next is the group of emotions related to *loneliness*. Loneliness is the feeling that no one cares, that you are separated from someone you love, that you have been abandoned. Related to loneliness are feelings such as alienation, isolation, and the sense of being ignored, rejected, or unloved. Mulling over a strained relationship, sending your "baby" off to college, listening as the phone never rings—these are formulas for loneliness.

The fourth cluster is connected with the idea of *boredom*, that sense of listlessness, dullness, and indifference when you are disinterested in whatever is going on. With the busy pace of life today, it might seem that boredom would seldom be a problem. But we all have experienced that occasional sense of futility even when we are busy. Boredom can result when a party is called off, when your job seems to be a meaningless routine, or when you can't think of what to do with a little leisure time. Related to boredom are frustration, apathy, and discouragement.

At the center of the fifth cluster is the emotional pain of *worry*. When you are worried, you feel vulnerable and unprotected, grieving in advance over the loss of something precious. You are fearful of some threat to your security or the security of something or someone you hold dear. There are so many things to worry about. If it isn't a lump that shouldn't be there or a teenager two hours late getting in, it is that advancing swarm of killer bees reported in the news.

Guilt is the distress at the heart of the next cluster. Guilt means being at fault in some misdeed or crime or being chargeable under the law for your offenses. Guilt as an emotion, however, is that sense of remorse or sorrow at the realization of your wrong behavior. You can feel guilty for eating a candy bar, turning away from a beggar, or sleeping with your wife's sister. Feelings of guilt are connected to conscience, which may or may not be a faithful judge of moral uprightness.

The final group of emotions is identified with *discontent*. Usually expressed by complaining and griping, it indicates a dissatisfaction with conditions. When you are discontented, you are restless, uneasy, and alert to the irritants in your present situation. The feeling of discontent can be triggered by something as insignificant as a spot on the rug or as discouraging as a dead-end job.

The message in these emotions can range from a mild alert to a serious warning. Each is an interpretation of how circumstances and events affect you. Negative feelings indicate a perceived threat to your own needs and desires, while positive emotions signal that everything seems to be going your way. As you read the messages in your emotions, you can then trace them to your personal responsibility and determine how to respond effectively.

Each of the clusters of emotional pain relates to an area of responsibility that is inherently yours as a human being. In chapter 2 I will try to sort out the often confusing elements in your conversation with yourself about your feelings and responsibilities.

▼
—

T W O

Talking to yourself

▼

Waiting recently at a traffic signal, I noticed a woman in the car next to mine having a lively conversation with herself. I looked to see who else was in the car. Nobody. But that didn't seem to bother her as she expressed herself with enthusiasm. As the light changed she noticed that I was watching, tossed her head at my impertinence, and drove away.

Do you talk to yourself? We joke about talking to yourself as a sign of being mentally unbalanced. I recently heard, however, that at least one psychologist thinks talking to yourself is good for you. He said it helps release pent-up tension and verbalize possible solutions to your problems. The way you talk to yourself is basic to your emotions and their message.

Your private conversation reflects your effort to interpret life and to fit yourself meaningfully into it. Much of what you say to yourself concerns your own place in the scheme of things—how you relate to others, how you handle problems, how you compare to others in various ways, how others treat you, how circumstances affect you, what actions you will take to get what you want from life.

Your inner discussions are also the private laboratory for your own creativity. It is there that you put ideas together in new combinations for solutions to your problems. It is there that the light of genius comes on with a new thought you never considered before. It is there that you formulate your plans for dealing most effectively with your world. You can mentally experiment with various possibilities until you find the one which seems to work best.

You do not deal with your world as it really is but as you interpret it to be. So your response to reality can only be as good as your interpretation of it. Neither are your emotions tied directly to circumstances, events, and relationships. They are actually tied to the meaning we give to these things.

Your Basic Programming

What you say to yourself is the conscious expression of a complex system of "programming" similar to the programming of a computer. All your ideas, impressions, experiences, attitudes, information, and observations are filed away in your "memory bank" as a vast resource library for dealing with life. All this data gives you the unique outlook that makes you think and behave in the particular ways people have come to recognize as you.

Our interpretations of what is going on around us arise quite consistently from our assumptions, those things we believe to be true about the situation, the relationships, the circumstances around us. These are what we would call the "facts" as we see them. We assume these "facts" are correct; hence, they are our "assumptions." But, if your assumptions are incorrect, you may make a wrong interpretation, develop the wrong attitude, and choose a wrong response.

How do we arrive at assumptions? We look things over and note familiar patterns based on our programming from the past. In other words, we assume the "facts" *we believe to be true*, based on *what we think we see*, assessed in light of *what we think we know*. It all sounds rather uncertain at best, doesn't it? Nevertheless, this is generally the way we deal with our world.

Look closely at the diagram below. Notice that the basis for all our reasoning process is a pool of information that makes up our *programming*. This data bank is everything you have "learned." That does not mean that what you "know" is all accurate. But that is beside the point to your reasoning processes. If it makes sense from your personal viewpoint, it is "true" whether it's accurate information or not.

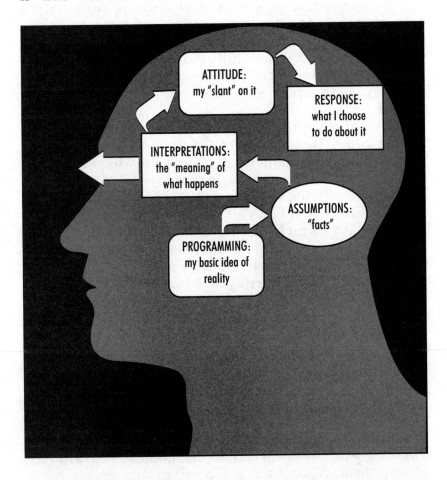

This programming is your basic idea of reality. It is your encyclopedia of how things really are. From all that information you have come to some conclusions. You have some ideas about the best way to behave in certain situations. You have some ideas about what certain behavior tells you about others. You have a philosophy of life, though it is probably unwritten and rather loosely organized. Nevertheless, this is your "wisdom," the general idea you have about the best decision to make when you face one.

The Monitor

The interpretive process is your ongoing conversation with yourself. It is out of this secret conversation that your emotions mysteriously arise. A way to picture this process is to imagine that there is a security guard on duty at the control panels of your mind. This Monitor watches everything that is going on and interprets it for your best interests. Here is how he operates.

He sits there at the control panel keeping watch all your waking hours. He is on guard for threats of any kind and quick to sound the alarm when he sees one. His control center includes a view screen to observe everything going on around you, with full sound as well. He operates out of a computer data bank that holds all you know. His sole purpose is to warn of any threat by setting off an alarm designed to provoke the "fight or flight" response we mentioned earlier.

The key factors for determining threat are your own human desires. I am not referring to physical desires like hunger, thirst, warmth, shelter, etc. The emotional signals may be triggered by a threat to these needs as well. But here we are dealing with much more subtle psychological and spiritual needs that are a mystery to most of us. The Monitor watches for a threat to your self-worth, to your desire for control, to your need for companionship, for achievement, for security, for integrity, and for peace.

These desires arise in the seven areas of interaction common to all of us. It is these seven areas that form the basis for this book, with the seven clusters of emotional pain associated with them. When a threat is posed to your desires in one of these areas the Monitor sees it and releases the appropriate emotion. Like signal flags on a ship, like a bugle call in battle, like a warning light in your car, these emotional signals carry a message to you that a threat to your well being has been detected.

So, as we have said, there is a message in your emotions. The feelings that mysteriously arise of their own accord are the natural work of your basic instinct for survival. As you become more aware of the function of these emotions, you will learn to read their messages. Then you can decide how to deal with what is perceived by your inner security guard as a threat. The Monitor is not infallible. All he has to work with is what you know and your outlook on life. But he is faithful, and you can use his uncomfortable signals to call your attention to one of the seven areas and your responsibility there.

Interrupting the Conversation

Even though most of us give our thoughts free reign, we don't have to. You have the power to take charge of your own thinking. You can deliberately interrupt with a new line of thought that will express much more appropriate attitudes. You can learn to guide that silent conversation away from self-defeating paths.

You are responsible for your own thinking. Though you may have unknowingly allowed yourself to be programmed with ideas that do not work well, now you are responsible to make the necessary changes. "Do not conform any longer to the pattern of this world, but be transformed by the renewing of your mind" (Rom. 12:2). You can intentionally reprogram your thinking with the truth of God.

Remember this: the ideas you have are the source for all your attitudes and behavior. Those ideas can be left to flow like a line of traffic down a highway. Or you can decide to monitor your own thinking. You can set up "checkpoints" and ask questions to make sure these ideas don't express themselves in some response you did not deliberately choose.

To make a real change will require overriding the process at several points. To override means to put a normally automatic process back under manual control. It is like turning off the "cruise control" and consciously doing the driving. Unless you deliberately decide to respond in new ways, you will follow the natural pattern. But you can intervene at several points.

▼ You can override at the point of your programming by introducing new ideas.

▼ You can override at the point of assumptions by carefully examining the "facts" for accuracy.

▼ You can override at the point of interpretation by analyzing whether the meaning you give to your situation squares with reality.

▼ You can override at the point of attitude by asking whether your feelings match the situation or reflect some unrealistic fear you have.

▼ Finally, you can override at the point of response by carefully choosing to act in the most appropriate way.

Your Hidden Handicap

I have always been fascinated with Robert Louis Stevenson's novelette, *The Strange Case of Dr. Jekyll and Mr. Hyde*. The genteel and proper Dr. Jekyll had secretly led two lives, practicing strange vices in secret. He became obsessed with the idea that men have two personalities, one good and one evil. He reasoned that these two natures could take on physical beings so he developed a drug which would transform his body to express his evil self.

At first Dr. Jekyll had control of the process and could change from one to the other at will. Then the change came without notice as his evil nature, Mr. Hyde, began to take over. Though he realized what was going on, he could not keep the monster from emerging in him. He left a letter telling his sordid story and finally locked himself in his laboratory. There he tried one drug after another to finally do away with Mr. Hyde. He was unsuccessful and poisoned himself as friends broke into his lab.

This story, as horrible as it is, is nonetheless a parable of our dilemma. Though we know there are two natures in us struggling for dominance, there seems to be little we can do to control the process. Men have attempted a number of strategies to deal with this problem. Some have denied the existence of the monster and insisted that man is inherently good. Others have recognized that the monster is there but have thought to tame him with therapy. Some have claimed that the monster is alone in us and have seen nothing of the image of God in man. Others have claimed that the dark side of human nature is the fault of our parents or the evils of society.

The problem we face is basically a divided self. In the beginning man understood himself in terms of God. He was placed in the garden in an intimate and unhindered fellowship with his Creator. But with the coming of sin, his understanding of himself shifted from God to self. He became independent and self-centered. He was, however, made in the image of God. There was still that nobility of his divine creation. He became a divided self. The self-centeredness drew him away from God, but the longing for intimacy with God was still there.

Our handicap guarantees that the Christian life is a struggle. It can only be lived intentionally. Paul writes of this inner conflict for the believer, "For the sinful nature desires what is contrary to the Spirit, and the Spirit what is contrary to the sinful nature. They are in conflict with each other, so that you do not do what you want" (Gal. 5:17). Here is a picture of war in your own inner being, as one nature is set over against another.

Def•i•ni'tion: The Handicap

The handicap refers to the self-centered nature of man which limits his ability to decide and act according to God's plan for him. It is a disability inherited by all human beings. Man is made in the image of God but corrupted by sin. He has a divided nature and must carefully monitor every desire and inclination. He is incapable of overcoming the handicap without the grace of God.

Because these two natures are in conflict with each other, "you do not do what you want" (Gal. 5:17). You cannot automatically follow the desires that emerge in your thinking. This is the handicap, that you and I are not in full control of our desires or the attitudes and behavior they promote. We are left with but one answer. We must discipline ourselves. We must watch carefully every word and action that presents itself at the door of our thoughts. We must ID every thought and attitude before we let them pass into the world of action and speech.

If I do not intentionally choose to operate out of the new nature in Christ, I will automatically revert to the self-centered patterns of the fallen nature. I cannot trust the desires that arise in me because they may well be from the dark side of my nature. They may be disguised as morally acceptable, and they may seem so right, but unless they pass the test of biblical truth, I dare not let them be expressed.

Of course there are ideas that are not morally and spiritually significant. I must deal with these thoughts and impressions all day long. My struggle is not with what to eat for breakfast, how to shave my face, the simple and routine functions of my job. My struggle is with the attitude I bring with me to work. It is with the words which come to my lips and must be tested before I speak. It is with the way I interpret what is taking place around me.

The Drift Factor

We often experience the handicap in terms of the "drift factor." When I lived in Oregon I went drift fishing for salmon with some friends. We took the boat upstream and drifted down the river without a motor, fishing as we went. Occasionally one of us would have to use an oar to move the boat to one side or another in the river. But all the time we were drifting wherever the river took us. While we were concentrating on hooks and bait and lines and fish, our direction was left to the river.

The "drift factor" in the lives of Christians refers to the tendency to pay no attention to where we are going and what is carrying us there. Believers can be so preoccupied with the ordinary tasks and interests of daily living that they forget the handicap. They forget that unless they intentionally choose to walk in the Spirit, they will drift. That drifting is never toward God. We always drift away from God.

The conflict of the divided nature is not only experienced in the moral and spiritual dimensions. There is a battle for self-control that touches every area of life. On the one hand are the good intentions of our higher ideals. You know the person you want to be and what you want to do. But the *drift factor* comes into play with a downward pull from within us, an inertia that is hard to overcome.

It is easier to make the soft choices, to give up the effort at better habits because there is resistence. But beware! Making the soft choices can become a lifestyle. Self-mastery is a key element in the development of Christian character. The call of Jesus involves self-denial. You cannot say "Yes" to your best if you will not say "No" to the easy path.

It is the hard choices that firmly establish new behavior patterns and character qualities. When the hard choice is made in the heat of conflicting desires, the positive effect is even greater. You send a signal to your inner self that a new direction is being taken. The greater the struggle, the stronger the signal. As the new pattern is established, however, the resistence weakens. You take a bit of new territory in the battle for self-mastery.

You've been through these battles. You know what I am talking about. You have decided on a healthier diet. You have started an exercise program. You have resolved to quit smoking. You have planned how to better manage your time. You have decided you must not watch so much television. What happened to all those good intentions? Self-mastery for a Christian is only workable under the lordship of Christ. The only way that can be done is to counter the drift factor by the grace of God.

Deciding and Acting

Life turns out to be the sum total of your choices. Decisions are tied to one another like links in a chain, each one giving rise to or excluding the possibility of many others. Of course, choices by others in the past have laid the foundation for who you are today. But beyond the decisions of others, your own choices of the past have shaped life as you find it now. And the actions you take now will shape your future.

The key to exercising your power of choice is action. You never really choose one alternative of several possibilities until you act. You never really decide until your action reveals your decision. Procrastination is actually the distance between intention and action. That distance can become so great that one's intentions are no more than meaningless wishful thinking.

There is a dynamic about action that thoughts and words do not have. Action speaks. Action changes things. Action confirms your choice. Action will even bring your emotions into line where no amount of thinking can. You may not transform your world overnight. But when you decide what to do, even the smallest action will get you started.

This truth is especially important as you deal with the emotional signals that call for changes in behavior. Real change will come when you act out your new behavior, no matter how your emotions seem to object. E. Stanley Jones is quoted as saying, "It is easier to act yourself into a new way of thinking than to think yourself into a new way of acting."[1]

Your inner programming, the "handicap" of your divided self, the Monitor, the "drift factor," decision and action—all of these elements are involved in your conversation with yourself. They are a part of the complex system from which your emotions come. The more you understand of this system, the less of a mystery your emotions will be to you.

▼

T H R E E

Understanding responsibility

▼

In the tropical forests of South and Central America lives a fascinating animal about the size of a large cat. It is called a sloth. These slow-moving mammals get their name from the fact that they usually appear lazy and sluggish. The toothless sloths live in trees, feeding on leaves and tender shoots and rarely descending to the ground. They move with great difficulty on the ground because their feet, equipped with long, hooklike toes, are adapted to their habit of hanging upside down from the limbs of trees.

There are two varieties of these small animals, the three-toed sloth (Bradypus tridactylus), and the two-toed sloth (Choloepus hoffmanni), so named because of the number of claws on each front foot.

Another interesting variety of sloth is the five-toed sloth (Homo sapiens), which inhabits most areas of the civilized world. They are also known to be sluggish and lazy. They are toothless, thus having no bite, and spend most of their time up a tree. From their habit of hanging around out on a limb they get a peculiar upside-down view of the world. They hardly ever get down to earth and move with great difficulty there when forced to do so. The mortal enemies of the five-toed sloth are responsibility and self-discipline.

This interesting animal is often mentioned in the ancient literature of the Hebrews, where he is called a "sluggard" and looked upon with disdain. The five-toed sloth is often found under the circumstances. In fact under most any pile of circumstances you are likely to find one of these timid creatures. The cry of the five-toed sloth is a miserable whine that sounds something like "I couldn't help it," or "Why did this have to happen to me?"

Unfortunately we all suffer from a likeness to the five-toed sloth. It is characteristic of human nature to avoid responsibility, get a cockeyed view of life, make excuses for why we are irresponsible, and see ourselves at the mercy of circumstances.

Even though we recognize our tendency to be less than we can be, we also recognize our dream for greatness. Within each person's heart lies a spark of potential just waiting for the needed fuel to bring the flame of fulfillment roaring to life. We are made in the image of God and intended to reflect His character. Even where Christian principles are not taught, human beings know instinctively that they are destined for a life better than their natural slothfulness. One key to that better life is personal responsibility.

Before going further, let's explore what we mean by "responsibility."

Defining Responsibility

The word *responsibility* comes from the Latin word *responsabilis* (requiring an answer) and that from the word *responsum* (answer). It means basically a condition that requires you to answer for yourself. If you are responsible you are answerable.

In the first place being responsible means you must give an *accounting* for your behavior. This implies, of course, that someone will at some time require you to report on your activities and justify what you have done.

None of us like being "called on the carpet." We naturally don't like others telling us what to do and demanding that we report on how we do it. Like it or not, however, responsibility suggests an accounting to someone who has a right to require a report.

De•fin•i'tion: Responsibility

Responsibility means to be "answerable." It is understood in terms of accountability, position, cause, maturity, and trustworthiness. Responsibility is the foundational quality of good character. For the Christian, responsibility can mean "my response to God's ability."

There are seven areas of God-given responsibility in which humans have inherent desires. As these desires are threatened, emotional pain signals that threat. These negative emotions carry a message that can direct us toward responsible action.

We also use the term responsible to describe the *position* of one who is in charge of something. We talk about a person being given a "responsible position." This means that by virtue of the role or title one has, the individual is expected to perform to certain standards. One premise of this book is that you and I are given a position of responsibility just by virtue of being human. To be human means we are expected to live up to a certain standard.

Responsible also means that you are answerable as a *cause* of some effect. We sometimes ask, "Who is responsible for this mess?" We are asking who caused it, who is behind it. This points to the issue of consequences. We are not only responsible for what we do, we are responsible for the outcome of our actions. It is natural to want to avoid this direct tie to the results of our behavior. This may be why our society seems to prefer operating by committees. Then no one person has to accept responsibility for the results.

We also use the word responsible to indicate that a person has the *maturity* to distinguish between right and wrong. We hold children responsible only for what they are mature enough to handle. Responsibility thus implies adequate understanding and knowledge to fulfill your obligations. Accepting responsibility means you think you know what you are doing and understand the ins and outs of the project. A serious source of stress is being held accountable for an assignment you don't understand.

Finally, we use the word responsible to describe a person who is *trustworthy* and dependable. This takes the idea of accountability inside yourself. You require an answer of yourself. You hold yourself accountable. You develop a reputation for being reliable because you require it of yourself. It is in this sense that responsibility is a character trait at the heart of all good character. Until you decide to demand something of yourself, other aspects of character are weak.

So in the common usage of the word *responsible* we mean accountability, a significant position, causing some result, a level of maturity, and trustworthiness. Living responsibly requires following the basic teachings of Scripture. These are foundational principles necessary to responsible living in this world. They will shape your attitude and your basic pattern of thinking.

God made the world and placed human beings in it to operate within the framework of of these laws. They are the guarantee that responsible living is possible. They are the essential elements that must be present as we operate in every area of human interaction. Within the framework of biblical teachings we can accept full responsibility for our lives.

Getting Rid of Responsibility

For the past hundred years the "experts" have tried to help people with their emotional distress by doing away with responsibility. Sigmund Freud declared that all behavior is caused by factors for which we are not responsible. This led to analysis that sought out the deep dark causes for our irresponsible behavior so that we would understand how it isn't our fault, and thus feel much better about being irresponsible.

The Behaviorists, a group of psychological theorists, wrote that all behavior is reflex, caused by stimuli from outside ourselves. The basic unit of behavior is identified by the stimulus-response connection or bond. Since all behavior is a predictable response to specific provocations, personal responsibility is irrelevant.

More recently, a theory called "sociobiology" has been hotly debated. Though not essentially a psychological model, this view claims that all human behavior comes from genetic formulas. Even the most noble and selfless of actions are a part of the evolutionary instincts of the human animal. Though we may think we are acting in a reasoned and moral way, everything is already determined by our genes.

Theories like these are called "determinism." They claim, in one way or another, that some force beyond our free will is pulling the strings. We are merely puppets, no matter how free we may think we are. Though these theories have promised freedom from old taboos and superstitions, they have failed to square with real human experience.

In spite of this obvious conflict with reality, determinism has dramatically affected the basic assumptions of modern society. In the social service efforts at various levels of government, there is an accepted understanding that people cannot help themselves. Their poverty, their ignorance, their criminal behavior, their self-destructive vices—all these are not their fault. Forces beyond themselves cause them to behave this way, and the only solution is to eliminate those causes.

In the criminal justice system of today, the defense for the most heinous crimes is usually to show the defendants as victims of forces beyond their control. It was not their fault that they murdered their parents, that she drowned her babies, or that he slaughtered his wife. What they need is not punishment but understanding and treatment. They need psychiatric help. They need rehabilitation. Again, the underlying determinism sets the agenda.

Most of us know that these theories are not valid. We do not live our lives according to such philosophies. In spite of our tendency to try to let ourselves off the hook, we have to live in a world where responsibility is built into the very fabric of creation. This tendency to avoid responsibility may well be the driving force behind continuing efforts to formulate a theory that eliminates it. Look now, however, at the value of accepting responsibility.

Accepting Full Responsibility

Like it or not, however, we human beings are responsible. We are held accountable for what we do by the way the world is put together. Our actions produce results that can be traced back to us. However we might wish it to be different, this is the way things are on planet Earth. Our Creator has made a universe in which responsibility is a fact. Each of us must determine how we will deal with this reality.

A necessary beginning point for dealing with your world is to accept full responsibility for it. I know that may be hard to swallow at first. How can you accept responsibility for your world when all but a tiny part of it is beyond your control? You might not mind accepting responsibility for your world if everything in it—people, situations, events, sickness or health, accidents, machinery, your feelings—went according to your direction.

By "your world" I do not mean, of course, the whole of planet Earth. I mean *your* world, the world of your unique and individual involvement. It includes your own traffic pattern of relationships and activities, your own interaction with what goes on around you. It is that moving circle of life in which you are the central figure.

Accepting responsibility for your world doesn't mean you expect to have everything go your way. Rather, it means you realize that you are the center of your little world and accept full responsibility for the impact you have on it. No matter how difficult the circumstances, you know you can make a difference by the way you deal with them.

Our natural inclination is to look for an "out" when things go badly. "It wasn't my fault." "I couldn't help it." "It was the other people, the events, the circumstances. That's where the fault lies. I was innocent." "My motives were pure. I gave it my best. I am the unfortunate victim of circumstances beyond my control." This "victim" outlook is quite popular today, but it is not a happy lot. God never intended it for you.

Responsibility means I take an entirely different view of anything that comes my way. After taking a sober and honest look at a problem I can say, "Nevertheless, I am responsible." The impact of this acceptance is immediate and amazing.

That simple affirmation, "I am responsible," changes the appearance of everything. It refocuses my attention to what I must do to deal with it. Instead of dwelling on the problems, I begin to consider the possibilities.

No matter how hard you try, you will sometimes find yourself overwhelmed. There are too many uncontrollables. When my boys were in Little League they would become discouraged because of what they called "the breaks." I told them they should expect to face four opponents on the field—the other team, the officials, the breaks, and their own errors. This is life. Get used to it. If you realize this in advance you are accepting responsibility in spite of the uncontrollables.

I must accept responsibility for my life, no matter how poorly it was handled by my parents and others in my childhood. Whatever my scars, now I can make the decisions. Now it is up to me. Now I can refuse to go on living in terms of the failure and irresponsibility of others who have shaped my life. Whatever I have to work with, I am responsible. This means looking at values and priorities in life. What do I stand for? What do I believe? What kind of person am I? What is my philosophy of life?

Responsibility and Faith

Accepting responsibility is a faith venture. I believe that God Himself made me responsible and will hold me accountable for what I do with my life. I also believe that as I accept full responsibility for my life, I will have His grace to meet every challenge. In this faith sense, responsibility is my response to His ability. The Bible says, "I can do everything through him who gives me strength" (Phil. 4:13). He is "able to do immeasurably more than all we ask or imagine, according to his power that is at work within us" (Eph. 3:20).

The Creator intended humanity to take charge of this world and rule it under the sovereignty of God. Accepting responsibility means dealing faithfully with my part. However small the beginning, I can know that if I am faithful with a small responsibility, I will be prepared for a larger one. Jesus said, "Whoever can be trusted with very little can also be trusted with much" (Luke 16:10).

Though accepting full responsibility for your world doesn't mean you can control it, it does mean you refuse to be controlled by it. You are looking beyond this world to a Controller who never fails. You refuse to allow your life to be driven by the shifting winds of circumstance. You cannot control everything that happens in your world, but you can respond wisely in faith to what happens. In the long run your response can be the key factor in how things ultimately turn out.

My special abilities come from the image of God in me. I have reason, self-perception, imagination, creativity, person-hood, a sense of purpose. Accepting responsibility means accepting myself as God has created me and as life has shaped me thus far. I cannot accept full responsibility for my life unless I fully accept myself. I cannot become the person I want to be unless I accept the person I am.

Growth is necessary to responsibility and faith. Without change there can be no growth. I can welcome change and refuse to cling to my old ways and old ideas. I must not make my goal to protect my ego and preserve the status quo of my present stage of development. God's pattern for growth will lead me on to the path of becoming the person in Christ that He intended.

I do not limit myself to what I perceive as my abilities and limitations. I know that I know only a little. I also know that God's vast and unlimited power is at work in my behalf. My life cannot be defined in terms of myself. I have to reach beyond myself because God has promised to be with me and enable me, to guide me and empower me. My ability to decide and act responsibly is the key to tapping into His resources.

My life has significance far beyond the little place where I stand, the people I can see, the moment in time in which I live, and the meager abilities I have. I am in touch with the God of the universe. I know that my life can make a difference but only as I remain in harmony with the Reality beyond appearances. I know that the farther away I get from that Reality, the farther I get from the real world and the real me.

Seven Areas of Responsibility

In seven basic areas of human nature we can see God's original intention and our present condition. Humans were created in the image of God in harmony with His grand design. But the Fall brought about a basic change in our nature. In each area notice the *given* of our inherent nature and the *responsibility* that follows. Then look at how the Fall has affected our present condition.

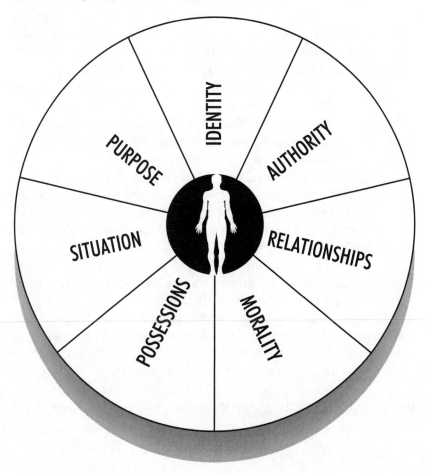

Identity

God, the I AM, made man *worthy* and holds him accountable for his *value*. Psalm 8:5 says of man, "For You have made him a little lower than the angels, and You have crowned him with glory and honor" (NKJV). Here is the inherent worth that is basic to the nature of man. None of us can really understand who we are without beginning with this high view of our worth in the mind of God.

With the Fall, however, the center of our identity shifted from God to ourselves. Adam and Eve began to think of themselves independent of God. Since the Garden of Eden, all of us have doubts about our own worth. Like Adam and Eve, we see our nakedness and want to hide. We naturally try to boost our self-esteem with the approval of others, with externals, with achievement. The only answer, however, is to follow the servant role of Jesus and pay the dividends of selfless service.

Authority

God is sovereign, so He made humans *autonomous* and holds them responsible for their *rule*. The psalmist writes, "You have made him to have dominion over the works of Your hands; You have put all things under his feet" (Ps. 8:6, NKJV). The given of autonomy must be expressed in the responsibility of this rule. In their exercise of God-ordained authority, humans were to represent God for the establishment of His authority on earth.

With the Fall, however, the source of our authority shifted from God to ourselves. From God's viewpoint this rebellion "is as the sin of witchcraft, and stubbornness is as iniquity and idolatry" (1 Sam. 15:23, NKJV). The issue we struggle with here is control. We strive to control our lives, but we find them plagued with loose ends and uncontrollables. We naturally try to demand our own way but have trouble enforcing this self-centered authority, resulting in anger, resentment, and bitterness. Only as we yield to God's authority will we gain control.

Relationships

Since God is personal, He made us *personal* and holds us responsible for our *treatment of others*. God intended us to have the joy of personal relationships. He said, "It is not good that man should be alone; I will make him a helper comparable to him" (Gen. 2:18, NKJV). So He made man a communicator, social, gregarious. He intended him to live in harmony with his fellow man as an expression of the harmony of God's creation.

The motive in our relationships shifted, however, from God to ourselves, from giving to grasping. As a result humans found little real love in relationships as compared with what God intended. Instead we experience conflict, alienation, and loneliness. Without the love of God, we remain ill-equipped to love another. Our natural inclination is to seek love by attention from others. The answer for the Christian is to give love by caring for others.

Purpose

God is purposive and made us in His image as *purposive*. He holds us responsible for our own *dreams* in life. "There are many plans in a man's heart, nevertheless the Lord's counsel—that will stand" (Prov. 19:21, NKJV). So man is a dreamer, an achiever. He was intended to be a participant in the grand purpose of God on earth, so that His will might be done.

With the Fall, however, the source of our purpose shifted from God to ourselves. We sought to pursue our dreams apart from God. This resulted in an emptiness in the pursuit of our own aims. The Christian can never be satisfied with a self-centered aim in life. Self-centeredness will only result in frustration, apathy, and boredom. Though we are inclined to seek fulfillment by pursuing our own dreams, we are fulfilled only by pursuing God's plans.

Morality

God is holy and righteous. Based on the moral absolutes of His own character He made us *moral* and holds us responsible for our *actions*. In giving the Law through Moses, God began with the charge, "You shall be holy, for I the Lord your God am holy" (Lev. 19:2, NKJV). God created us with a built-in moral guide we call "conscience." We are able to judge morality and see the difference between good and evil behavior.

In the Fall, the standard for morality shifted from God to ourselves. So, apart from God, we become confused in our moral understanding. "Woe to those who call evil good and good evil, who put darkness for light, and light for darkness" (Isa. 5:20, NKJV). Our natural inclination is to seek our own pleasure by satisfying our appetites. As a result we suffer from guilt, regret, and shame. Christians will rather want to seek purity by obeying God's law. They will reject the demands of their fallen nature.

Possessions

God, as the Owner of all that is, made us *possessive* and holds us responsible for our *management*. God intended for us to serve as stewards of his creation, carrying out the policies of the Owner. The Bible offers a clear picture of the intention of God for our stewardship on earth, for "it is required in stewards that one be found faithful" (1 Cor. 4:2, NKJV). So we, territorial and a collector by nature, are to manage what God puts in our hands as His stewards.

With the entry of sin, however, the ownership of our possessions shifted from God to ourselves. We are no longer clear about our role as managers of God's resources. Rather than stewards, we thinks of ourselves as owners. We try to acquire and secure possessions for ourselves. But a Christian can never gain security in temporal possessions. He or she will feel insecure, will worry, be greedy and materialistic. Instead of seeking security by protecting his treasure, he is to gain security by faithfully managing God's treasure.

Situation

God is the Creator of everything that is. We marvel at the variety and beauty of His creation. He also made us *creative* and holds us responsible for our *situation*. "Then the Lord God took the man and put him in the garden of Eden to tend and keep it." (Gen. 2:15, NKJV). Man is the gardener, the fixer, the reshaper, the changer of his world. God intended that he be creative in shaping the world for God's purposes.

In the failure of responsibility, however, the plan for man's situation shifted from God to himself. As a result, in our independence from God, our world seems hostile to our happiness. No matter where we turn, trouble breaks out to spoil our situation. In response we seek happiness by escaping our circumstances. Christians, however, gain joy by living beyond circumstances. They know that they can deal creatively with any circumstance. They remain content whatever their situation because their happiness is not tied to present conditions.

This survey of the seven areas provides an overview of the entire book. It shows how Christian responsibility can be approached with a clear understanding of our true nature. For most of us this scheme resolves many a mystery. If this is how human nature functions, no wonder we have been confused about what was taking place in our own thinking.

▼

	Identity	Authority	Relationships
Made in the Image of God	God made man worthy and holds him responsible for his value as a person	God made man autonomous and holds him responsible for his rule.	God made man personal and holds him responsible for his relationships.
Inherent Desire	Personal Value	Control	Companionship
Self-Centered Nature	Center of identity is self instead of God, so man has doubts about his worth as a person	Source of authority is self instead of God, so man vainly seeks to establish his control.	Focus of relationship in self instead of God, so man fails to find unconditional love.
Faulty Thinking	"I must establish my worth by performing in a way that gains others' approval."	"I must try to get every area of my life under control to have things my way."	"I must try to find someone who will really care for me and meet my needs."
Emotional Pain and Symptoms	Embarrassment, Self-doubt, Self-hatred, (low self-esteem, arrogance, pride, perfectionism)	Anger Resentment Bitterness (rebelliousness, lack of self-control)	Alienation Loneliness Isolation (hostile, critical, manipulative, insensitive)
Natural Strategy	Seeks value through recognition in comparison with others	Seeks control by demanding his own way and manipulating others	Seeks love by getting attention and affection from others
Biblical Strategy	Gains value by serving without recognition.	Gains control by yielding to God's authority.	Gains love by giving attention and affection.
Faith Application	Secret selfless sacrifice	Choosing grace over control	Unconditional love in action

Purpose	Morality	Possessions	Situation
God made man purposive and holds him responsible for his dreams	God made man moral and holds him responsible for his moral choices	God made man possessive and holds him responsible for his management of what he has	God made man creative and holds him responsible for dealing with his circumstance.
Achievement	Integrity	Security	Personal Peace
Designer of purpose is self instead of God, so man lacks fulfillment in his selfish pursuits	Standard for morality in self instead of God, so man follows self-indulgent impulses.	Ownership of possessions in self instead of God, so man cannot secure his possesions.	Desire for situation in self instead of God, so man sees the world as hostile to his happiness.
"I must pursue my purpose for my life by achieving what I can for myself."	"I must maintain the appearance of integrity, even though indulging selfish desires."	"I must increase and protect my personal resources in order to be secure."	"I must remove all trouble from the circumstances of life to find personal peace."
Frustration Boredom Apathy (stubborn, selfish, competitive, or indifferent, lazy)	Guilt Shame Remorse (hypocritical, deceitful, self-indulgent)	Worry Insecurity Fear (materialistic, stingy, suspicious, greedy).	Discontent Restlessness Uneasiness (complaining, negative, critical, gloomy)
Seeks fulfillment in the pursuit of his own dreams and goals.	Seeks pleasure by indulging his natural appetites.	Seeks security by increasing and protecting his possessions.	Seeks personal peace through changes in circumstances
Gains fulfillment by pursuing God's will for his life.	Gains purity by obeying God's law by His grace.	Gains security by faithfully managing God's treasure	Gains peace by living beyond the circumstances.
Working with God	Living in the light of openness	Yielding ownership to God	Gratitude and creativity

F O U R

What is my real value?

▼

It was not a happy period in my life. I was thirteen and a student at MacArthur Junior High, an impressive city school for a country boy. Though fairly comfortable with myself in my few previous years, I had begun to feel self-conscious. Being thirteen is a tough time. I was growing so fast that some of my features outran the rest of me. My nose was two or three sizes too big for my face, prompting one of my more alert classmates to name me "Nose." I was also thin. No, let's call it painfully skinny.

Then there was the tooth. My eyetooth on the right side stuck out from the rest. This provoked another creative nickname: "Tusk." When I looked in the mirror at my bony self with the oversized nose, I could almost accept it all, until I tried to smile. Then that tooth would shatter my frail self-esteem with its mocking white salute in the mirror.

All of these obvious evidences of my inferiority seriously affected my attitude. I just knew that everyone could see how very awkward and foolish I looked. I suspected that they were all rolling their eyes or chuckling every time I came into view.

Well, that was a long time ago, but the memories are as clear as though it all took place yesterday. I know now that, in spite of my appearance, most of my classmates paid little attention to the features that bothered me. They weren't really laughing at me, but I was so self-conscious that I was convinced of it. It was the first time I had struggled over my own value as a person. I didn't think about "self-worth," but it was a major issue in life for me.

Later, in high school, a teacher played a recorded speech by Earl Nightingale about making something of yourself. Though I missed essential parts of the message, what I latched onto lit a fire of determination among the dry kindling of my self-doubt. The orthodontist had the tooth straightened out with braces by that time, and I had finally grown tall enough to match my nose. I was ready for a different kind of self-consciousness—arrogance. And I was really good at it. I read books on success and was convinced I was destined for greatness. I made a transformation from being shy and embarrassed to being pushy and obnoxious.

What I experienced as a youth was a crisis of self-esteem. In the younger phase I was plagued by a painful self-doubt based on my appearance and all the biological turmoil of puberty. Later I moved to an equally painful (for others) arrogance based on a "positive mental attitude." Though apparently opposite in their effect, both attitudes were rooted in the same idea, a self-centered misunderstanding of legitimate self-worth.

In this chapter we are considering the emotional pain of *embarrassment* and *self-doubt*. The message in your emotions here is the warning of a threat in the area of *identity*. The issue is self-worth, a basic desire every person has. First we will define these emotions. Then we will look at the challenge of self-esteem problems as many of us have experienced them.

Experiencing Self-Doubt

Several levels of emotional pain generally are connected with self-doubt. They all relate to a doubt about the significance I have as an individual. My desire to be somebody, to be recognized as worthwhile, is inherent in me as a human being. When that desire is not fulfilled, the inner Monitor sends up a signal of distress through emotional pain. That message tells me that my personal worth is threatened in some way by circumstances or events around me.

The normal occasional feeling is *embarrassment*. As a warning of threat to my personal value, embarrassment is relatively minor. It is the more active expression of emotional pain from this cluster. Once Sharon and I were guests at an after-church youth gathering. While she was reaching for bread at the buffet, the paper plate tilted and her tacos slid off onto the spotless white carpet. Everybody in the room immediately saw what had happened. The Monitor saw as well and hit the embarrassment button.

The degree of embarrassment is dependent upon the nature of the event, the number and kind of people around, and your attitude about your own self-worth. You are seldom embarrassed when you are alone. Embarrassment has to do with your self-worth in the minds of others. It is a public matter. You suddenly feel conspicuous (everybody is watching), dumb (of lesser value as a person), and, that old standby, have a strong inclination to run away (remember fight or flight?). This event is a direct threat, though minor, to your identity, your personhood. It seems to demonstrate that you are a lesser-quality person.

The degree to which you feel the embarrassment is directly proportionate to the degree to which you are self-assured. Since Sharon is fairly self-assured, she immediately made some self-depreciating remark like, "Well, look what I have done. Alice, I have ruined your carpet." Her sense of self-worth was strong enough to stand some evidence that she was a klutz and not be affected.

If, on the other hand, a person spilled the tacos who was already suffering self-doubt, she would have been mortified. She would have seen the event as proof that she was a complete loser and commented again and again about how sorry she was about it.

This very strong embarrassment might be called *humiliation*. But notice something here. Humiliation suggests being brought down, being humiliated. One is only brought down from some height. Humiliation is only possible for a proud person. For one who is truly humble, humiliation can't happen. This indicates that low self-esteem is a function of our natural self-pride.

So embarrassment is normal. It is a simple signal that your self-worth seems threatened by some event taking place around you. Instead of the food spill, we could discuss the time Jerry brought up with his parents the story of Barbara's pie, the one that burned to a crisp, filling the house with smoke and prompting a 911 call. It is bad enough that the thing actually happened, but even worse that your husband laughs about it in front of your uppity in-laws. The emotion in this case is an equal mixture of embarrassment and anger. It takes a pretty self-assured person to join in with the laughter and enhance the tale with further details.

Self-doubt is the term we are using for an emotion which goes beyond embarrassment. Whereas embarrassment is an occasional problem connected with a specific event or set of circumstances, self-doubt is an ongoing uncertainty about yourself as a person. Self-doubt can be a direct result of the attitude of others as you were growing up. Parents, teachers, and other adults in your life can put you down until you finally believe them. Over time you begin to notice evidence to "prove" what your mother always said about your not being too bright.

Self-doubt is what I am calling *disease* instead of an *injury*. By *injury* I mean something that comes upon you from outside, that wounds you in one of the areas of responsibility. *Disease*, on the other hand, is some flaw in your thinking that causes ongoing trouble for you and provokes emotional pain signals when the threat is really not real, or at least not serious. A healthy sense of self-worth is relatively free of the misconceptions that cause you to be vulnerable to such threats.

Extreme self-doubt can become *self-loathing*. You see yourself as so worthless that you begin to hate yourself. You may not think you are even worthy of life. This is the state of mind behind some of the self-destructive behavior that is so difficult to treat. Self-hatred is a very serious problem, beyond the scope of our discussion here. The person who hates himself has lost the natural instinct for self-love and survival. This may stem from unresolved guilt over a moral failure or over some unresolvable condition that you feel is your fault.

The Self-Esteem Challenge

How does a person come to suffer the emotional pain we call self-doubt? The contributing factors are numerous—how parents and other adults treated us as children, the circumstances of our background, life-changing experiences, physical and mental capabilities or handicaps we were born with, and, of course, wrong thinking. More than we often realize, each of us is the product of our past experiences.

Though we cannot change the past, we can take full responsibility for life as we face it now. No matter what baggage we bring with us to this moment, we can accept it as part of the stuff of which we are made. We can interpret these factors as excuses for our weaknesses or see them as opportunities for character-building as we work to overcome them.

Self-esteem is the respect and value with which a person thinks of himself. Chronic problems with low self-esteem are a signal of the failure of responsibility in the area of identity. Consider some of the symptoms of the person with this ongoing self-doubt.

▼ He often compares himself to others, mostly unfavorably.

▼ He feels that others do not really appreciate him as they should.

▼ He is probably dissatisfied with some feature of his appearance.

▼ He is highly sensitive to the disapproval of others.

▼ He has little self-confidence and avoids making decisions or doing new things in which he might fail.

▼ He has difficulty cultivating friendships because he assumes people will not like him.

▼ He is resentful and critical of others who seem to be "superior" to him.

▼ He sees himself as a victim of forces beyond his control and excuses himself from responsibility for changing.

Most of us identify with some of these feelings. It could be that all of us have been self-doubters at some time in our lives. While low self-esteem may at first seem to be a form of humility, it is actually a function of self-centeredness and self-pride.

Since most of the "evidence" of one's inferiority has to do with appearances or competency, the self-doubter may try to compensate for this poor value by trying to get the approval or recognition of others in self-defeating ways. He or she may concentrate on appearances—clothing, makeup, fashion—to find acceptance in some group. Young people often are drawn into gangs and other groups of rebels just to find acceptance and affirmation.

Another strategy may be to compensate for self-doubt by trying to excel in some particular skill. This may not be a bad or destructive strategy, but if it is pursued in order to "prove" one's value, it will not resolve the misunderstandings at the root of low self-esteem.

The most tragic strategy is seen in various forms of self-destruction. Teens, who are most susceptible to self-doubt, have the highest suicide rate for any age group. The strategy of self-destruction also has been recognized in the causes behind anorexia. Though long a mystery to most physicians and therapists, new success is being achieved with even the most severe cases by recognizing that anorexia is an effort at self-destruction.

A somewhat surprising strategy for hiding low self-esteem is the arrogance and bravado some cultivate. This swaggering and boasting may be a cover for self-doubt even though it seems to be the opposite attitude.

Remember that emotional pain is built into the human psyche to motivate us to correct our thinking or behavior. The emotional pain of self-doubt can be a positive incentive to make needed changes in our lives. If a person can understand what is going on in his own thinking, he can begin to deal with his self-doubt. Whether his poor evaluation of himself is chronic or only occasional, understanding God's point of view will offer positive answers that make a significant difference.

Misunderstandings about Self-Esteem

The thinkers of this generation seem to see self-esteem as the cure-all for whatever ails the country. It seems the most important need is for everyone to "feel good about himself." But our natural approach to self-worth is self-centered and founded on several fatal misunderstandings.

The first misconception about self-worth is that it can be improved simply by positive education and affirmation. We hear education touted as the solution to crime, poverty, problem behavior, poor job performance, and so on. This implies, of course, that the basis of these ills is ignorance.

When applied to the challenge of low self-esteem, educational efforts often resemble Jesse Jackson's affirmation when he was doing the Operation Push rallies. He would stand before a largely black and poor audience of children and young people and admonish them not to let anyone look down on them. He would have them chant, "I am somebody." Though he would give some challenge about behavior, the main thrust was a recovery of personal pride, based solely on one's determination to assert himself.

This approach, with little or no emphasis on the costly development of character, is common among well-meaning educators today. The results of such a view were seen in a 1994 international math competition involving the best American math students and those of six other nations. The Americans finished in last place. When surveyed about how they felt about themselves, however, the American students came in first. They performed the poorest but felt really good about themselves.

It is true that each human being is of inestimable worth simply by virtue of being human. But this value should not be taught as self-pride separated from a humble acknowledgment that life is a gift from God. The result of the "I am somebody" emphasis is often nothing but a change from one form of self-doubt to another, from a lack of confidence to a swaggering arrogance.

Understanding that one is made in God's image and consequently of great worth is the beginning point for encouraging healthy self-worth. But it is only the beginning point. This "given" of inherent worth is confirmed in the hard work of character development. Education at this point must take the form of character training and not simply empty affirmation. Healthy self-worth comes with responsible behavior.

A second misconception about self-esteem is that it can be improved by removing the possibility of failure. Any experience of failure makes us think less of ourselves, at least for a time. Persons who experience failure after failure may then come to see themselves as losers and of little value.

I am sure it was thinking along this line that first inspired educators to come up with some of the new strategies for removing most accountability from the classroom experience. School systems have changed grading from A's, B's, and C's to interesting new designations like "L," meaning "learning in progress." When grades on the SAT tests continued to plummet, the conclusion was obvious—the test had to be made easier. Because the traditional "spelling bee" resulted in mostly losers, it was abandoned in some schools as unfair to those who could not win.

The idea that removing opportunities for failure will create healthy self-esteem is a grievous error, not only for education as a whole, but for the self-doubting students as well. Creating a situation insulated from any failure teaches students that someone should protect them from negative consequences. It teaches them that those who excel are out of step and should be punished for making the poor performers look bad. It teaches them that they need do nothing at all to feel good about themselves, that this is someone else's responsibility.

These new educational strategies seem to reflect an effort to institutionalize the poor performance of public education in the United States. Since the scores keep going down and students do not feel good about themselves, they change the expectations instead of challenging the students.

The basic problem with these ideas is that they do not square with real life. Everybody knows that. Losing is a normal part of life. Dealing with failure is an important aspect of a child's training. If we try to protect the individual from all failure and its disappointment, we are creating the impression one should never have to experience it. Character development requires realistic understanding and personal responsibility in success and failure alike.

A third misconception concerning self-esteem is that it can be healthy without reference to character and moral values. For those seriously concerned about self-esteem, the problem of morality and character is a big one. Do you tell a person that his or her behavior is immoral, that their character is not acceptable? How can you do this in today's pluralistic and permissive culture, especially within the education establishment? Since the prevailing view seems to be that there are no absolute moral values, we cannot define morals for others. Therefore, whatever people feel is right for them must be right.

Self-esteem is necessarily tied to morality. Individuals who behave without self-restraint and discipline will have difficulty thinking well of themselves. Too many bad consequences come of such behavior. The reason that so many people doubt their own worth is because they have a pattern of worthless behavior. To try and talk a person whose behavior is not worthwhile into "feeling" good self-esteem demonstrates an obvious misunderstanding of the human psyche.

A fourth misconception about self-worth is that it can be enhanced simply by gaining the approval of others. We can easily see how this idea could seem reasonable. When others approve of us we feel better than when they disapprove. The approval of parents and teachers is a powerful tool for directing behavior and developing character.

Being others-directed may be normal for a child because of being under the charge of parents and being too immature to be self-directed. The aim of child training is to move the child, through careful development of character, from control by parents to self-control by the child. The development of good character traits allows the child to internalize a set of standards for acceptable behavior. Finally, as an adult, the person may look to parents for counsel, but he is guided primarily by his own inner convictions and values.

Many an adult, however, seems to be stuck in an adolescent mode in which the individual still finds worth as a person only in the estimation of others. Seeking the approval of others may be an unconscious effort to please his parents through the approval of others around him. This can be caused by the failure of parents to provide affirmation in childhood, as well as a failure to develop character appropriate to adult life. The person never gets past that teenage dependence on the approval of others.

Bob was a sad example of this stalled development. He worked at a small radio station where I did a weekly program. He was a twenty-nine-year-old chain smoker and drank too much. His foreign-born wife left him from time to time. On one occasion when she was gone, I went over after work for a visit. He served Coke with something extra in his. He opened up to me about his drive to please his father who had never been satisfied with him.

He spoke as though he saw his father's approval as the key to every task. The more he talked, the more I could sense the pain in his preoccupation with that bad relationship. It had left him evaluating himself almost totally in terms of what he might do finally to get a positive word from his father. Thinking perhaps something could be done to reconcile them, I asked about his relationship with his father now. He replied, "Oh, he's been dead about five years." He was still trying to please a father who no longer knew or cared what he did.

Seeking self-esteem through the approval of others is not only a disappointing method, it is a trap. Instead of being self-directed by Christian character, the others-directed person is constantly checking the signals to determine what others expect. Even if he correctly interprets their wishes, he sacrifices his own personal freedom. Like the teenaged boy whose girlfriend said "spiked" hair was "cool" until he spiked his, he could well misinterpret the desires of others and try to comply with mistaken wishes. What a fool's errand!

These mistaken ideas about self-esteem affect our efforts to build a healthy self-image in others, but they are most damaging when an individual tries to live life according to these misunderstandings. We are all responsible for our own self-worth. Whether we accept that responsibility and act wisely will determine the extent to which we suffer the emotional pain of self-doubt. Our handicap, that divided and self-centered human nature, sends us automatically down the wrong paths.

In the next chapter we will look further into the practical steps for recovering a positive self-esteem. We will discover the keys to feeling great, and even better, the keys to *being* great.

▼

F I V E

Reaching out to greatness

▼

It is quite impressive. An event in the Rose Garden of the White House has all the trappings of greatness. The Marine Band plays as dignitaries gather. Members of the press corps prepare their cameras and strain at the limits of their assigned area. Secret Service agents stiffly take their positions, grimly scanning the crowd. Then the president and his honored guests arrive from the White House, announced by the band and saluted by an honor guard. The cameras flash and whir at every step as he smiles and approaches the microphone.

At the National Prayer Breakfast, February 3, 1994, a figure who seemed out of place stepped into this arena of greatness and power. Mother Teresa spoke there, with the president and vice-president present, along with the cabinet, international dignitaries, and others of importance.

Mother Teresa's world is nothing like the pomp and circumstance that surrounds the White House events. In Calcutta, India, she leads the work of Missionaries of Charity, an order of nuns who ministers to the dying, lepers, and orphans gathered from the filthy streets of that city. Born in 1910 of Albanian parents, she grew up in Yugoslavia. Today her name is known throughout the world as a symbol of service and love.

Encountered at her work in Calcutta, a visitor will find her barefoot, an old woman less than five feet tall, somewhat stooped, wearing a sari-like habit, white with blue trim. She has rather large feet, very crooked, and hands quite strong and large for a woman her size. Her voice is low and strong. She is quick to smile and her eyes sparkle with energy and interest in her deeply wrinkled face. She looks intently at whomever she speaks with, convinced that in every human being, especially the poor, Jesus comes to her disguised.

What is greatness? Is it to be recognized by the presence of Marine bands and reporters? Is it to be measured by the number of people and resources that one commands? Is it determined by position and power? Or does true greatness come from within, from character that shows itself in service, in selflessness, in humility? Is greatness content to hold the hand of a dying man, offering him the dignity and respect of a clean place to lie and the delight of being loved in his final hours? How shall we measure greatness?

In the responsibility each of us has for our self-worth, we must face the issue of greatness. Is it possible that the drive to feel better about ourselves completely misses the essence of personal value? No matter what we do to manipulate our emotions toward self-esteem, the key to human value does not lie in how we feel. Neither can we help others come to a healthy self-esteem without addressing the deeper issues of identity and character.

The Basis of Personal Value

At the root of the personal self-esteem problem lies the deeper question of the value of human life. The Bible teaches that man and woman are made in the image of God (Gen. 1:27), that they are placed "a little lower than God" (Ps. 8:5, NRSV), that God carefully directs the development of the unborn in his mother's womb (Ps. 139:13–16), that whoever takes the life of man is to be executed at the hands of men (Gen. 9:6).

Many of the most critical issues facing the nation today are rooted in the sanctity of human life. The "sanctity of human life" means that human life is holy, not to be violated. Abortion has divided the nation as nothing has since slavery. Child abuse is at an all-time high. In the fall of 1994 the state of Oregon was the first to pass a ballot initiative legalizing physician-assisted suicide.

Responsibility for Identity

God is personal, so He made humans personal, aware of their uniqueness as individual thinking beings. With this aspect of their nature came the desire for *self-worth*. A threat to this desire is signaled by the emotional pain of *embarrassment*, *self-doubt*, and *self-hatred*. Responsible behavior in the area of *identity* will require understanding and applying the principle of self-giving service.

It is no wonder Americans suffer uncertainty about our own self-worth when a million and a half of our brothers and sisters are exterminated every year for mere convenience. No wonder child abuse is rampant, when the parent knows that he or she could legally have chosen to dispose of the child only weeks before it was to be born. No wonder indeed, when the parent is often suffering from a painful sense of worthlessness.

The value of a particular person can be assessed in many different ways—beauty, physical skills, intelligence, artistic abilities, wealth, position, popularity, and so on. But a human being should be valued in different terms. Let me suggest three basic ways we may assess our worth as human beings. In these three kinds of worth we will also see keys to our desire for self-esteem.

Inherent Value

On November 11, 1994, at Christie's in New York a notebook of drawings and scientific writings was sold at auction for 30.8 million dollars. What made those seventy-two pages of illustrations so valuable in the eyes of the winning bidder? They were hand-drawn by Leonardo da Vinci. You and I might look at the notebook and wonder why anyone would want it. Would you place it on your coffee table? To someone who knows little about art or science there may be a thousand books that are more attractive. But this is a Leonardo da Vinci original. That says it all. Its value is inherent because of the artist.

In the same way each human being is a "God original." Whatever your attractiveness to the untrained eye of the brutish masses, you are made in the image of God. All the common ways in which we size up one another are of no account when we see that the Creator of all the universe has planned you and crafted you as an expression of His own love and purpose. With David, the king of ancient Israel, you can exclaim in praise,

> You created my inmost being;
>> you knit me together in my mother's womb.
> I praise you because I am fearfully and wonderfully made;
>> your works are wonderful, I know that full well. . . .
> All the days ordained for me were written in your book
>> before one of them came to be.
>> Psalm 139:13–14, 16

Your inherent value means that you are of great worth simply because you are human. God thought it was a good idea to make you in the first place. Whatever the circumstances of your birth, you are still made in the image of God, sacred to Him, the highest expression of His creation. This truth is the beginning point of understanding your self-worth. What a difference it would make if we taught all the children in our homes and schools this great truth.

We cannot teach public school children that they are God's masterpieces because that might offend some nonbeliever and his lawyer. So the children grow up being taught that they have evolved from a one-celled life form that emerged from the primordial slime millions of years ago. Is it any wonder that human life seems to have little value today?

A child is a priceless treasure even as she swims in the safe haven of her mother's womb. He is an invaluable work of art even in a high chair with oatmeal on his face. She is the highest expression of God's creation as she closes her tired eyes to this world for the last time.

The *inherent* worth of a human being is the beginning point for understanding our identity. It is a "given" apart from any value placed on us by others or any accomplishments on our part.

Attributed Value

A second type of value by which we might assess the worth of a person is *attributed value*. This has to do with the value placed on an object or even a person by the opinion of others. Most of us think of our own self-worth in terms of the value placed on us by parents and other adults as we were growing up. If your parents continually affirmed your value and gave you every indication they believed you were worth a great deal, then you came to believe it as well. But not all parents have operated this way toward their children. Many parents themselves suffer from a lack of self-esteem and pass along the same sense of condemnation to their children.

In a book titled *Pygmalion in the Classroom,* Robert Rosenthal describes an experiment with the "self-fulfilling prophecy." His theory was that parents, teachers, supervisors, and others in positions of influence actually create in those with whom they work a level of performance and a sense of self-worth. It is the attitude of the parent or teacher toward the child, even though not openly expressed, that produces in the child a certain self-understanding and confidence about his or her abilities.

Rosenthal's study involved teachers at a San Francisco elementary school who were told that tests indicated certain children in each class were gifted. Each teacher was given a list of those unusually gifted children, but was instructed to treat all the children in the class the same way. They were not to call attention to the gifted children or do anything to give them special help with their work. At the end of the school year, grades indicated that the gifted children had excelled just as expected. They were better liked by the other students, looked upon as leaders by the rest of the class, and generally thought of themselves as capable and likable. This report was, of course, no surprise to the teachers. They had fully expected the gifted children to excel.

The surprise came when they were told that the children on the list were actually chosen at random. They were not any more gifted than other children in the class. The only difference in those children and the rest of the class was in the minds of the teachers. The teachers were shocked at this new information, insisting that they had treated the "gifted" children no differently from the rest of the class. In subtle ways, however, they had communicated to them an expectation that they should excel, that they were unusually capable, that they were liked and of unusual value as persons.

What we see in the self-fulfilling prophecy is the amazing power of *attributed value*. When a significant person in your life believes profoundly that you are of great worth and that you have outstanding capabilities and potential, you will tend to function in terms of that person's faith. You will live up to his prophecy about you. If, on the other hand, someone of great influence in your life thinks that you are not talented, that you probably won't amount to anything, this becomes a self-fulfilling prophecy as well. Depending on the influence of the other person, you will tend to become what is believed about you.

Attained Value

A third kind of value for assessing the worth of a person is what we may call *attained value*. We have noted that *inherent* value comes by virtue of your being human, and that *attributed* value is based on the estimate others have made as to your worth. *Attained* value is what you earn by the contribution you make in your life. It is the investment of your ideas, your abilities, and your energies for the good of yourself and those around you.

You have no control over your inherent value. It is a given that you accept or do not accept as true. You have some control over your attributed value, the price tags others have placed on you. But the kind of value you can really work with is your attained value. You can prove yourself a productive person, one who works to develop your own character, honor your God, and serve your fellow man. You can use what you have to the best advantage.

Have you ever heard a person referred to as "good for nothing"? If you have, you know what it means. It is an assessment of value based on a person's track record. We do not speak of infants and children as "good for nothing." They have to have time to prove their value with their performance. It is not politically correct today to admit that some people are better than others. Nevertheless, we all know it is true. We believe fervently, as the Declaration of Independence says, that "all men are created equal." We are all "created" equal. This is inherent value. But what we do with our potential is finally up to each of us.

For parents, an understanding of these three kinds of value can serve as a guide in building positive self-esteem in children. In the first place we can teach them about their inestimable inherent value by virtue of their being made expressly by God in His own image. Then we can also let them know our own confidence in their potential, while warning them about the emptiness and danger of seeking the approval of others. We can also teach them that they are responsible for what they do with the tremendous potential God has invested in them.

Because of the environment in which a person grows up, along with his natural self-centeredness, he will likely choose strategies for dealing with self-worth that are ultimately self-defeating. Though they do not come naturally, the individual must learn those understandings and strategies that will result in positive self-worth, strategies which are in harmony with the world in which he lives. To lay the groundwork for such strategies let's consider the views of Jesus on true greatness.

Jesus' Secret to Greatness

"I have a request of you," she said, bowing respectfully and looking closely at Jesus to try to read His mood. "What do you wish?" asked Jesus, looking beyond her to her two sons, James and John, who stood a few paces back, trying to watch the conversation and look disinterested at the same time.

"Appoint my two sons," she said, with a slight movement of her head toward the young men, "to be on Your right and left as key officials in Your government."

Jesus leaned back against the tree and looked at Salome intently, then looking again at the sons. He then raised His voice as though ignoring the woman, "You do not know what you are asking for." He stood slowly and asked in a grave tone, "Are you able to drink the cup that I am about to drink?"

The two young men stepped forward eagerly, glancing at one another. "We are able," they replied, sensing that the appeal might be going well.

Jesus sighed and looked away as if into the days to come. "My cup you shall drink," He said slowly and then turned to look squarely at the men. "But to sit on My right and on My left is not mine to give; it is for those for whom it has been prepared by My Father."

The others heard this last comment and realized what the conversation had been about. They became indignant and grumbled to one another about this flagrant attempt by James and John to get ahead of the rest of them. Jesus quieted them and motioned for them all to draw near.

Looking from face to face, He said, "You know that the rulers of the nations lord it over them, and their great men exercise authority over them." He paused to let that picture sink in, then continued: "It is not to be so with you, but whoever wishes to become great among you shall be your servant, and whoever wishes to be first among you shall be your slave; just as the Son of Man did not come to be served, but to serve, and to give His life a ransom for many."

With this interpretation of greatness, Jesus turned the normal thinking of His followers upside down. Using Himself as an example, He sketched a path to greatness that runs directly counter to our natural inclinations and experience. Look at the principles revealed in His comments.

The common understanding of greatness among men will not be acceptable for you. You must not trust your own natural inclinations or the common patterns of society. These ideas of greatness are rooted in the self-centeredness of the natural man. Besides being foolish from the viewpoint of God's grand design, they will only leave you empty and more self-centered. Do not think to achieve greatness through position, authority, or acclaim, however "normal" this may seem to the world around you.

If you really wish to become great, you can achieve it only through servanthood. It is not a bad thing to wish for greatness. Built into each human spirit is the longing to have a significance in this life beyond one's place and time. But you must not concentrate on greatness itself as your goal. You must abandon any visions of authority, position, and acclaim. Instead, follow the steps of the Son of God in servanthood. Set out to pay dividends on your Creator's investment.

So greatness is not measured in terms of how many you command but how many you serve. The trappings of greatness are not a military band and a bank of microphones but a tray and a towel. The path to greatness is not in surpassing others but in serving them. The Christian heritage in America even dictates that we call our political officials "public servants." Even those in positions of governing power can achieve genuine greatness only by serving well.

The chief question at this point is how we are to apply the principles of servanthood that Jesus gives. The next chapter will offer His practical prescription for self-doubt, along with positive steps for building self-esteem.

▼

The secret to self-esteem

▼

In Lloyd C. Douglas' novel *Magnificent Obsession*, Dr. Wayne Hudson, a famous brain surgeon, drowns. The death of the beloved and skillful doctor shocks the community. At the funeral there are floral memorials from people all over the country, mostly strangers to the family. As the weeks pass, his young widow, his second wife, begins to receive visitors who tell her of her late husband's kindnesses.

These callers recount story after story of how Dr. Hudson helped them in a time of crisis. They offer various sums of money in repayment for his help, indicating Dr. Hudson would never let them pay it back. Their stories also include his charge that they never tell anyone about the arrangement. Each of the well-wishers is somewhat conspiratorial, as though they and the doctor were a part of some secret society.

The callers also tell of a mysterious comment Dr. Hudson made when refusing to let them pay him back. He would say something like, "I can't take it back, you see; for *I've used it all up myself!*" Neither they nor the widowed Mrs. Hudson can imagine what the comment means.

The fascinating story continues as this mystery is slowly uncovered. At a time of crisis in Dr. Hudson's life he himself was told a secret that promised to change his life. And it did. Clive Randolph, a friend he met just after the death of his first wife, saw his despondency and told him the secret. From that point on his whole life was transformed.

Though the secret is never spelled out specifically in the book, it is clear as the story unfolds. When a person does a good deed he naturally tells others about it, and thus collects the credit for it then and there. When he does something selfish and petty, he hides it from others, thus allowing the negative "credit" for these deeds to accumulate. At any moment, then, his net worth as an individual is overbalanced on the negative side. The result is an insecurity about having to settle up, of being found out. This deficit affects all his life—his energy, his attitude, his abilities.

The secret Randolph told Dr. Hudson reverses the natural strategy: admit and be rid of your weaknesses, follies, and sins, while hiding your virtues, good deeds, and kindnesses. The result is an ever increasing net worth of virtue. With it comes the confidence and security of personal wealth, not in money but in character. This secret knowledge of such worth gives energy, optimism, enthusiasm, and hope. It literally transforms your life.

Is this but a fantasy cooked up by Lloyd Douglas to make a good story? No. It is a secret directly from the pages of the New Testament. In the novel Clive Randolph explains that he came upon the secret as a minister read a Scripture text. In fact there are two passages that, taken together, lay this amazing secret before us. This is the secret to self-esteem.

Servanthood and Self-Esteem

The previous chapter briefly sketched Jesus' formula for greatness in the kingdom of God. Greatness is found in servanthood. The one who would be great must be the servant of others. But there is more. The service of the believer is actually service to God. Jesus makes clear that "'whatever you did for one of the least of these brothers of mine, you did for me'" (Matt. 25:40).

The question now is *how* this service is to be given. Let's look at Jesus' prescription for how to perform good deeds. As you follow His instructions, you will not only prove yourself great, you will feel great.

In Matthew 6:1–18, Jesus introduces three kinds of actions that believers should engage in. The three arenas of positive action are directed toward *others* (giving), toward *God* (prayer), and toward *self* (fasting). He warns that they must not be done in the wrong way or from wrong motives. As we have already noted, following our natural inclinations leads to self-indulgent behavior that disregards others and dishonors God. If we do the right thing, we will have to go against the grain and make deliberate choices based on the wisdom of God.

The central point of Jesus' warning is that we avoid doing our good deeds to be seen of men. The word here for "to be seen" is the one from which we get the English word *theatrical*. Jesus also warns us not to "be like the hypocrites" who do everything for show. This word essentially means "actor." Being motivated by the desire for others' approval has you constantly on stage, playing for the applause.

This "acting" is the natural strategy of the self-centered human nature in the desire for positive self-esteem. We think we will feel better about ourselves when others approve of us. For the person suffering self-doubt, the fleeting notice of others is like a sip of cool water to a man dying of thirst. But it is gone so quickly, leaving him no better off, still unsatisfied.

Jesus says that when you do the right thing, let it be for the eyes of God. When your selfless actions are for His eyes only, He will reward you. But when you sell out for the attention of others, He will withhold His reward. It is just that simple. You can act in service because it is the right thing to do and seek only God's approval. Or you can act for the approval of the crowd and their notice is all the reward you get.

When you act selflessly for the eyes of God only, He sees what you do and He rewards you. What is God's reward? The Bible usually calls it being "blessed." Perhaps the greatest blessing is His approval. For the Christian there is great satisfaction in the knowledge that you have pleased God. Jesus worded it this way, "'Well done, good and faithful servant! . . . Come and share your master's happiness'" (Matt. 25:21).

The Chamber of Secrets

Jesus places three conditions on right actions in order to receive God's reward. First, they must be *secret*, not for the eyes of men. Second, they must be *selfless*, seeking no personal advantage. Third, they must be *service*, aimed at returning a benefit to God. These three requirements all run counter to our natural inclinations. They will not be done, then, without deliberately intending to act. We never just drift into secret, selfless service.

Remember Dr. Hudson's secret. Instead of keeping our good deeds to ourselves, we tend to tell others so they will recognize how wonderful we are. In doing so we "spend" the thought of that good, to get credit for it right then. On the other hand, we like to keep our embarrassing actions secret so that others will not know how foolish and selfish we are. These are the deeds we "save" in our memory that remind us every day who we are.

The opposite, however, is what the Bible teaches. Do the right thing and keep it secret (Matt. 6:1, 4). Admit your wrong actions and make them public (James 5:16). In doing so you get rid of what lowers your value and keep what raises it.

The secrets you keep will feed your self-esteem, one way or the other. No matter what others think of you, only you know what is stored in the chamber of secrets in your mind. If, in a quiet moment, you go to the door of that inner chamber and look over all the secrets stored there, what will you see? What will your secrets tell you about yourself? What will they do for your self-esteem? How will they affect your energy, your motivation, your creativity? How will they affect your fellowship with God?

If what you see there is a supply of memories that shame and embarrass you, your self-esteem will plummet. Evidence that you are self-indulgent, demanding, manipulative, and morally impure is right there in your chamber of secrets. Those are the memories that remind you of the kind of person you are.

The answer to that problem is confession: exposing your shameful secrets to God and, as they may be involved, to others. Confession cleans the shameful stuff out the chamber of secrets. Actually, confession of your sins can become an ongoing pattern. It is just a matter of being open, of admitting your mistakes, of laughing at yourself. This openness keeps a clean slate and clear conscience. We will look in detail at the power of confession in chapter 18.

If, on the other hand, your chamber of secrets is well stocked with memories of selfless service, your sense of worth will be enhanced every time you visit it. But remember, if you expose your service secrets for the fleeting recognition of others, you spend the value. As you serve for the eyes of God only, you store up a good supply of evidence of who you are. He sees what you do in secret, and you see it. And the memories of those actions stay in the chamber of secrets as a reminder of who you are. Your secrets will feed your self-esteem.

Is this just a gimmick for feeling better about yourself? Or is this a plan for building real character? Responsibility in the area of your own identity calls for actually being a person of real worth, not just trying to act like one. Though your embarrassment and self-doubt bring you a message about threats to your self-worth, your aim is not to correct the emotions. Your aim is to change the attitudes and behavior behind the emotions. Your aim is to be responsible in the area of identity.

In Jesus' instructions in Matthew 6, he talks about this secret, selfless service in three areas: toward *others,* toward *God,* and toward *yourself.* These are areas of personal discipline that reveal your character. They cover the whole of your opportunities to exercise your commitment to the lordship of Christ.

Helping Others

The first area of service to God is in serving others. This is represented by Jesus' instructions about your "giving" (Matt. 6:2–4). Very specifically, He means your giving to help the poor. But giving has a broader dimension for all of life. It is God's intention that the flow of our lives be in the *giving* direction instead of the *getting* direction. Our natural self-seeking must be overcome in favor of self-giving, which benefits others around us.

This *giving* finds a point of contact in the needs we see in others. We are not to serve others on our own terms. We do not, in other words, "do our own thing." We watch carefully for needs to arise and do what we can to address the need. As we set out to be available to God as a channel of His help, He will show us those needs we can meet.

Following this plan means you cannot get by cheaply in being kind and helpful to others. It will cost you. Sometimes it will require more than you can afford. It will take more time, more energy, more money, and more attention than you can spare. But when you are in business for Christ, you are only planting seed, investing in His purposes as you deal with needs He wants to meet.

Remember Paul's analogy of sowing and reaping: "Whoever sows sparingly will also reap sparingly, and whoever sows generously will also reap generously. . . . And God is able to make all grace abound to you, so that in all things at all times, having all that you need, you will abound in every good work" (2 Cor. 9:6, 8). You will reap what you sow. You will always reap more than you sow. You will reap later than you sow.

Time is always at a premium for me. If I don't have five or six "irons in the fire" I am bored. On one occasion I was overloaded and could not see how to get all the work done. There were classes to teach, papers to grade, and a major administrative assignment to complete. On top of all that, I really needed to mow my lawn. So I was grumbling as I put on my work clothes and got the lawn mower out.

Then I looked across the street where my neighbor, with his two young sons, was about to spread a huge pile of topsoil on his lawn. I went over to speak to him and learned he was in a rush to beat a coming downpour. As I walked back across the street, the thought came to me that I should go over and help him. What a ridiculous idea. He has no more to do than I do, probably not as much. I am already behind. So my arguments with myself went.

Then a new thought came to me. I need more time, so I will invest some time by giving time to my neighbor.

Obviously the math won't work for this line of reasoning. But from the viewpoint of biblical wisdom it makes perfect sense. So I got my gloves, shovel, and wheelbarrow and helped spread the dirt. We got the work done in no time and beat the rain. It was a little experiment, but I was definitely the winner. Somehow all I had to do got done, and with a much better attitude on my part.

The sacrifice of such ministry will tempt you to fish for recognition for your kindness. But don't do it. Remember that you are serving God, for His recognition alone. And He always sees that you are amply rewarded. So file the deed away in your chamber of secrets. Then let it energize and motivate you as you "use it up" like Dr. Hudson.

Fellowship with God

The second area of service Jesus mentions is exemplified by *prayer* and represents our efforts to maintain an intimate personal relationship with God. Again, our praying is to be in secret, going into our own rooms and shutting the door. This is not a prohibition against public prayers, but it is a warning against prayers designed to impress men.

Our personal fellowship with God is another indication of what we value. The worship of God not only honors Him, it strengthens us as we spend time in His presence, seeking His will and joining Him in the spiritual battle for overcoming evil and establishing good. Every day is best begun in fellowship with God through prayer and Scripture reading, planning your day in communion with Him.

In this section on prayer Jesus includes the model prayer. This prayer represents how Jesus thinks we should pray. It may also represent what Jesus thinks our greatest needs are. Surely He would have us pray about what we really need. If that is the case, the prayer seems to suggest that we really need, first, an awe in the presence of the holy God. He says, "Our Father in heaven, hallowed be your name" (Matt. 6:9).

As the prayer continues, we find ourselves praying for the will of God to be done and His rule established. Then we pray for our daily bread. God wants to do personal business with us every day, even about the food we eat. We then pray for forgiveness of our sins. But this forgiveness is tied to our own forgiveness of others.

Jesus expands on this forgiveness of others as a condition of our own forgiveness by God. He makes it clear that if we do not forgive others, God will not forgive us. The heavenly Father is so serious about our relationships with our brothers that He will not receive us until our relationships are right. Our sins are not forgivable if we refuse to forgive. But if we forgive, we start the flow of grace and find forgiveness for our own sins as well.

Imagine, though, what is in your chamber of secrets if you keep a grudge against someone for some long-past offense. You may well have good reason to be bitter, but remember that if you are storing that bitterness among your secrets, it will contaminate everything else. You will never overcome it. You can only get rid of it. We will look more closely at the miracle of forgiveness in chapter 9.

Discipline of Self

The third avenue of selfless service is fasting. If we are to be faithful servants, we must discipline ourselves. Fasting is going without food for a higher purpose. It is intentional self-denial, postponing our own pleasures for the greater good that comes from spiritual devotion. Whether your "fasting" takes the form of an exercise program, managing your time, marshaling your eating habits, or controlling your speech, it is a service to be offered to God, for His honor and approval.

As we have already considered in chapter 2, self-discipline is crucial to Christian responsibility. The battle of a divided nature rages in our lives. We are pulled downward by the force of sin. We are drawn upward by the image of God in our natures. But as new creations in Christ we have a new nature. We don't have to be in bondage to our appetites anymore. We can make a choice for obedience with the confidence that God will enable us to carry through with it.

A minister friend used to say, "I've never met anyone who jogs or gets up early who doesn't brag about it." We laughed because his observation was so true to life. We really feel proud of ourselves for exercising the personal discipline necessary to get up early. Sleep is so inviting, especially in the early morning hours. And maintaining a consistent exercise program is also an achievement.

No matter how pleased you are with yourself for these feats of character, don't cash it in for credit just to impress someone else with your self-mastery. Keep it to yourself. Laugh at your inconsistency and let others laugh with you. But save your successes for the chamber of secrets. There you not only offer them up to God, you relish them for some time to come. It is not just the deeds themselves, it is the consistency of character that is important.

In these three avenues of service we prove our value as human beings made in the image of God. It is His purpose that we serve others, relate intimately to Himself, and discipline ourselves in thought and action. Neglect of any of these disciplines leaves you out of balance. Serving faithfully in these areas not only demonstrates your worth to others, it creates a sense of self-esteem within you.

Action Plan

You are responsible for your identity as a human being made in the image of God. Whatever your experiences in the past, you are responsible now for what you do about your worth as a person. When the message in your emotions signals a threat to your self-esteem, here are some summary ideas for responding positively to the emotional warning.

▼ Remember your inherent value as a "God original."

▼ Accept full responsibility for your attained value.

▼ Be an affirmer of others by attributing value to them.

▼ Accept your servant role with a humble spirit.

▼ Remember Jesus' prescription: selfless, secret service.

▼ Keep your "chamber of secrets" stocked for greatness.

As you put these ideas to work in the area of your own identity, you will experience the positive spirit of Christian greatness God intends for you.

▼
—

S E V E N

Who's in control here?

▼

Sam was a very unhappy man. His family physician had prescribed antidepressants for the gloom he had experienced for several months. The problem seemed to be his job. He had to decide whether to keep it or find another. His job was so unpleasant that he dreaded facing the day. It was a real struggle just getting up in the morning to go to work. He would awaken in the middle of the night unable to sleep in dread of the day to come. He was irritable with his family, losing his temper and arguing heatedly over minor matters.

The job wasn't all bad. He liked the planning, design, and development of the electronic products his company manufactured. What he did not like was management—the politics, indecision by administrators, having to start over on a project, various reorganizations, new managers. He did not want to be in management or in any leadership position. But he felt he could not trust those in management. His supervisors seemed largely to be victims of circumstances beyond their control, because of their supervisors who made every decision on the basis of profit.

He confessed that he had become disliked by his coworkers, by those he supervised, and by his own supervisors. He felt their coolness when he entered the room. They saw him as a troublemaker who was sullen and uncooperative. He was repeatedly disappointed when his suggestions and input were not implemented. By delay and other means he would deliberately resist implementation of ideas contrary to his own opinions.

As we talked it was obvious to me that a major factor in Sam's trouble was his anger and bitterness. Without realizing it he was unable to relate properly to the authority systems and personnel at his company. He was at an impasse. His own vision of how the company should be run brought him into continual conflict with the way things really were and the people who were in charge. He couldn't seem to adjust.

His anger and resentment had deepened to depression, a sure signal he had despaired of finding a solution to the conflict. His attitude had affected his family life, his personal life, his relationship with others at church, and now it threatened his job. He was completely stymied as he tried to find a solution to his situation at work. No matter how hard he tried he only found himself losing more control and growing increasingly angry and depressed.

Anger is the central emotion in a cluster of feelings that relate directly to the issue of control. It is the signal of a perceived threat in the area of authority. It can indicate an unwarranted demand for control. To Sam it signaled that he was out of step with the real world and failing in his responsibility for relating to authority.

In this chapter we will examine the symptoms and causes of anger. We will trace this emotional pain to personal responsibility in the area of authority. The pivotal issue is control. How can we get control when things seem to be out of control? The message in your anger can help answer that question.

Understanding Anger

The cluster of emotional pain related to anger includes *anger*, *resentment*, and *bitterness*. These emotions are signals from the Monitor to warn you of a threat to your desire for control. In some matter where you feel you should have control, there is a violation, a trespass on your rights.

Anger is a volatile combination of annoyance, hostility, and aggression. You feel aroused and irritated. You feel upset, with the "fight or flight" impulse charging your system and putting you in a battle stance. Anger can range from mild irritation to uncontrolled rage. The provocation can be another person, some circumstance, or even your own mistakes. The thinking behind anger seems to be, "I am angry because I deserve better than this."

My anger overflowed when my son flushed a stopped-up commode for the third time, after being told twice that it was out of order. I shouted at him and proceeded to clean up the mess in a fury, visualizing a ruined ceiling downstairs if I didn't get the water up quickly. The look on his face told me that my offense was much worse than his. He had merely forgotten, but I had lost control.

Anger is recognized worldwide by characteristic facial expressions. Human beings don't often growl and bare their teeth. But their faces tell the story—the penetrating stare, the tense eyelids, the eyebrows often lowered and drawn together, the lips pressed together or pushed forward. Other body language can also signal anger—arms crossed in defiance, stiff posture, hands clenched into fists. Just by glancing at you, others recognize your attitude.

Whereas anger is the more active expression of these emotions relating to authority, the more passive expression is *resentment*. While *anger* focuses on the offense, resentment focuses on the offender. It carries a more relational meaning. *Resentment* seems to take the matter much more personally, suspecting that the perpetrator intentionally set out to cause trouble. *Resentment* is more of a long-term and seething wrath.

We express our anger and resentment in different ways, depending on our temperament, the situation, and the nature of the provocation. When a person loses his temper, he is actually losing control of the *expression* of his anger. Some try not to express anger at all. They hold it in, perhaps while pretending to be happy. Others express anger with a quiet and sullen withdrawal from interaction with the circum-stance. With family members or coworkers they may use the "silent treatment." They close the invisible door of fel-lowship and freeze others out with a formal and stiff indif-ference.

Def•i•ni'tion: Anger

Anger is the feeling of hostility and aggression in reac-tion to some circumstance or event that poses a threat to one's control. Anger can range from irritation to rage. It is the center of a cluster of emotional pain in the area of au-thority.

While *anger* is the more active emotional expression from this cluster, the more passive is *resentment*. If left un-resolved, anger and resentment can develop into *bitter-ness*.

With some people anger is like a firecracker. It doesn't take much to set it off. When it blows up it's over pretty fast, but it leaves a ringing in your ears. For others anger is like a volcano. It takes a long time for the magma to move up into the cone, but look out when the pressure builds to an erup-tion. After the eruption the hot lava flows and does damage for quite some time.

If the causes of anger and resentment go unresolved, the emotion will evolve into *bitterness*. At this level the feeling becomes an attitude toward the offender. *Bitterness* is anger that does not go away with time but becomes a grudge. It moves beyond hostility to hatred, from wrath to revenge, from passion to plotting. The offender is seen as an enemy who must pay for his crimes. The bitter person is emotion-ally fixated on the wound he has suffered. Even though he may suppress the memory, the pain is still there, waiting to surface.

There is a message in these emotions about a threat to your control of your life. It signals that your rights have been violated. It may remind you of old wounds—wounds that still cause you quickly to become upset. It may call at-tention to faulty thinking in the area of authority. Whatever the complex message contained in anger, you can decipher it and respond wisely to deal with the underlying problems.

Expressing Your Anger

Should anger be expressed or restrained? On one side of this argument are the "ventilationists" who believe it is unhealthy to bottle up anger. They say the old Puritan restraint should be overthrown in favor of "blowing off steam" and releasing the tension of anger. Go ahead and shout. Tell off the offending person. Hit something, throw some furniture around, or clobber a bucket of golf balls. This is a commonly held view, a bit of folk philosophy passed along from generation to generation.

Jack Hokanson of Florida State University experimented with students by checking the effect on blood pressure of various methods of dealing with anger.[1] He found that an aggressive response helped young men when the provoker was a fellow student. When angered by a professor, however, aggression only created more stress. For women students an aggressive response was more stressful, even toward another student.

Hokanson's research indicated that an aggressive reaction to anger is a learned response. Even though screaming and throwing things may relieve some of the tension, it may also create a habit for the future. Since any emotional arousal will calm down with time, an aggressive venting of your feelings may only prolong the anger. The age-old advice of counting to ten may work much better.

Social psychologist Leonard Berkowitz of the University of Wisconsin found that ventilation by yelling does not reduce anger.[2] It actually intensifies the anger. A minor annoyance, if vented in language and behavior, stimulates a person to make more of the annoyance than is warranted. Efforts to talk out your anger may only rehearse it and keep it stirred up. Very often the best choice with anger is to do nothing at all. Most provocations will turn out to be trivial and will be soon forgotten.

Expressing anger is something we learn to do. As children, we express our anger in ways that work in getting what we want. Whether it is a simple case of pouting or a kicking, screaming fit in the floor, children find out what works and become good at it. They can also learn not to express their anger aggressively. We bring to the complicated world of adulthood whatever childhood strategies for anger worked for us as children.

As adults, we learn that kicking and screaming is no longer appropriate. But some adults cannot overcome those old habits. They release their fury by stomping, yelling, and throwing things. If you are an important basketball coach, you can go into a rage at the games. It will undoubtedly influence the officials. What the fans see, though, is an overgrown little boy having a fit because he didn't get his way.

We learn to restrain ourselves with those people and in those situations when it just doesn't pay to let ourselves go. Most of us soon learn that the boss is not our mother. He or she does not respond to our tantrums the way our mother did. We are most uninhibited in our expression of anger when we know we can get away with it, when we think it may get us what we want. So we rage at our families, our subordinates, hapless store clerks—anyone unlikely to retaliate.

Occasional flashes of temper may not be a problem. Long-term and chronic anger, however, calls for learning new strategies for handling it. Ray Novaco of the University of California at Irvine suggests learning three skills for dealing with chronic anger: (1) thinking about your anger; (2) controlling arousal of your anger; and (3) behaving constructively when angry.[3] It is at these three points that you can override your negative emotional responses with deliberately chosen, positive responses.

Assumptions of an Angry Spirit

Though we all experience anger from time to time, some people develop a chronically angry spirit. For them, anger is a lifestyle. This is an indication of a failure of responsibility in the area of authority. In their effort to get control of life they operate on the basis of several mistaken assumptions. Perhaps you will recognize some of this faulty thinking.

The person with an angry spirit sees outside provocations as the cause of his anger. This assumption places the reason for anger "out there" in external factors rather than "in here" in his own attitudes. It is easy to see how this idea develops. Since anger arises in reaction to some provocation, he assumes that if all such irritations were removed, he would never be angry. It is the external provocation that causes the anger.

He does not see his reaction to people and circumstances as the problem. Since he feels so strongly about it, his feelings must be valid and appropriate. As long as he sees the problem with his anger as outside himself, he never has to take responsibility for it. He never has to question whether his attitude is the best way to deal with a particular situation. The only challenge the angry person faces is trying to control the expression of his anger to his own advantage.

The person with an angry spirit sees herself as a victim of forces beyond her control. She sees the world as filled with irritations and threats. On every side is someone or some circumstance threatening to trespass on her rights. She sees a conspiracy against her by those in authority.

Symptoms of an Angry Person

▼ Prone to displays of anger at minor irritations
▼ Resents those in authority and is suspicious of them
▼ Has difficulty cooperating with those in charge
▼ Carries an attitude of independence and rebellion
▼ Cites faults of leaders as the reason for resisting
▼ Blames outside provocations for angry outbursts
▼ Is resentful and argumentative receiving instructions
▼ Provokes anger in those under his or her authority
▼ Thinks of those who disagree as enemies
▼ Is often sullen and resentful in attitude

She struggles for control of her life and often feels herself a victim of her own emotions. Her anger seems to have its own agenda. It boils over with little or no notice. She may lash out at those she loves best for what she knows was a trivial matter. The angry person may be most angry at herself as she occasionally catches a glimpse of the truth about her attitude.

The person with an angry spirit assumes he has a right to have his way. He seems to carry the unconscious thought, "I have a right for things to go my way." This idea, of course, is directly related to his unconscious belief that he is the final authority in his life. When he finds himself in conflict with someone else, he immediately assumes that the other person is striving, as he is, to get his way.

The emphasis on his "rights" will always put a person in conflict with the world around him. If he does not get his way, he will usually see the problem in the attitudes of others. He thinks they don't like him, that they are just stubborn, that they are jealous of his superior ideas. Surely there is something wrong with those who resist him; his mother never did.

The person with an angry spirit sees those who provoke her as enemies. She has a hard time relating to those who do not please her. She has an "enemies list" in her mind and sorts out others as those who are for her or against her. She may even plot the downfall of those who oppose her. She will find a kindred spirit in other rebels and prefers their friendship.

When there is no one immediately available to blame for circumstances that displease her, she may accuse God. This can lead to bitterness toward God because He is the only One finally responsible for whatever happens. Since God has let her down, He must not be a God worth worshiping. "I'll show Him!" the angry person says. "Just see if I do anything for Him." She may even try to punish God by denying His existence.

As irrational as some of these attitudes seem, they are common with chronically angry persons. They seem reasonable from the viewpoint of the angry spirit. In these faulty assumptions is an underlying attitude of independence and self-centeredness. The person with an angry spirit is generally rebellious and expects to be in control of everything that touches his or her life.

This sketch of the assumptions of a chronically angry person may seem extreme. Most of us will find ourselves dealing with the issue of control in more subtle ways. We may have learned how to mask our childish demands, but the emotion inside is still telling us that we are being denied the control we expect to have. The signal of anger is a message from your inner self. The Monitor is telling you that your control of a matter is being threatened.

Training an Angry Adult

A person does not develop an angry spirit overnight; it takes years of training. The angry person believes he has a right to be in control. He was allowed to think that way as he grew up. Children naturally resist the control others would exercise over them. It isn't long before even an infant will demand control by resisting a diaper change or screaming his protest over not being held. From that early beginning, the parents must decide how they will deal with this natural demand for control by their little angel.

Rather than requiring the child to comply with their wishes, many parents try to reach some accommodation to keep the child happy. They avoid directly confronting his resistant spirit by attempting to manipulate him in some way. They may try to divert his attention or just put up with his anger. In the meantime, they are teaching the child to demand control and to make trouble for those who do not yield to him.

By the time this child grows up, he has come to believe that everyone should comply with his wishes, a belief that he learned from his parents. Maybe that belief was reinforced by slack discipline at school. Even though he has found himself in trouble on the job, with authorities of other kinds, and in relationships, he blames that trouble on others and continues to forge ahead with the mistaken idea that he is to be the final authority in everything that affects him.

The person with an angry spirit who demands his way finds often enough that others will yield. They do not like his anger, his pushiness, his blindness to any view but his own.

So they just give up and let him have his way to avoid a confrontation. This only reinforces his habit of expecting the world around him to accommodate itself to his wishes.

It is normal for a person to become angry when he feels he is not being treated fairly. Most of us, however, realize that we will not get everything we want. We grow up with enough experiences at the hands of our parents to learn that we do not get our way every time. We come to the conclusion that happiness does not depend on getting our way. If what we want is not possible at the moment, we happily move on to other matters.

The person with an angry spirit will almost surely raise children with the same attitude. In his demand to have things go his own way, the parent will expect his children to comply with his every wish. His goal is not to train the children but to demand their compliance with his wishes. The children, of course, will rebel against this kind of treatment and learn early to resist authority, resenting the attitude they see in that parent. So another generation of angry persons is produced.

There is enough of this angry spirit in each of us to see ourselves in this chapter. Even though you may not be chronically angry, you can still profit from the message in your emotions at this point. So let's move on now to an understanding of what anger is really telling us and how we can respond with biblical wisdom.

▼

EIGHT

Living under authority

▼

The two young black men stood on the Olympic medal-ist platform wearing gold and bronze medals. The national anthem of the United States played. The American flag was spotlighted. It was the 1968 Summer Olympics in Mexico City. The event was the 200-meter race. As they stood on the winners' riser before a cheering crowd in the arena and a vast television audience, Tommie Smith and John Carlos bowed their heads and raised their right arms, fists clenched in defiance.

Political demonstrations by participants are forbidden by Olympic rules. These two American men defied that rule to protest what they saw as injustice toward Blacks. They got the attention they wanted, though they were suspended from the games and thrown out of the Olympic Village. The clenched fist they raised is a symbol of rebellion in most of the world today. It represents anger, defiance, and resistance against authority or injustice.

Rebels through the generations have been looked up to as heroes or vilified as demons. There is something in human nature that rejects authority, particularly when that authority is perceived as restricting a person's control over his or her own life. The young Olympic athletes had to comply with Olympic rules even to be allowed to compete in the games. Ironically, they could never have expressed their rebellious defiance had they not submitted to authority to get to that winner's spotlight.

So it is with us all. We have that inherent rebellious streak. We want to have control of our own affairs and the freedom to do as we please. But to have that freedom we must also submit to authority. It is a tension we all must live with. Authority is built into the very fabric of creation. At every level there is order and subordination. In his fallen nature, man chafes against such restrictions and defies those who would compel his obedience.

This tendency toward rebellion is at the heart of our desire for control. A normal expectation for control can become a demand for authority over everything that touches your life. The message in your anger warns of a threat to your control at some point.

Anger may also bring a message about *injuries* caused by past experiences with authority or the *disease* of wrong thinking on your part. Either way there are practical steps you can take to deal responsibly with authority. In this chapter we will look more closely at authority, control, and anger. Then we will suggest a practical plan for responding to the message in your anger.

A Biblical View of Authority

The Bible makes clear that God is the Lord and Ruler of all that is. He is sovereign. As such, He answers to no one, seeks no counsel, receives no instruction, accomplishes in heaven and earth whatever He pleases. In poetic descriptions of His sovereignty the biblical writers assert that His "is the greatness and the power and the glory and the majesty and the splendor, . . . exalted as head over all" (1 Chron. 29:11). He is "the blessed and only Sovereign, the King of kings and Lord of lords. It is he alone who has immortality" (1 Tim. 6:15–16, NRSV).

Though the principle of authority is built into creation, it is not essentially a religious issue. With or without any acknowledgment of God, man has learned that order in society requires systems of authority. Even though some exercise of authority has been brutal and tyrannical, the necessity for authority is obvious. The alternatives to legitimate authority are anarchy, chaos, and the complete breakdown of human society.

In the biblical view, all earthly authority proceeds from God. Paul writes, "Everyone must submit himself to the governing authorities, for there is no authority except that which God has established. . . . Consequently, he who rebels against the authority is rebelling against what God has instituted" (Rom. 13:1–2).

Since authority, as a principle, is established by God, so all authority should be respected. "Submit yourselves for the Lord's sake to every authority instituted among men: whether to the king, as the supreme authority, or to governors, . . ." (1 Pet. 2:13). In honoring authority, the believer is honoring God.

We are to give respect to those who are in positions of authority even though they don't deserve it. "Slaves, submit yourselves to your masters with all respect, not only to those who are good and considerate, but also to those who are harsh" (1 Pet. 2:18).

Believers are to make a distinction between the *position* of legitimate authority and the *person* who holds that position. Even though the person may not be worthy, the position is to be honored. They must also distinguish between authority as a principle and its evil expressions, such as slavery. Even though slavery is inherently evil, the Christian slave is to respect his master.

So neither the injustice of human social structures nor the unworthiness of those persons who are in positions of authority is an acceptable reason for a Christian to disrespect authority. Respect for authority is basic to the believer's attitude as he honors God.

A Christian must not give way to the natural inclination toward independence and rebellion, even when he suffers at the hands of human tyrants. "For it is commendable if a man bears up under the pain of unjust suffering because he is conscious of God" (1 Pet. 2:19).

Responsibility for Authority

God is sovereign and made us in His own image as autonomous, to rule over creation under God's authority. With this limited autonomy, we were also given a desire for *control* of our lives and circumstances. A threat to our control is signaled by the emotions of *anger, resentment,* and *bitterness.* Responsible behavior in the area of authority calls for accepting and implementing the principles of *submission.*

When a conflict arises between human authority and the commands of God, however, the authority of men is respectfully rejected. The believer gladly accepts the penalty of disobedience to men rather than disobey God. Peter and John were faced with such a dilemma when commanded by the Jewish Council to stop preaching the message of Christ. They answered, "We must obey God rather than men!" (Acts 5:29). The men were beaten but rejoiced that they had been counted worthy to suffer disgrace for the name of Jesus.

Critical to our understanding of authority is the connection between authority and power. Though we may use the ideas of "power" and "authority" interchangeably, they have distinctive meanings. While "authority" is the right to rule, "power" is the ability to act. In our discussion of control, the two ideas come together. "Control" really means the ability to see that things go your way. In that sense it is the same as power. Authority is the legitimate right to have things go your way. If you have authority, you expect to be in control.

The principles of authority revealed in the Bible can guide us in a practical plan for dealing with anger. Basic to such a plan is the full acceptance of personal responsibility in the area of authority. This means, simply, that you are saying, "I am responsible for my attitude and response when things do not go my way." You can refuse to blame the chaos in your life on someone else, on circumstances, or on any other factor in a situation. You can accept full responsibility for your own attitudes and actions, even though you cannot control every aspect of your world and your life.

The Desire for Control

The basis for anger is our desire for control over our lives. By nature, made in the image of God, we have been given a degree of autonomy. We are commissioned to "subdue the earth." A part of our responsibility as human beings is to bring some order to the part of this world we touch.

Though the desire for control was initially a good quality, it went bad in the Fall. As we have already noted, man's understanding of himself shifted from God-centeredness to self-centeredness. Instead of serving as agents of God's control on this earth, we naturally try to establish our own independent control. Instead of seeking to please God with efforts at control, we seek to please ourselves. Instead of seeing our control as an expression of God's authority, we see it as our own rule.

So it is the independence in our desire for control that is the root of anger. If we are the center of control, we are responsible to establish control in our world. We are not counting on the sovereign God to establish control. We are attempting to be in authority without being under authority.

The world is designed for proper structures of authority. So we ultimately find it difficult to be in charge. We immediately run into the *uncontrollables*, those factors that keep breaking loose, popping up, falling down, getting in the way, generally gumming up the works. These uncontrollables touch our lives in two forms.

First, there is something built into creation that resists control. Even though God created the best of all possible worlds and saw that it was "very good," He also built an element of disorder into it to keep it interesting. Scientists have discovered this randomness in the most basic levels of matter. We experience this resistance to control every time something in our control goes wrong.

Plenty can go wrong. And it does. There are so many ways things can be fouled up. There is no end to the creative and imaginative possibilities for something to go wrong. NASA is famous for careful planning and backup systems for trouble. Even so, in the spring of 1995 the launch of the next shuttle flight was delayed because environmentally protected woodpeckers were pecking holes in the insulation on the booster rocket. Think you thought of everything? Surprise! This kind of thing keeps all of us very busy trying to establish control in our little corner of the world.

The second factor challenging your control of your world is the many other independent control centers out there vying for dominance over the same space and circumstances. I mean, of course, other people.

Each person is a moving control center, seeking to establish control of matters touching him, according to his own desires. When you run into another control center with aims in conflict with yours, what happens? I saw this illustrated recently when a young friend tried to claim control over the same piece of highway as another driver. Both cars were destroyed and both drivers seriously injured.

Experiencing the issue of control from the other side, you may encounter attempts by others to control you. This is *manipulation*, a blatant control device.

Here are some of the sounds of manipulation (and their control messages): "You don't love me" (or you would do as I want). "You have hurt me" (and you need to make it up to me). "I am ill" (and you are the cause of it). "You don't appreciate all I've done for you" (so you should do something for me). "I don't want to live" (and I might even kill myself if you don't make me happy).

The element of chaos and the competition of other roving control centers make establishing control a challenge. Enter the Monitor, that hidden defense agent who mans your inner communication center. When he sees some threat to your desire for control of your world, he pushes the warning button called "anger." The alarm goes off, sending you a rush of irritation and resentment. The message is simple: "Alert! Alert! Control threatened! Take aggressive action to repel intruder!"

That is exactly what you feel when the anger alarm sounds. Aggressive. Ready to attack. At full alert. You feel that your own rights have been trampled on. Some circumstance, event, or person has entered your territory and threatened your control. Like a dog in his own yard, you feel like snarling, barking, and crying alarm so that the trespasser is driven away.

The threat may be a violation of your self-respect, your things, your space, your plans, your schedule, your convenience, your comfort, your peace and quiet, your relationships, your money, your ideas, your reputation—anything over which you feel you have a right to exercise control.

Servanthood and Control

We begin relating responsibly to authority when we accept the role of a servant. A servant has submitted himself to the authority of God and is no longer attempting to establish his own independent authority. A servant understands that control (power) is something God must exercise and that He will do so only where His authority is established. Christian servants, then, do not see themselves as independently in charge of anything. They are responsible, as servants of God, to exercise a positive influence at home, at work, and in other relationships in their personal lives.

Jesus demonstrated the servant role in the dramatic gesture of washing the disciples' feet. He made it clear that He was indeed their Lord and their Master. But He also made clear that what He had done to them, acting as a servant, was exactly what He expected them to do for one another. So the Christian must be a servant in all circumstances and with all people.

A parent's responsibility for her children demonstrates the struggle for control. The parent's role with the child must be that of a servant. This does not mean that she is to comply with the child's wishes. She is the servant of a different Master. Since the Lord Jesus is her Master, she answers only to Him for command and instructions. But her service to her Lord must be implemented through service to people. Her role as a parent is a servant role, even though she is in authority in the lives of her children.

She will ask, "How can I best serve these children through the training and discipline God has instructed me to give?" The needs of that child at that moment set the agenda for the service. Does the child need affirmation? Does he need discipline? Does he need tenderness? Does he need firmness? Does he need instruction? Does he need punishment? All of these questions are answered in terms of the goal, which is training the child in godly character.

In every aspect of a Christian's responsibility for authority, the servant role is appropriate. An employer asks, "What do these employees need from me in order to be the best employees they can be?" Not only does the employer serve his employees, he serves them as human beings made in the image of God. This is the servant leadership Jesus modeled.

An Agent of Control

A neighbor couple was keeping two little boys, ages four and six, while their parents made a visit to the hospital where a new nephew had just been born. A firm word by the hostess had set the tone when the children became a bit rowdy soon after their parents left. From that time on, the children were very responsive to whatever the adults required. They played quietly on the floor with a Lego set for most of the evening.

About nine the doorbell rang as the parents returned for the boys. Immediately the children tensed and looked at the door. As the young parents came in, the children began pleading with them to stay longer. Their mother apologized to the hostess for any trouble the boys had caused and thanked her for keeping them. The hostess tried to assure her that they had been no trouble. Meanwhile the boys were clamoring to tell their mother that they were not ready to go home.

The parents were invited to sit down for a moment and report on the new baby. But it was almost impossible to talk. In one instant the atmosphere in the room had gone from quiet and serene to chaotic. The young mother was sure the boys had been a bother. The father was trying to instruct them. They were ignoring him and besieging their mother with unceasing pleas to stay longer. The host couple was amazed. What had happened to these compliant little boys? Why had they suddenly become noisy and disruptive?

The answer was simple. They had sensed in the older couple a control and stability, and it affected them. It served as a warning against disruptive behavior and an assurance of security. When their parents arrived, however, they knew that control was gone and they immediately responded by creating chaos. This is not to say the parents were disruptive. They seemed calm enough. But they were not clear about authority in the home. Rather than taking charge as parents and training the boys in character, their aim was to keep them happy.

Some people, like the older couple, are agents of control. Their presence helps to create a climate of calm and security. While this may seem to be a matter of temperament, it is often really an expression of authority. If a person is under authority, he is in authority. Where authority is established, control will prevail. Control means peace and order.

God intended each of us to be agents of control. It is obvious that those around us need a good dose of peace and order from time to time. Situations get out of control. Tempers flair. Where is an agent of control? Where is the peacemaker who will bring a sense of serenity and calm? It will be the person who has settled the authority issue, the one who chooses grace over control. It will be the ones who know they can be in control only as they are under control.

Are you an agent of control? Does peace and order follow where you are? Or do you seem to be surrounded continually by chaos? Consider the issue of authority. Allow God to establish His authority and control in your life. Allow Him to use you to bring order out of confusion and peace out of conflict. But it means giving up your control. Not only will you be blessed as His grace works in your life, you will be a blessing to those around you.

Anger is a warning that there is a threat to your control somewhere in your present circumstances. But anger can also warn of faulty thinking about authority. Your anger can be an alarm to remind you that it is God, not you, who is ultimately in control. When the message in your emotions signals a warning that you are trying to control circumstances and other people, it is time to take action to address the control issue. The next chapter offers a plan of action.

▼

NINE

The miracle of forgiveness

▼

The war had touched the family already. The younger brother had received his draft notice just after the death of their father in October of 1942. Now Richard was leaving for the merchant marines. His young wife was expecting their first child. He had to make sure she was cared for before he left.

Daddy had left three apartments to provide a rental income for Mama. One was in the house, making it a duplex, the other two in a garage apartment next door. Richard and his brother had finished the garage apartments after their dad died to make sure Mama was set up since they both would be off to the war.

Richard had always been something of a mama's boy. When he tried to get his wife settled so he could leave, he naturally turned to his mother. Could his wife live in the apartment in Mama's house? She would be company for Mama. He would pay the rent. The two most important women in his life could take care of each other while he was gone.

Mama said no. Nobody ever knew the reasons she gave or the details of her conversation with Richard. She had always seemed to resent the sons-in-law, and maybe her one daughter-in-law as well. Richard was disappointed, embarrassed, and angry. It was a blow he almost couldn't bear. His young wife took it very badly, feeling personally rejected.

Hurt and perplexed, Richard made other plans and left for his merchant marine duty. Thus began over thirty years of bitterness. They never spoke again. Mama had little or nothing to do with her grandchildren. Brothers and sisters in the family alternately tried to make peace or joined in the dispute. Richard came to Mama's funeral but didn't sit with the family, and most of the family members didn't greet him. When he died at seventy-three one of his last words was "Mama."

The tragedy of this story is that it happened. The ripple effect even spread to later generations, though most of the children refused to keep the grudge going. Who was right? Who was wrong? What difference did it make? Pride and hatred prevailed. The joys of family gatherings and watching grandchildren grow up were lost. All that and more was the toll of bitterness.

In this chapter, I want to spell out a specific remedy for such bitterness. It is the miracle of forgiveness. Bitterness indicates that the cause of the anger and resentment was not resolved. First let's look at specific insights for dealing with anger.

Assumptions behind Anger

The first step in dealing with anger is to identify the expectations that lead you to anger. If you expect to keep your stuff in order, it angers you for someone in the family to rummage through it. If you expect your car to start, it angers you when it doesn't, especially if you are late. If you expect to be treated with respect, it angers you to be accused and mocked.

Anger is understandable in cases like these. But we also tend to get angry when our expectations are not reasonable. We claim rights that are not really ours. We refuse to allow for the disorder in this world and the imperfection in those around us. As a result our anger may be connected more to our attitudes than to what happens to us.

If I am angry that my lawn mower won't start, I am assuming I should be able to control it at all times. But is this a reasonable assumption? Am I forgetting that the real world contains an element of chaos? When something doesn't work properly the Monitor flashes a warning that my control is threatened. But is it possible that this is a threat to my control only because I am expecting too much?

The same examination of my expectations is necessary when dealing with people. When another person angers me, here is the question, "Do I have a reasonable right to expect this person to comply with my wishes?" If I am a military officer and that person is under my command, then I do have such a reasonable right and will insist that he comply with my instructions. As an officer, I am in control. I won't sense any threat to my control because I know I have authority and expect to be obeyed.

Parents, on the other hand, don't expect to maintain military control of their children. They are responsible to train their children and to guide them. They are responsible to protect them from their own foolishness and to provide such control as is necessary for their particular level of maturity. Even so, parents cannot actually control their children's lives. Children can be very creative in resisting such efforts at control.

Early in life, children express a desire to take control of their own activities. Even an infant will show this inclination when she kicks and screams to resist having her diaper changed or her nose wiped. But since she is an infant, her mother must exercise a great deal of control. She is not able to control herself (hence dirty diapers) so her mother must control most of her activity. The mother cannot, however, maintain that level of control as her child grows up. Her purpose as a parent is to see her control diminish as the child assumes greater and greater control of herself.

Freeway driving is another vivid example of our need to examine our expectations. There are few human experiences so likely to provoke anger as driving. Of course, it is the other drivers who cause the trouble. They cut in front of us. They drive too slowly. They drive too fast. They do not seem to pay attention. They drive in the wrong lane. You are probably thinking that it's okay to get angry when other drivers behave that way.

Questioning Your Anger

▼ Can I reasonably expect to be in control in this matter?

▼ If so, how can I maintain it in the most sensible and productive way?

▼ If this is not a matter under my legitimate control, why am I angry about it?

▼ Does my anger indicate a demand for control that I had not realized I felt?

▼ Am I in error in assuming that I should have my way in this matter?

▼ Am I feeling angry because I am upset about some unrelated matter that poses a threat to my control?

Here is the question: "Can I reasonably expect to be in control of the highway, including all of the other drivers?" If so, I will do even better than emergency vehicles. They are supposed to have the right of way. But often we see them struggling to get through traffic where inconsiderate or inattentive drivers are not yielding. But you and I do not drive emergency vehicles. We cannot reasonably expect all the other drivers to give us the whole highway. Anger in traffic says we *think* we have a right to have our way on the highway. Once you confront yourself with the foolishness of such an idea, you will find your anger fading.

So, when I become angry, I can immediately ask myself whether I have a reasonable right to expect control in the situation that has angered me. If the answer to that question is yes, then I have no need for anger because it will only frustrate my efforts to exercise properly the authority and control for which I am responsible. If the answer is no, then I can realize that my anger is out of place and smile to myself as I relax and release my anger. If there is no reasonable right of control, there is no reason to react to the loss of control.

Choosing Grace over Control

Even in the heat of an angry response you can choose *God's grace* over *your control*. Grace and control are mutually exclusive. *Control* is the exercise of your power to force compliance with your wishes. *Grace* is God's exercise of His power to enable you to respond properly in any circumstance. You cannot have God's grace and your control at the same time.

When you choose grace you are automatically yielding control because "God opposes the proud but gives grace to the humble" (James 4:6). The demand for control is an expression of pride. You are trying to establish your own independent authority. You are rejecting God's authority when you demand control. You are forcing your desires, by your own strength, and you are refusing God's help. God resists this prideful independence in man. So you are on your own.

Grace gives power, freedom, and peace to the person yielded to God's authority. God longs to give His grace in every circumstance. We Christians live our lives by grace. But this grace is available only as we put our trust in God and yield to Him.

When you feel the tension of anger, you can make a conscious choice to choose *grace* over *control*. I find that it helps to acknowledge my desire for control by clenching my fists. Then I express to God that I am choosing grace over control, and I relax my clenched fists and open my hands to receive His blessing. This simple exercise can make an immediate difference in the tension of anger. We can decide to override the natural demand for control by choosing to express faith and receive grace.

God has built into our systems the emotional pain of anger to signal a threat in the area of authority. When anger arises we can know that it is time to examine our desire for control and our attitudes about authority. Though your desire to influence what takes place around you is normal, anger will remind you that *influencing* and *controlling* are two different aims. An objective analysis of the entire matter can cast it in a different light and allow you to respond wisely.

Anger will often show you your own attitudes in a way you would never otherwise see them. It will show you how childish and demanding you are to think you can control the people and circumstances around you.

I am often embarrassed when anger calls my attention to attitudes in my own heart that I know are out of order. These attitudes reveal me as being a demanding, pushy, unyielding person. Were it not for the anger, I might not see this faulty thinking and therefore might not be aware of my need to deal with it. So anger can be a helpful signal to me, a warning about my attitude. I can turn anger to my benefit by thanking God for showing me what is in my heart.

If I will examine my anger, it will give me an opportunity to ask God's forgiveness for my spiteful, petty demand for control. I can see the message in my anger and heed that message. I can reorient my thinking and attitude so as to comply with the authority of God, to allow Him to be in control of me and my circumstances.

The Poison of Bitterness

Most of us have been deeply hurt at some time in our lives. As you read the story of Richard's experience that opened this chapter, I am sure you could recall occasions in your own life when you were hurt. Everyone does not become bitter over such experiences. Bitterness over past wrongs is a deep, long-term form of anger. It is like a poison in your system, like a cancer of the soul spreading deadly cells throughout every aspect of your attitude. The Bible warns that a "root of bitterness" will spring up and trouble everyone around us (Heb. 12:15, NRSV).

Bitterness over past mistreatment is a complicated emotion. It can involve anger, resentment, guilt, and hatred. When you hear stories of perceived injustices, you hear some that make anger and revenge seem appropriate. I listened to two grown sisters who separately told me of abuse by their father when they were children. Through their tears they related the same story of how their bitterness had poisoned every relationship since those tragic events.

Others have told of verbal abuse, bullying, and intimidation by parents and others. Some have described neglect and indifference by family members, particularly fathers who were too busy and distracted to give the love and attention children need. Abortion forced on young girls has left them guilty, resentful, and bitter toward parents who wanted only to cover the embarrassment of a teenage pregnancy. In all these cases bitterness seems justified.

Many a Christian has been hurt over mistreatment by fellow church members. In research with the unchurched, John Savage learned that most church dropouts have been offended in some way.[1] For some it was burnout—working hard at too many assignments in the church while no one cared that they were overloaded. For others, some slight by another church member, or even the minister, caused them to leave. In most cases they still carried the bitterness that developed from the injury.

The trouble with bitterness like this is that it harms the injured person the most. The one responsible for the injury is often indifferent or unaware. Bitterness is a form of anger that seethes and boils with the desire for revenge. Bitterness means you want the guilty person to understand and experience the hurt he has caused. It is a hatred that refuses forgiveness and leaves emotional tension unresolved where that person is concerned.

There are many cases, however, when the bitterness seems unjustified. Bitterness can come because of misunderstandings. The bitter person believes he has been injured deeply. But upon hearing the story you might see that most of the offense was in his own interpretation of it. But whether warranted or trivial, the perceived injury is taken as a serious offense in the thinking of the person suffering with bitterness.

Each of us is responsible for our own attitudes. Whatever our experiences of the past, we must deal with life as it comes to us. We must accept responsibility for today's attitudes. This is the only way we can deal effectively with the baggage of yesterday's trouble.

Retelling Your Story

The most common irritants for occasional anger and long-term bitterness are other people. Without even realizing it, those around us, even loved ones, can trespass on our space. In some matter over which we feel we should have control, someone can speak too sharply, forget an appointment, laugh at something we are sensitive about, misuse a borrowed item, or do any number of other evil deeds. Some will even set out to anger us by needling, criticism, or practical jokes that aren't funny.

More serious are those offenses that leave wounds. Most of us can remember vividly those occasions in our past when we have been hurt deeply, even though some of these wounds may be years, even decades old. The old saying, "Time heals all wounds," isn't always true. When another person is at fault there is no remedy but forgiveness.

Forgiveness actually means canceling a debt. When another person offends me, I feel he is indebted to me to make it right. The anger or resentment at such a trespass is, in a sense, a demand for satisfaction of the debt. We feel the other person should make reparations, realize the harm he has done, even suffer as we have suffered. We feel we cannot just forget the hurt until some effort is made to settle accounts.

In one sense, we are trapped by our own bitterness. The guilty party may have no awareness of the hurt nor any intention to make amends. The only one stewing over the offense is me. I am the one who can't forget what happened. I am the one who goes over and over that painful story in my mind. I am the one who rehearses conversations in my mind in which the guilty party finally learns of the damage he has done. I am the one whose relationships now are affected by what happened.

Sometimes old hurts can be covered over so well by our minds that we do not remember them. Your mind tries to hide the memory so that you do not have to relive the pain. Then something will trigger a surfacing of the old story and you will realize that it has never been resolved. If that happens, go through the same steps to forgive and cancel the debt. I have seen counselees suddenly shocked as memories long buried suddenly flood to the surface, demanding attention.

The only answer is forgiveness. But by forgiveness I do not mean you are to say the misdeed is of no importance. Real forgiveness must take the offense seriously. Forgiveness does not mean covering up the wrong done. If anything, forgiveness requires you to uncover it and look at it in all its ugliness and evil.

I recommend that you write out the story of your hurt in vivid detail. So take a few pieces of paper and tell the story. Describe how it made you feel at the time and the trouble you still experience from what happened. Writing the story will usually bring back all the old emotions. The bitterness will spill over in tears and anger. You will feel a mixture of rage, self-pity, and hatred. Let the tears come. Express your bitterness in the most vivid way you can.

After you have written the story in all its sordid details, then what? You must review the biblical basis for forgiveness.

Canceling the Debt

Jesus made very clear that forgiveness is not just a virtue; it is a necessity for His followers. He taught in the Lord's Prayer that we are to ask the Father to forgive us just as we have forgiven those who have offended us (Matt. 6:12). He explained that if we forgive others the Father will forgive us (v. 14). But He went beyond that to say that if we do not forgive others, the heavenly Father will not forgive us (v. 15).

Jesus even told Peter he was to forgive without limit (Matt. 18:22). Paul then gives the basis for forgiveness, "Be ye kind one to another, tenderhearted, forgiving one another, even as God for Christ's sake hath forgiven you" (Eph. 4:32, KJV).

So our forgiveness of others is made possible by Jesus. Because He has paid the debt for all sin, including the sins of others against you and me, we can forgive. We can cancel the debt and write it off. The debt is paid, if we are willing. And just as we could never do anything to make up for our offenses, so our forgiveness can be given without requiring any restitution of the one who has hurt us.

When you finish writing the story of your hurt, move to the next step. Pray and thank God for His forgiveness and for the horrible debt paid on the cross to make it possible. Since the sins He has forgiven are covered, you need not go back over them in detail. But it is important to see where you stand as to sin and its offense. Where would you be if God had not forgiven you in Christ? Thank Him for His forgiveness as you recall just what that means, just why you needed forgiveness, and still do.

Now call upon God to witness your canceling of the debt against the one who has offended you. Visualize that person in your mind. Thank God that He loves him and that Jesus died for him. Now reach out to him and say, "I forgive you. It's over. I hold nothing against you. You are frail and sinful just as I am. Our debt is paid only by the sacrifice of Jesus. You need never know how much this has hurt me. You need never apologize or try to make it right. It's over. All the debt is canceled forever. I forgive you."

Now thank God for His grace and love to you. Thank Him that it is over. The transaction is finished. The debt is canceled. Take the written account of your hurt, write "FORGIVEN" across it, and tear it up. You may even want to burn it. By faith you have claimed the grace of God. This simple ritual will help confirm the transaction in a physical way.

Now you can have a different attitude toward the person who hurt you. You can have new freedom within your own heart and mind. Though you will not likely forget the offense, the anger will be gone. Like a wound that becomes infected, an unforgiven offense will not heal and will remain painful. But when you forgive, the infection of bitterness is gone and the wound can heal. The scar may still be there and the place may be a bit sensitive, but the pain and infection are gone.

Since emotions follow interpretation, it may take your feelings a while to catch up with the new condition. Even though you have forgiven and it is over, you may yet feel a pang of bitterness again. If you do, just affirm in prayer that you have forgiven that person completely and that it is over. Eventually your emotions will adjust to the new reality and the memory will lose its sting. Eventually you will not think of it at all.

Thinking about Control and Anger

Your natural desire for control is a God-given motivation to be responsible for authority. God intended you to take control of your world in order to establish His authority there. But your self-centered human nature aims for control that is independent from God. When that demand for independent control is threatened, your emotions of anger, resentment, and bitterness send you the warning.

Here is a summary of suggestions for dealing with the emotions in the anger cluster:

▼ Identify anger, resentment, and bitterness as threats to your own control.

▼ Honestly assess your tendency to press your control.

▼ Avoid misconceptions about the cause of anger and your responsibility for it.

▼ Recognize that anger is basically an authority issue.

▼ Ask the "reasonable expectation" questions about your anger.

▼ Deal with bitterness by following the forgiveness exercise.

Anger is a common problem. The message in the emotions of anger can help each of us deal responsibly with control. The next chapter deals with *loneliness, alienation,* and *isolation.* The message in these emotions is also vital to Christian responsibility.

▼

T E N

Does anyone really care?

▼

John Erwin was a loser. When he was six his mother gave him and his sisters up because she could not care for them. They were placed in a foster home where the father abused John's sisters, and no one would believe John when he reported it. When the truth was discovered, they were moved again.

From there he and his sisters were separated, and he was shuttled to eight different foster homes. After threatening one set of foster parents with a rifle, he was sent to an orphanage.

In the orphanage he learned to fight and became part of a gang of boys who specialized in stealing. At age fifteen he was sent to an institute for problem children, where his life was controlled by a tight schedule, a leather strap, and backbreaking work. After a year there, he was sent to the Indiana Soldiers' and Sailors' Children's Home. There he was well treated, but he had become perpetually lonely and isolated from others.

It was at this home that he found his one comfort, music. He learned to play the trombone and played in various bands and musical groups. When he received his high school diploma through the home, he got a job as a power lineman and rented a room in a small Indiana town. He was totally alone and frightened.

He received one piece of first class mail that year, his draft notice. Just as he was about to get used to his job and room, that was all taken away.

He was stationed at Fort Gordon in Augusta, Georgia. In his anger he obeyed orders just enough to get by. He spent most of his evenings and weekends alone and half-drunk, cursing the army. Six months into this lonely drudgery he noticed an ad in the paper calling for musicians to play in the Augusta Civic Orchestra. At the first rehearsal he met David Pitman. He felt drawn to him, sensing a peace and stability he had never encountered in others.

After a few rehearsals together, David invited John to his home for lessons. There he met David's wife, Rozzie, and was made to feel welcome.

John visited once a week. Then they prepared a bedroom where he could stay weekends and gave him a key to the house. They sensed the tragic loneliness and insecurity in John. He made up stories about his background because he couldn't bear to tell the truth. The Pitmans accepted whatever he told them, and they loved him.

News of the death of two of his half brothers caused John to tell the Pitmans the truth about his terrible past. They listened quietly. Finally David told him, "John, you seem to think you must straighten yourself out before you can turn to God and ask forgiveness for the hatred you've had for Him and for other people. It's not so. God loves you because you're John Erwin."

This was the first time John had heard of unconditional love. All he had known before was that you are treated well only if you earn it by behaving well. To think that you could be loved simply for yourself, without having to perform or earn it, was revolutionary to him. That night everything changed. Dave and Rozzie knelt on either side of John and prayed for him. He prayed too, receiving God's forgiveness and surrendering his life to Christ. He said that the key to his faith at that moment was the love of David Pitman, which to John was a taste of the love of God.

Somewhat to his surprise, John's conversion brought a dramatic change in his life. Over the months, his fear and anger were gone. He started to think of serving others. He enrolled in a Bible college and began to work part-time at the Cook County Jail. Then he was employed as Protestant chaplain at the jail. From the needs he saw there, he eventually established PACE Institute, a program to provide education and encouragement for inmates. "I've learned one thing in this jail," he said. "Anybody from any culture at any time can understand the power of love."[1]

The power of love. To those who are lonely and isolated from others, that phrase is just romantic fancy. To them, real life is not unlike the experience of John Erwin. Too many stories do not have happy endings. Millions of lonely people spend day after day cut off from the warmth and nurture of loving companionship. Though most of us do not experience such a radical isolation, we all feel the alienation and loneliness from time to time.

In this chapter we will examine the cluster of emotional pain associated with loneliness. The key issue is *companionship*. How can we find love and care, that sense of belonging and acceptance we long for? There is a message in those feelings of loneliness, alienation, and isolation.

The Pain of Loneliness

The primary emotions in the loneliness cluster are *alienation*, *loneliness*, and *isolation*. These feelings carry a message of threat to the intimacy and nurture in companionship. The Monitor, ever diligent where your interests are concerned, spots some circumstance or event that threatens this desire for companionship. So he triggers an emotional alarm that you are threatened in that area.

We have all experienced it, being cut off from the companionship that we desire. An argument takes place, with angry words, and even though you move about in the same house the companionship is broken. Or physical separation distances us from the touch, the laugh, the idle conversation of the ones we love.

Def•i•ni'tion: Loneliness, Alienation, Isolation

Loneliness is the sadness and self-pity we feel in the absence of companionship. This is the more passive form of emotional pain in the area of relationships.

The more active form of this distress is *alienation*, the sense of distance and loss, perhaps hostility, when a companionship is threatened by conflict.

The unresolved ongoing form is the feeling of *isolation*, a sense of abandonment and desertion in which no one seems to care whether we live or die.

The more active form of this emotion is *alienation*. This is a feeling of sadness, and sometimes hostility, we sometimes experience when we are "at outs" with someone else. At this point we can deal with it before our relationships deteriorate even further.

You have a serious argument with a good friend and the Monitor sends out a warning that you are threatened with the loss of a friendship. In normal relationships this kind of trouble will arise from time to time. Though the threat can be real, the rift between yourself and someone you care about can serve to strengthen the relationship.

There were harsh words between you and your wife this morning. You felt that mixture of anger and sadness when you left for work. There was no kiss. Not even much of a good-bye. The emotional signals come in waves. After a while you realize that the argument was over nothing of importance. But now you cannot do your work. There is a wall between you and a beloved companion. You know you love her. Even though you do not ordinarily see her all day, you miss her. The barrier has come between you, whether she is present or not.

Another form of emotional pain in the relationship area is *loneliness*. Whereas alienation is a sense of brokenness in a relationship, loneliness is the more passive sadness of missing companionship. While alienation relates more to specific conflict with others, loneliness can arise with or without conflict. Loneliness is that sadness you feel in the absence of companionship. Loneliness is not only the feeling of *wanting* another, it is the feeling of *not being wanted* by another.

Loneliness can come over you just because you come home and there is no one there. You wanted to tell him about what happened today but he is off golfing, completely unaware that you need him close just now. Loneliness involves an element of self-pity. You feel sorry for yourself because you are alone and no one seems to care that you are alone. This occasional sense of abandonment is normal. Our desire for companionship naturally means that the loss of it is a threat. If you realize what is taking place in this process, you can identify why you feel the way you do.

If alienation and loneliness are not addressed, the distress moves into a more troubling level. The unresolved trouble becomes a sense of *isolation*, of being forsaken by others. This is the case for many elderly people who are shut in or live in nursing homes and wait day after day for someone to visit or call. In one study almost half the widows over fifty said loneliness was their worst problem. Researchers discovered that elderly men are loneliest of all, particularly those with some infirmity who live alone.[2]

Psychologist Robert Weiss has identified three basic forms of isolation. The first form he calls *emotional isolation*. This refers to that lack of a psychologically intimate relationship with another person or persons. This is that sense of utter aloneness or abandonment. The second form is *social isolation*, when a person has no supportive network of friends. He feels left out, on the margin of life, without a sense of significance. A third form of isolation is *existential isolation*, the feeling that life has no meaning, that one is alienated from God. This is described vividly by existentialist writers who picture man alone in all the universe as a thinking being.[3]

The cluster of emotional pain centered in loneliness is familiar to us all. *Loneliness*, *alienation*, and *isolation* are the normal results of the loss of meaningful companionship. Understanding the dynamics of these emotions and the message they carry can open the way to dealing responsibly with relationships.

Symptoms of Alienation

The cluster of emotions around loneliness signals a threat to your desire for companionship. Sometimes the threat to companionship may go beyond the occasional conflict with a loved one or unwanted hour of solitude. The emotional message may also indicate a failure of responsibility in the area of relationships. Instead of being occasional, the trouble can become chronic. In order to understand the emotional pain that results from a failure of responsibility in the area of relationships, let's consider some of the symptoms of the chronically alienated person.

The chronically alienated person normally experiences tension and stress in relationships with others. Satisfying and meaningful relationships are characterized by peace and freedom. When relationships are strained, the sense of peace and freedom is gone. Peace in relationships is the settledness and serenity that accompanies good companionship. Freedom in relationships is the joy of not having to be on guard with another person. These are the positive experiences in relationships that are missing for the chronically alienated person. He or she instead experiences tension and stress in one or more ongoing relationships.

The chronically alienated person often is in conflict with others. It is not uncommon for us to have differences of opinion and short-term stress in fellowship with other people. This conflict, however, can become a normal and ongoing experience. When this happens a person can realize he or she is experiencing a failure of responsibility in the area of relationships. If I encounter recurring conflict with various people, the attention should focus on the one who is the common factor, me. It means that at some point I am failing to deal properly with relationships.

The chronically alienated person blames loneliness on the "fact" that no one cares for him or her. As with each of the other areas, one of the common symptoms is denying responsibility and blaming the problem on others. This is a mistake that cuts to the very heart of loving relationships. To expect the other person to provide the necessary attention, care, and acceptance for a positive relationship is to fail to accept personal responsibility for that relationship. As we have said repeatedly, we are responsible for every area of our lives, including relationships. Shifting the blame to others, however they may have failed, denies the need for a change on our part and insures that the troublesome conflict will continue.

The chronically alienated person longs to be loved but is repeatedly disappointed in others' failure to meet his or her needs. Meaningful relationships meet both persons' need for acceptance and understanding.

Many young couples think that getting married will fulfill these needs. The husband thinks his wife will be able to meet his needs, and vice versa. The young bride says, "I just know I am going to be so happy." The groom may put it, "She's everything I've been looking for." While this sounds very romantic and complimentary, these comments may reveal that each one sees the other as the answer to his or her needs. Though they want to meet each other's needs, each runs into trouble when demanding that the other meet their needs. That never works.

Symptoms of Alienation

▼ Tension and stress in relationships with others
▼ Often in conflict with others
▼ Blames loneliness on others' lack of care
▼ Longs to be loved but is repeatedly disappointed
▼ Approaches relationships in terms of own needs
▼ Resents the neglect of those who should meet his or her needs
▼ Little or no success maintaining close friendships
▼ Sees self as a helpless victim of others' rejection

The chronically alienated person has little or no success maintaining close friendships. Friendships take place on several levels. At the deepest level, the person who is my best friend can know me at my worst and accept me anyway. This kind of relationship is demanding, requiring self-giving and mutual availability. Most friendships, however, are not at that level. They are more casual, involving less disclosure and requiring less attention. The person who does not want to get involved in the ongoing responsibility of real friendships will back away when friendships become too demanding.

The chronically alienated person approaches relationships with others in terms of his own needs rather than the other person's needs. No one wants to be friends with people who approach relationships only for what they can get from them. Not only are these people boring and self-centered, they tend to drain the energy of everyone around them. They are "social vampires." As they try to draw care and love from people around them, they further alienate themselves as others withdraw from their presence. Eventually they experience the rejection they have come to expect. Instead of learning to give friendship, they are always seeking to take it.

One strategy of the "social vampire" is to overwhelm a new acquaintance with friendship through phone calls, gifts, cards, and special outings. It does not take long for the other person to realize that she is being smothered and cannot fulfill that level of exclusive friendship. She will have to back away, usually provoking a series of manipulative comments like, "I thought you were my friend. But I guess I was wrong."

The chronically alienated person most often sees herself as a helpless victim of others' rejection. The person who suffers the symptoms of alienation and loneliness will often be the last one to know why her relationships are not fulfilling. The self-centeredness that tries to draw everything from others is the same outlook that causes her to be blind to the fact that she herself is the problem in the relationships. She is convinced that she is lonely because no one cares for her. This wrong thinking is a vicious trap that brings misery to many a lonely and alienated person.

How We Get This Way

A description of the alienated and lonely person gives each of us a glimpse of ourselves. Even though we don't see all these symptoms in ourselves, we see ourselves to some extent in the symptoms. The basic assumptions, the attitudes, and the distress experienced by the lonely person are all too familiar. But how do people get on the wrong track in their approach to relationships? Consider some of the causes.

In the first place, it is *our nature to be self-centered*. We bring to all our relationships a natural tendency to use people for our own satisfaction rather than give something to them. We set out to find someone to love us, to care for us, to meet our needs. Though there are instincts for self-giving, these do not often prevail. Unless we are trained in the qualities of unselfishness, gentleness, and kindness, giving will not come naturally.

The corrupted nature of man naturally tends to shift the focus from God to self. In seizing independence and autonomy by taking the forbidden fruit, the original couple lost that intimate relationship with God in which they were loved and nurtured. Ever since Adam and Eve were forced from the garden, their children have searched for the love that was lost. So they try to find it in human companionship, latching onto others with a relational hunger that cannot be satisfied.

Your approach to relationships is not only corrupted by a self-seeking nature, it is further *warped by faulty programming*. All you have experienced to this point is in your mental computer as "the way things are." Your background determines who you are and how you deal with your world. The way you grew up and how you were treated as a child have shaped your approach to relationships. You will be wary of any approach that is inconsistent with what you think you already know.

Children have three basic needs in their development if they are to be prepared for healthy relationships. (1) They need to feel attached, that they belong. (2) They need to feel accepted and affirmed in their value. (3) They need to learn social skills. When children grow up in a family where there is little expression of affection, they will have a hard time expressing affection as adults. If they are not accepted and affirmed, they will be unsure of themselves in relationships. If they do not have good models for social skills, they will be awkward and ill at ease.

We relate to others in the way we have learned. And "learning" is the key word here. Though our natural inclinations move us in certain directions, we can learn to relate to others in more fulfilling ways. If young parents want to be courteous, thoughtful, and self-giving for the sake of their children, they will have to break new ground, and it will be a difficult task. But it is the only way to provide their children with the demonstration of a fulfilling relational model.

A background of abusive relationships can cause an adult to be closed and distant with friendships. She fears to make herself vulnerable again to the hurt and disappointment of being used. On the other hand, some respond by searching so diligently for the love they never had that they are suckers for more abuse. Remember the woman at Sychar? Jesus said to her, "You have had five husbands, and the man you now have is not your husband" (John 4:18). The longing for nurturing and intimacy is a powerful force, but the foolish reactions of human nature make it a destructive force as well.

Many a couple has learned the lesson of "the twig" in adopting a child out of an abusive background. A child no older than five or six is already proof that "as the twig is bent, so grows the tree." In spite of the new environment and the affection of the adoptive parents, these little ones sometimes are not capable of receiving affection and nurturing. It does not compute with their programming; it is a foreign experience, an unrealistic idea. Change may take some time, but love can eventually prevail.

Now that we have reviewed the emotional pain of alienation, loneliness, and isolation, we will move on to God's answer. We will see that what we long for cannot be found until we accept God's love and set out to be agents of that love for the needs of others.

▼

ELEVEN

Keys to companionship

▼

Gloria Gaither has a poem entitled "When Did I Start to Love You?" In it she describes the caring and attention her husband has given through the years, the shared joys and sorrows that have drawn them ever closer together. It is a wonderful picture of loving companionship.

I would like to feel every day as I feel when I hear that poem. I would like to be able to draw upon that feeling and be my best giving, caring, loving self. But the inspiration dissolves at the first challenge, and I find myself with a different set of emotions. I quickly become distracted and inattentive. The people around me become more the objects of my irritation than my affection.

After all, just think of the way people are. They are hard to love. Some people are unlovable only some of the time. Some are unlovable almost all the time. Even those we love best are often irritating and disagreeable.

In this chapter we will examine the nature of love from a uniquely Christian viewpoint. The premise is that love of the sort the Bible describes does not come naturally to us. It is contrary to our self-centered bias, even the opposite of our normal inclinations. When the fall of mankind shifted the center of human relationships away from God, real godly love was lost. Now it must be learned and intentionally applied. Instead of creating love, we are to be agents of the love of God.

If we are to pursue companionship with others in a uniquely Christian way, we will need to understand Christian love and see how that love behaves. We need to know how love thinks and how it expresses itself in the very human situations we each face day by day. We must take the mystery out of the idea of Christian love and see it in the real terms God uses.

"This is how we know what love is: Jesus Christ laid down his life for us. And we ought to lay down our lives for our brothers" (1 John 3:16). This verse says we can know what love is by looking at Jesus Christ. In Jesus we can see how love relates to others. In Jesus we can see the motives and attitudes of love. In Jesus we can see love's basic method of operation in the serious business of life and its challenges.

Paul also sought to define love. In 1 Corinthians 13 he describes love as "the most excellent way." The greatest gifts of God and the most complete dedication of the believer are nothing without love. Love is described in terms of its attitude. It is patient, kind, does not envy, does not boast, is not proud. It is not rude, nor self-seeking, nor easily angered, nor vengeful, nor delighting in evil. Rather love delights in the truth. It always protects, trusts, hopes, and perseveres. It never fails.

Jesus spoke often about love. He also lived out the meaning of love. As His own execution drew near, He met with the disciples for a private time at the Passover meal. To their amazement, He got up from the table, took off His robe, wrapped a towel around His waist, and began to wash their feet (John 13).

This was His example to them, more eloquently spoken than words could have done. He, their Lord, took on the role of a servant and treated them like His superiors. He ministered to them, addressing their needs, getting His hands dirty with their uncleanness. This was love acted out so that they would never forget it.

Responsibility for Relationships

Because God is relational, He made us *relational*, able to interact in a meaningful way with other persons and with God. With this aspect of human nature came the desire for *companionship*. A threat to this desire is signaled by the emotions of *alienation, loneliness,* and *isolation.* Acting responsibly in the area of relationships calls for learning and implementing the strategies of self-giving *love*.

So a Christian must not think that being kinder or nicer or sweeter is what this new love is about. The Christian life is not just a better *quality* of life; it is a different *kind* of life. It turns our natural self-centeredness inside out. Ours is a new identity centered in Christ instead of ourselves. From that perspective, our desire for companionship takes on a new meaning.

The Desire for Companionship

Built into our human nature is the desire for companionship. God made us in His own image, personal as He is personal. The Creation account says that God said it was not good for the man to be alone. To address this problem He made the woman to be his companion. His intention was that they experience not only the intimacy and nurturing of His love, but that Adam and Eve also find fulfillment in their relationship with each other. They were to love each other as He loved them.

Man's God-given desire for companionship was meant to be satisfied by giving love. But the contamination of sin corrupted his whole being and he became self-centered instead of God-centered. So now, twisted and confused about his own needs and their fulfillment, he sets out to find companionship for his own good. His view of life is so restricted to self that his natural inclination is to use others to meet his needs. He tries to find someone to love him, friends to care for him, someone to provide that affection and attention he longs for. But this self-serving approach proves frustrating because others do not want to be used.

There are all levels and kinds of companionship—from the very casual relationship with a neighbor you hardly know to the very intimate one with your wife or husband, from the structured association of fellow workers to the accidental company of a seatmate on a plane, from a formal involvement with the board chairman to the easygoing fellowship at a family gathering. In every case, however, we have an inherent need for human companionship.

Our inherent desire for companionship is actually a longing for what it brings with it, the good we derive from good relationships with others. Let me suggest four qualities of companionship that we all need: *belonging, acceptance, trust,* and *intimacy.* Relationships that do not involve these benefits are tasteless and empty.

The Need for Belonging

Relationships with others give us a sense of social identity. The groups or individuals we associate with reveal who we are. The old saying, "Birds of a feather flock together," is an acknowledgment of this desire. If I am around a group of people with whom I have little or nothing in common, I feel out of place, defensive, and isolated.

I can tell you who I am by naming my circles of belonging—evangelical, academic, conservative. But more significant than these is the sense of "owning" and being "owned" in the relationships I have. In my family I belong. In my neighborhood I belong. Among my colleagues in teaching I belong. Whatever the level of companionship I have in these connections, I derive a sense of identity and place from them.

The Need for Acceptance

A second benefit of companionship is the sense of acceptance I receive. Others with whom I am associated accept me as I am. Whatever their judgment of my personality and character, they receive me. In doing so they endorse me as a person and attribute value to me. They affirm me as a worthy person to know and be associated with.

Just as *belonging* gives me a sense of place, *acceptance* gives me a sense of value. Acceptance is obviously tied to self-esteem. Companionship dramatically affects my own sense of self-worth. People have recognized this need for companionship for centuries, using the ban of companionship to punish those who violated society's laws. Those under a ban were considered nonpersons, not to be acknowledged or associated with in any way. In primitive cultures a violator would often feel he had ceased to exist and would eventually wander off in the jungle and die. Acceptance by others is necessary to life.

The Need for Trust

Companionship meets a third need in every person, the need to *trust* others and *be trusted*. In healthy relationships there is an implied covenant of expected behavior. Your neighbors expect you to honor their property and their peace and quiet. Your coworkers expect you to carry your part of the work load. Your family expects you to be consistent, supportive, and caring. Even strangers in public places expect certain behavior of one another. This often unspoken social covenant is an important element in companionship.

We need to be trusted, and we need to be able to trust others. This is why we experience such anger and grief when close friends turn against us. Unfaithfulness in marriage is a blow as serious to the wronged partner as he or she can experience. It is not only a rejection of the faithful spouse's love, it is a violation of the trust they shared. Relationships of trust give a sense of security, a confidence and fortitude against the threats to our well being that loom all around us.

The Need for Intimacy

A fourth benefit of healthy companionship is *intimacy*. The depth of relationships is measured in intimacy. My best friends are those with whom I am most intimate. Before we are willing for a relationship to move to an intimate level, we must be assured of the belonging, acceptance, and trust described above. The familiarity and freedom you have with another is a matter of intimacy. It is only with my wife that I have such intimacy that our relationship has blurred the borderline between "I" and "we."

In one sense the key to intimacy is mutual disclosure. Of course disclosure alone does not make for intimacy. Sharon met a young man in a physician's waiting room who told her his whole life story and all his problems, though she did not even know his name. This disclosure on his part was a desperate effort to find intimacy such as he might have with a parent or wife. Real intimacy calls for disclosure by both persons because they belong to one another in some way and they accept and trust each other. It is a delicate process of blending their lives to the degree the relationship requires.

The benefits of companionship are what we generally call love—the belonging that gives a sense of place, the acceptance that gives value, the trust that gives security, and the intimacy that allows oneness. For all these desires the ultimate fulfillment will come only through a personal relationship with God through Jesus Christ. This relationship with God has the qualities of belonging, acceptance, trust, and intimacy. It also creates such a change in the heart of a person that he is able to relate to others in more meaningful ways.

Misconceptions about Relationships

Companionship, as we are using the term here, refers to a wide range of relationships. It is the intimacy and love of a good marriage. It is the casual fellowship we enjoy sitting on the same bench with a stranger at the mall. It is the camaraderie of coworkers on a team project. It is family laughing around the dinner table. We are made for such companionships, whatever their level of intimacy.

There are a number of misconceptions about companionship that reflect our natural biases. Our self-centeredness causes a warped approach to life, which, in turn, results in a set of ideas about "the way things are." Some of these ideas are faulty and will keep us from the companionship God intended for us. Let's consider some of these misconceptions and their results.

Loneliness is caused by being alone. Though this sounds right at first hearing, it is not true. Being alone can often be a refreshing retreat to think and meditate. On the other hand, you can be in a vast crowd and still be lonely. Working downtown in a big city can put you in contact with more than twenty thousand people every day. This overexposure to others can actually cause you to shut them out and begin not to see them as persons at all. So it is not the presence of others that dispels loneliness; it is companionship with others that does it.

Love is a "spell" that comes over you, and you have no control over it. The popular idea of falling in love portrays love as something that happens to you. It is seen as fully emotional, with little reason or volition involved. Other cultures are often amazed at the American concept of "falling in love." In *The Road Less Traveled*, psychiatrist M. Scott Peck says that falling in love is irrational, a suspension of the normal boundaries of the self.[1] But the experience of "falling in love" is not what I mean by love. Real love has a reasoning and deciding element as well as an emotional element. It is not something that happens to you so much as something you express in action toward another person.

Good relationships, even in marriage, should be a fifty-fifty arrangement. There is much truth in this idea. If we mean a sharing of the load and helping each other across normal job assignment lines, it is surely true. Marriage should be a partnership in which both husband and wife carry their weight. But if we mean that my share in the relationship is only 50 percent, then we are wrong. If I limit my effort to wait and see what my partner will do, I am reacting instead of acting. If I try to carry my load 100 percent of the time, I might be successful 50 percent of the time in meeting my partner's needs. My commitment to the relationship must be 100 percent. I am wiser to focus on my responsibilities rather than measuring the efforts of my partner.

Conflict means that a relationship is not right for you and should be ended. Normal relationships will suffer conflicts. No two people can get along perfectly all the time. There will be misunderstandings and offenses. The goal is not to avoid conflict at all costs but to resolve conflict as soon as possible, whatever it takes. Relationships grow through hard times in ways they do not when all is harmonious. Though we should never give up trying to maintain harmony, neither should we give up when conflict comes. The real test of love may be how we respond when we are in conflict with the one we love.

If you do not love a person anymore, it is wrong for you to stay in that relationship. The basis for this idea is that love in a marriage is based on emotion. When the emotion fades, the romance is gone and the real basis for the marriage is over. I have counseled many a person who said something like this, "He has killed all the love I ever had for him." Or maybe the explanation was, "I don't know what happened, Pastor. Somehow we have just drifted apart over the years." If marriage is based on the emotional level of affection, it is easy to see why half of them end in divorce. Marriage is hard work. Love calls for planning and sacrifice. Emotion will follow commitment and investment.

If you really love someone, you will try to make him or her happy. On the face of it, this is obviously a true statement. Love for another person will call for doing the good things that please that person. But the idea runs aground when used as an effort to manipulate another. Here is the reasoning: "If you love me, you will make me happy. Now here is what I want. If you love me, you will do it my way." Another failure of this idea comes when parents set out to make their children happy instead of training them in character. Sometimes the most responsible and loving thing parents can do will make their children very unhappy. So the happiness test for loving action will not work.

In relationships it is best to let your heart guide you. There are times when your "heart," meaning your emotions, can guide you in the right direction. But if you follow your heart all the time, you will get into serious trouble. Emotions can take relationships on a roller coaster ride of uncertainty. A more stable and dependable guide is a clear understanding of the responsibilities of friendship and love. Sometimes we must act in direct conflict with our emotions. The true story in the film *Tough Love* is a clear example. With hearts breaking, the parents locked their rebellious son out, refused to help when he was jailed, and let him live in poverty. Emotionally wrenching as it was, this approach finally brought him home to responsible behavior.

Physical intimacy is an indication of real love. There are two sides to this idea. On the one hand, those who are promiscuous would admit that "one-night stands" are not love. Their reasons for being promiscuous may be related to their own unwillingness to make a commitment. To them one night of pleasure does not require responsibility. On the other hand are those who confuse the passion of physical intimacy with love. This is the stirred-up teenaged boy's reasoning: "If you love me, you'll go all the way with me." If his date is not better prepared with moral standards of her own, she may fall for that line.

Physical intimacy is a wonderful aspect of the marriage relationship. God intended it for that covenant alone. For any other relationship it is out of order. Sex as the sole means to self-satisfaction is never what God intended, even within marriage. It is meant to be a sharing of the most intimate physical experience for the delight it brings to each partner and the expression it gives to their oneness and their commitment to each other.

When our desire for companionship is threatened, the alienation, loneliness and isolation warn us to address the problem. Though our self-centered human nature will respond in self-defeating ways, we can learn to love. In the next chapter we will examine biblical principles for the love God intended for us.

▼

TWELVE

Learning to love

▼

James Marsh just couldn't love his Aunt Alice. He couldn't even like her. On his trips back home, however, he felt an obligation to make a call on his father's sister. But his Christian intentions seemed to wilt every time she answered the door of her apartment. Instead of greeting her nephew with a smile, she would open the door with her customary scowl. She was naturally abrasive and chronically critical.

"Oh, it's you," she would say. "C'mon in." Then she would immediately begin to berate James about the rest of his large family, complaining that few of them came to see her, and the ones who did wouldn't stay. Inevitably he would find himself reacting to her complaints and accusations. Within minutes he would be snapping back at her and wind up leaving upset.

Back home in Atlanta, James put Aunt Alice out of his mind. He then attended a conference where the speaker talked about giving up resentment and asking God to forgive you. He prayed for his aunt and asked God to help him love her. She had criticized him last time for sending her Scripture references to read. On his next visit he was determined to refuse taking the bait of her critical remarks.

He took a deep breath before her apartment door and prayed that God would allow him to love her in spite of her caustic personality. She greeted him with the same sarcasm and accusations. "Oh, it's you," she said. "Come on in. Your father hasn't been down in months. Why?" As she went through a list of uncaring relatives, James refused to take the bait. He suggested they have the usual Irish soda bread and tea and play some Scrabble.

He asked her to tell him about when she was a telephone operator. She began to tell stories of years gone by. Here was a strong woman who had been through a hard life. Instead of reacting to her irritating comments, James really focused his attention on his aunt as a person. Instead of backing away from her as he was inclined to do, he had moved toward her in love, and the results were amazing.[1]

This story presents us with two vital observations in the area of relationships. First, Aunt Alice had no idea why her family members did not visit her. She was obviously lonely but blamed it on everyone else, while they all knew why everyone stayed away. Second, James found that his natural response to his irascible aunt was not helpful and surely not what he wanted as a Christian. He had to plan a deliberate strategy that went against his natural reactions.

Alienation, loneliness, and isolation are painful emotions. But there is a definite message in them. For the chronically lonely like Aunt Alice, it is a warning of failure of responsibility in the area of relationships. Even for someone occasionally alienated like James, it was a warning of the same thing. Each of them needed a strategy for genuine love. Let's consider some elements of such a strategy. Since self-giving love doesn't come naturally to us, we will have to learn it.

Strategies for Love

The Bible's teachings about love are often dramatic in their contrast with our normal ideas about love. Let's consider five principles from Scripture to guide the attitudes and actions of love.

Christian love is an expression of faith rather than passion. At the very beginning we must recognize that the kind of love we are commanded to give is not natural to us. It is not an emotion of affection and warmth. It is rather an attitude in which you intend to do good to others, in spite of their actions toward you or your own feelings in the matter. This love is based on the confidence that God will ultimately set everything right.

The Bible says that "God has poured out his love into our hearts by the Holy Spirit" (Rom. 5:5). John writes, "Let us love one another, for love comes from God" (1 John 4:7). This love is supernatural, deposited in our lives by the Spirit. Ours is not to create it but to release it. We do so by acting in love. As we take the action, God will release the love. This means moving toward the other person, even when you want to withdraw. It means acting, even when you do not feel like it. It is a matter of faith, of trusting God to pour out His love through you.

Christian love calls for acting instead of reacting. Some of Jesus' most remarkable teachings about love are about loving your "enemies" (Luke 6:27–36). He describes them as those who hate you, those who curse you, those who mistreat you. He even pictures the situation in which you are struck in the face and your coat is taken from you by force. In all these cases, He instructs His followers to love, to bless, to pray for, and to give to their "enemies."

So Christian love cannot be held hostage to mistreatment. We are to act in love regardless of the way others treat us. If we can do this under such extreme conditions as Jesus describes, surely we can act in love with much less provocation. Our love too often withers before such minor matters as a sarcastic comment, a misunderstanding, a repulsive lifestyle, or an irritating manner. We are to stop before we *react* to such disappointments so we can choose how to *act*. We must override the natural system.

Christian love is others-oriented rather than self-oriented. It is natural for us to be preoccupied with our own personal concerns. These are the details of our life: work, family, health, children, marriage, home, car, entertainment, vacation, shopping, and so on. We have to keep up with all this, so it is normal to think about them much of the time. As a result, we bring the same agenda to our relationships with others. This is what we are concerned about, so this is what we talk about.

Strategies of Love

- ▼ Christian love is motivated by faith rather than passion.
- ▼ Christian love calls for acting instead of reacting.
- ▼ Christian love is others-oriented not self-oriented.
- ▼ Christian love addresses others' needs instead of your own.
- ▼ Christian love aims to give rather than to gain.

The problem is that other people are preoccupied with *their* own personal concerns. To act in love toward them, you will have to set aside your own personal concerns for the time and focus on theirs. Otherwise no ministry can take place. You must switch from your channel to their channel, deliberately paying attention to the details of their life. This is not hard with your children because their interests are yours as well. It takes real thought with those outside the family circle. It takes listening. It takes leaving your own worries in the hands of God so you can give attention to one who needs His love through you.

Christian love addresses the other person's needs instead of your own. Most of us think of love in terms of being loved rather than giving love. We know what love is, what it means to have someone else love us. We know because we have a need for such love, for the companionship that brings belonging, acceptance, trust, and intimacy. It is normal, then, for us to approach every relationship in terms of our needs. We desire companionship so that our own needs can be met.

The agenda for Christian love is the need of the other person. Since your own needs have been completely met by the perfect, unconditional love of Christ, then you are able to express Christian love for someone else's needs. You are the agent of God's love. Real ministry takes place when the grace of God in you touches the need in another. Love does not act only when it is convenient, but as the need requires.

A delightful older lady in the church was generous to help when there was a need. Her specialty was pies, so she inevitably made a pie for every occasion of need. Once a whole family came down with the flu. She went to see them, bringing a pie. The sick family gagged at the sight of the pie, but it didn't matter; she did pies. Real Christian love, however, will take a cue from the need of the other person.

Christian love aims to give rather than to gain. We usually see relationships as a "give and take" matter. Friendships, marriages, and other ongoing relationships are said to be a "two-way street" or a "fifty-fifty relationship." But Jesus' instructions place the full responsibility on us to give, even when there is no take. He says very simply, "Give to everyone who asks you, and if anyone takes what belongs to you, do not demand it back" (Luke 6:30). Here He expresses a basic principle that is essential to the Christian life, that our energy is to flow in the giving direction.

Jesus even goes so far as to say that we are to give to the person who forcefully takes our things from us. If we can maintain a giving strategy toward those who violently take what is ours, surely we can make giving our primary strategy with friends and family. His promise is clear that God will ultimately set it right. The real givers will be rewarded to overflowing (Luke 6:38).

A handicapped woman who was unable to get out began to write notes of encouragement to others in her church. It was something she could do, despite being shut in. Eventually she received letters, calls, and visits from those grateful for her love. She gave what she could and God kept His promise.

Four Levels of Love

It is helpful to think of relationships in terms of levels of intimacy. Sometimes it is difficult to know how love might behave in various kinds of relationships. Even though we may want to practice the attitudes and actions of love, the rather casual contact we have with most people makes it difficult. Let me suggest four *levels of love* that describe increasing intimacy and sacrifice on your part.

The Love of Acknowledgment

The first level of love calls for *acknowledgment* of the other person. This is simply some gesture that says, "I see you there as another person touching my life." This expression of love is for all levels of intimacy, but it is all that may be required at the most casual level. As you see another person you can smile, greet her, be courteous, pay attention to her.

Jesus said, "If you love those who love you, what reward will you get? Are not even the tax collectors doing that? And if you greet only your brothers, what are you doing more than others? Do not even pagans do that?" (Matt. 5:46–47) Here Jesus applies loving others to a simple greeting. As a Christian meets another person, he or she comes into contact with another individual made in the image of God. Even at a casual level, you can release the love of God by a greeting that focuses on the other person.

You are probably able to remember an occasion when someone greeted you in an outgoing and enthusiastic way, which, surprisingly, made you uncomfortable. You realized something was wrong but could not identify what it was. I have been greeted that way. As I think about it now, I realize that the person with the overenthusiastic greeting was not really paying attention to me. He was just being self-assertive and perhaps self-important.

I have also been greeted in another quite different way. This person spoke to me as though he had been looking forward to meeting me, though I knew that couldn't be the case. He looked me carefully in the eyes, not glancing about to see who else was there to talk with. He shook my hand and held it a bit longer than usual while he asked me about myself. It was obvious that he was actually giving me his full attention, as though at this moment I was the most important person in the world.

We often find ourselves so preoccupied with our own personal concerns that we do not even see the people around us. You know they are there, but you do not see them as human beings God wants to love through you. Instead of seeing the person in front of me at the checkout line as another person touching my life, I more often see her as someone who delays me by her presence.

Even in so mundane a matter as going to the grocery store you can pray, "Lord, somebody important to You will touch my life today. Who will be that person? Don't let me fail to be in touch with You and allow Your love to be released through me." Then, as you go about your activities, you will be looking at the faces, reading what you can see in the eyes, the expression, the body language, focusing the love of God in simple acknowledgment.

The Love of Acceptance

The second level of love moves in closer to a more intimate relationship. At this level the expression of love is *acceptance*. This has to do with receiving others just as they are, without placing conditions they must meet. This unconditional love is what Jesus commanded when He said, "You have heard that it was said, 'Love your neighbor and hate your enemy.' But I tell you: Love your enemies and pray for those who persecute you, that you may be sons of your Father in heaven" (Matt. 5:43–45).

Jesus is reminding His hearers that the normal human behavior is to love your family and friends but to hate your enemies. This is just the way things are. Everybody knows that. In light of the common view, Jesus' instructions were probably something of a shock to His hearers. Love your enemies? Who ever heard of such an idea? But in reality, relating to others is like buying used furniture. Most of the time the sale tag says "as is."

It is obvious that Christian love goes against the grain of our natural inclinations. Even in our relationships with family and friends, we tend to express self-centered love. Instead of accepting family members as they are, we often demand that they meet our expectations, and we withhold our affection any time they do not measure up. To accept others unconditionally means to allow a wide margin for error. It means that we do not demand that they be who we want them to be. We must accept them as they are, just as God has accepted us.

The Love of Affirmation

We have seen that love moves from acknowledgment to acceptance. Now we come to the third level in which the expression of love is *affirmation*. Whereas acceptance of others means you receive them as they are, *affirmation* means you endorse them with your own friendship. Affirmation does not require that you approve everything about the person, but it does risk your reputation by having you stand with him or her as a friend.

Jesus was criticized most for associating with the wrong kind of people. He ate with "sinners," that religious category of persons who did not observe the ritual requirements of the Law. Though He never condoned sin by anyone, He did affirm sinners and express His love for them. He said, even as He commented on His visit with Zacchaeus, "the Son of Man came to seek and to save what was lost" (Luke 19:10). He was on a mission to find just such "sinners" and bring them to the Father.

Whereas acceptance is receiving others into your life, affirmation is the idea of your moving into their lives. You enter their space and identify with them on their own territory. This is what Jesus did in going to the home of Zacchaeus for a meal with his friends. He was saying, "I am not too good for your house and your food and your friends. I do not stand aloof from you. I bring the love of God where you are."

Jesus said to His disciples just before He returned to the Father and left them with His mission on earth, "As the Father has sent me, I am sending you" (John 20:21). His was a mission into the world of sin to rescue those held in bondage there. To accomplish that mission He affirmed people by becoming one with them. He did not shout God's instructions from a safe distance. He walked off into the world's darkness with His arm around humanity's shoulder.

121

The Love of Atonement

Following the example of Jesus we express God's love in acknowledgment, acceptance, and affirmation. But Jesus went further yet to offer atonement for us. He sacrificed His own life to cover our sins and bring us to God. He said, "This is My commandment, that you love one another as I have loved you. Greater love has no one than this, than to lay down one's life for his friends" (John 15:12–13, NKJV).

In His atonement Jesus acted in a unique way we can never duplicate. Nevertheless, atonement is a model of our own calling to self-sacrifice in behalf of others. Jesus died for our sins. He also calls on every Christian to "deny himself, and take up his cross, and follow Me. For whoever desires to save his life will lose it, but whoever loses his life for My sake will find it" (Matt. 16:24–25, NKJV).

For Jesus, the cross meant intentional, vicarious sacrifice. Can it mean something else for us? "Intentional" indicates that He acted as a matter of personal choice. "Vicarious" means on behalf of others. "Sacrifice" points to the cost, even of life. If this is what Jesus meant by "take up your cross," it is the highest expression of Christian love. Atonement means our willing sacrifice for another to release God's love to him or her.

What will love as atonement mean for you? I cannot say. But it will involve giving up your own wants for the needs of another. It may involve giving up your needs for the needs of another. It may even involve giving up your needs for the wants of another. It will begin with those closest to you. You will take up the towel and tray of servanthood. You will allow the needs of others to set the agenda for your service. You will ask, "What does he or she need from me at this moment?" You will release the love of God for that need.

Acknowledgment might be visualized as a smile and a hand raised in greeting. Acceptance can be pictured as hands reaching out toward others to receive them. For affirmation, imagine an arm around the shoulders as the two of you walk off together. For atonement, there can only be the image of the outstretched arms of Jesus on the cross. Each progressive level of involvement calls for more commitment and service to the other person. Each releases God's love in a greater portion.

An Action Plan

Alienation, loneliness, and isolation are warnings of a threat to your companionships. They can also be a warning that your own thinking is faulty about relationships. They can be an alarm to remind you that companionship is found in seeking to give love, not find it. Love will come to you when you give it away to meet the needs of those around you. You are to be an agent of the love of God who poured out His love in your heart by the Holy Spirit.

If you are to act in love, you will need to apply these principles in your relationships with others:

▼ Receive the love of Christ and allow Him to meet all your needs through an intimate love relationship with Him.

▼ Determine to be an agent of the love of God.

▼ Love by faith and not according to your feelings.

▼ Decide how you will act instead of reacting to others.

▼ Be a good listener as you focus on others.

▼ Let another's needs set the agenda for your love.

▼ Give with no thought of return, trusting God.

▼ Practice acknowledging others in love.

▼ Accept others unconditionally.

▼ Give the affirmation that endorses others.

▼ Be ready to make sacrifices for the sake of others.

Remember, this prescription for the emotional pain of alienation, loneliness, and isolation is not a plan to get others to care. It is a plan for applying the strategies of Christian love. The next chapter moves to another cluster of emotional pain—frustration, boredom, and apathy.

T H I R T E E N

Why am I here?

▼

It makes a good science fiction plot. An intelligent race of beings is doomed to extinction by some impending catastrophe like the explosion of their sun. So they determine to spend their last years and resources in seeding the galaxy with primitive living material. They hope that out of this sowing, intelligent life will have a chance to evolve again. A plot very much like this was the theme of W. Olaf Stapledon's *Last and First Men*, published in 1930.[1]

Some prominent scientists have suggested that this is how life came to be on earth. Sir Fred Hoyle, Britain's best known astronomer, announced in January of 1982 that organic material he discovered in space was probably placed there by intelligent beings seeding the universe with life. This announcement was greeted with skepticism in the scientific community.

But one month later came a book speculating that life came to earth in a kind of interstellar Noah's ark sent out by a doomed civilization somewhere in the galaxy. This book was not intended to be science fiction. It was *Life Itself: Its Origins and Nature*, by Professor Francis Crick, one of the world's most distinguished biologists, a Nobel Prize winner in 1962 for discovering the molecular structure of DNA.

How did Dr. Crick come up with this idea? He said he was driven to it by the sheer improbability of the conventional biological theory. That theory speculates that life arose independently on earth in the primeval organic soup. "The origin of life appears at the moment to be almost a miracle," said Crick, "so many are the conditions which would have to be satisfied to get it going."[2]

Astronomer Hoyle offered the same sentiments, pointing out the unlikely chance that the random combination of amino acids would produce a single one of the 200,000 different protein molecules necessary to human life. He said the likelihood of this happening is like the probability of rolling five million successive sixes with a pair of dice. "I had a real shock when I realized it couldn't happen," said Hoyle.

So these two distinguished scientists came to the conclusion that the random and spontaneous emergence of life on earth is impossible. Conventional biological theory in the matter is wrong. Where did they go from there? How did they explain the presence of life on Earth? Did they recognize that it is indeed a miracle, one that could have been achieved only by God Himself? No! Any theory is better than the "God" theory. It must have been space creatures who did it!

A London reporter who wrote about the theory exclaimed, "God only knows what they might have looked like, these putative ancestors of ours who may have sent the spores out two or three million years ago."[3] Yes, God does know. He was there. But it wasn't space creatures who put life on earth. God is the Author of life.

Some of the most important questions people have raised through the centuries are, "Where did I come from?" "Why am I here?" "What is my purpose in life?" And these questions are necessarily connected. If there is no Creator, how can there be meaning in the uncreated stuff, even in my own life? If I was not created on purpose, how can I make a purpose of my own? If a Creator does not exist, these questions only lead to despair.

God is purposeful and made us with a sense of *purpose*. He also gave us an innate desire for *achievement*. With the coming of sin and the self-centered nature, however, mankind abandoned God's purpose in favor of our own independent purposes for our lives. Our desire for achievement drives us to pursue our own aims. The emotional pain we experience involves frustration, boredom, and apathy. After a definition of these expressions of emotional pain, we will review some misunderstandings about purpose.

Understanding Boredom

In the area of purpose we actively express the emotional pain of *frustration,* while *boredom* is the more passive expression of our emotional pain. If the message in these emotions is not heeded, the resulting distress is *apathy.* The message carried in these feelings is that we are threatened in our desire for achievement.

Frustration means "to bring to nothing," "to render of no effect," "to nullify." Frustration pictures a person striving toward some purpose to which he is giving his strength but being turned back; all his efforts are brought to nothing. It can mean the thwarting of some effort, or it can mean the emotion or attitude in which a person feels frustrated. Frustration as an emotion is a combination of anger and discouragement. You are angry because you are being kept from your goal, and you are discouraged because your efforts did not bring success.

Def•i•ni'tion: Frustration, Boredom, Apathy

The cluster of emotional pain related to purpose includes *frustration*, *boredom*, and *apathy*. These emotional signals warn of a threat to one's achievement.

Frustration, the more active expression, is that feeling of discouragement and anger at being hindered from a goal.

Boredom, the more passive expression, is the sense of indifference and weariness at having nothing meaningful to do with one's time.

Apathy, the aspect of this cluster that develops when threats to achievement are not addressed, means "no feeling," indicating a total lack of enthusiasm for anything.

When I think of frustration, my imagination immediately calls up a picture of myself sitting on the kitchen floor. I am wearing a stained jumpsuit, my hair is tousled, my hands are grimy. I am leaning against the wall opposite a dishwasher that is supposed to be built in, but isn't. The old dishwasher had died. So I bought a new one and set out to install it myself. But it doesn't fit—almost, but not quite.

So I have wrestled with the thing for over an hour. I am really not sure why it won't fit. I have growled and uttered appropriate expletives. Sharon and the children occasionally peep around a corner, but they keep their distance. I am discouraged—my shoulders slump, big sighs escape my weary body. I am angry. At this point I would like to throw the dishwasher out the back door. This is frustration.

Your natural response to frustration will be *fight* or *flight*. You will want to lash out at those people or circumstances that stand in your way, or you might abandon the project altogether. You might take the interference as a personal affront and redouble your efforts to accomplish your aim, come "hell or high water." This kind of determination can be positive as a character trait. On the other hand, it can be nothing more than selfish pride, an attempt to prove something to others.

Boredom is the emotional distress associated with a more passive approach to a lack of purpose. It is experienced when you are not sure about goals. You feel indifferent, in the doldrums, and listless because "nothing is going on."

Boredom, as an emotional signal, indicates you are threatened because you have lost sight of any meaningful purpose. The passive person is waiting for someone else to act or some circumstance to develop that will give him or her something interesting to do. Bored people do not strive to make plans and achieve goals. They tend to wait and see what happens next.

Not having anything interesting to occupy your time is seen as a threat in the area of purpose, so the Monitor pushes the boredom button. The natural reaction to this feeling is to find something interesting to do. Very often this takes the form of entertainment. When you find yourself living in anticipation of the next television program or movie or golf game, you can know you are reacting to the boredom message.

When the problems behind the emotional pain in the area of purpose are unresolved, the result is *apathy*. This is the feeling of indifference that becomes an ongoing attitude instead of just an occasional reaction to circumstances. The apathetic person doesn't care about anything. He has no initiative, no direction, no ambition. Picture the "couch potato" who has no goals, no projects, no energy. Whereas boredom suggests only a temporary indifference, apathy indicates an almost complete loss of interest. Frustration can also lead to apathy, when a person is so thwarted in his aims that he gives up.

Apathy means "without feeling." It means not caring. Apathy is a normal attitude when a person has no interest in matters that do not concern him. Every evening the newscasters report momentous events like a war in Africa or a flood in Bangladesh. But you may not be moved by these reports because they are too far away. They do not touch your life. On the other hand, a house fire just down the block awakens intense interest. It is close to home. Friends are involved.

Apathy becomes a serious problem when a person is indifferent about his personal affairs. This chronic apathy develops when the warnings in frustration and boredom are not heeded. It is a sure sign of the failure of responsibility in the area of purpose.

Symptoms of the Apathetic Person

The person who does not deal responsibly with his or her lack of purpose will finally become apathetic. Let's look at some of the attitudes and ideas that are characteristic of the apathetic person. Though you may not identify fully with this description, you may see some of your own thinking among these symptoms.

▼ He sees little meaning in his normal daily activities.
▼ He seeks to fill his hours with activities, recreation, entertainment, or idle socializing.

▼ He tends to blame his boredom on the fact that, "nothing's going on."

▼ He operates best in the security of a schedule directed by others.

▼ He often finds himself "killing time" until the next directed activity.

▼ He has no clear definition of his own goals and priorities.

▼ He may devote himself to temporal goals in the pursuit of personal achievement.

The apathetic person finds his life empty of meaning. He gets into a routine in daily living that does not reflect any identifiable purpose. He faces the same schedule every day, eating breakfast, going to work, doing the same job all day, coming home, watching television, going to bed, only to get up the next morning and repeat the whole schedule.

A clear symptom of failure in the area of purpose is the effort to "find something to do." You can see it in the disconnection between activity or "busy-ness" and any clear purpose for that activity. I have asked, "How are you?" and heard the response, "I'm staying busy." This simply means a person is finding something to do to keep active, whether that activity has any particular meaning or not.

The apathetic person tries to schedule activities and entertainment for as many hours during the day as she can. She does not want to think about the fact that she has nothing meaningful to do. The easiest and handiest way to keep herself occupied is to watch television. Most households have the television on an average of eight hours a day. Children of school age watch television an average of six hours a day. Very few would call this productive activity.

The question is not whether a person should spend any time at leisure. Leisure is a normal and healthy part of life. Leisure, however, is most healthy when it is a break from meaningful pursuits. It is a time away from work to rejuvenate, rest, and recover one's strength in order to return to productive activities. But for millions of Americans leisure is not a break from meaningful activities. Being entertained is the primary aim, and work is only a way to pay for the entertainment.

As in other areas of responsibility, the self-centered human nature does not see the problem as "in here" but "out there." Instead of looking at his own goals and the way he uses his time, he thinks his boredom is caused by what is taking place around him. This view is that we are victims of circumstances beyond our control. We are like spectators at a sporting event where there is a lull in the game. The apathetic person does not see himself as a player in the game of life.

The Apathetic Person

▼ Sees little meaning in his regular daily activities
▼ Stays busy to avoid thinking about his lack of purpose
▼ Spends inordinate amount of time with entertainment
▼ Blames his boredom on factors outside himself
▼ Prefers the security of a schedule directed by others
▼ Lives from one scheduled activity to the next
▼ May pursue goals reflecting materialism and pride

Apathetic people make the soft choices for themselves by refusing to apply discipline in their management of time and efforts. This tendency to take the easy and passive approach is a reflection of the natural man's self-centeredness. The laziness inherent in the self-centered human nature makes it natural for us to stir ourselves only when we must, rather than learning to plan our activities according to our responsibilities and purposes. We fall into a pattern of being externally directed. We prefer a job that does not require us to manage our time and organize our activities.

Not having a clear set of priorities and goals reflects irresponsibility in the area of purpose and will result in frustration and apathy. Four out of five high school students do not know what they want to do with their lives. Twenty years later many of them still have not decided. They have merely drifted along in thoughtless consent to whatever life brought to them. Many find themselves at midlife with no sense of direction and no expectations for the future.

Those who recognize symptoms of apathy in themselves will do well to examine their approach to purpose in life. A failure of responsibility for purpose leads to emotional pain and results in a forfeiture of the richness of life that God intends.

Misconceptions about Achievement

Not only do most people just drift along without any sense of purpose beyond self-indulgence, our society as a whole seems to encourage this lack of purpose. Consider some of the common misconceptions.

Each person should do with his life what he alone chooses. Personal autonomy and individualism are primary themes for understanding ourselves in the contemporary age. It is normal thinking that every one of us is his own final authority. We should not have to answer to anyone else for what we do with our lives.

This attitude is a natural expression of the self-centered nature of man. While we may achieve success with this approach, we will never find the fulfilling and productive purpose God had in mind for our lives. Only as we join with God in His purpose can we reach beyond the place where we stand and the moment in which we live to leave a lasting legacy.

A person's first goal should be to take care of himself. At one level, self-interest is a legitimate principle for guiding one's activities and efforts. If each of us is responsible for his own business and takes care of it in good order, that is not destructive to the community. When we work to enrich ourselves by providing some service or product others can use, that benefits everyone. It is the basis for commerce. But this self-serving approach to purpose is only productive at an economic level. For a Christian, life cannot be entirely devoted to personal concerns and self-interests. The very flow of life requires that one be a giver and a servant.

Setting goals just sets you up for the disappointment of not being able to reach them. This idea is one expression of the philosophy that has resulted in the "dumbing down" of the public school system. It is based on the belief that self-esteem is one of the most important factors in personal character and that failure destroys self-esteem. The conclusion is that it is better not to try than to fail. But this idea misunderstands human nature at several points. Any objective worth the energy will involve some risk. It is better to try for reasonable goals and fail than to make no effort at all. Even in failure there are lessons to learn that give the wisdom of experience and help to build character.

As long as a person is busy in a wholesome activity, he is purposefully involved. The old saying, "Idle hands are the devil's workshop," is true to some extent. A person with time on his hands and no plans for using it is much more likely to get into trouble than one who is busy, even if his activity has no serious aim. Purpose, however, has to do with a clear direction and the ends one hopes to achieve. Being busy may keep one occupied but not necessarily with purpose. I saw a bumper sticker that makes this point: "Support Bingo: Keep Grandma off the Streets."

Only business executives or control freaks set goals and make "to-do" lists. It is true that the majority of reasonably successful people set goals and make lists. Goal setting and other organizational techniques are helpful for those who must be responsible for their own work. When the goals and lists become ends in themselves, however, you may have a "control freak." But for the most part, everyone can profit from clear goals and lists of specific activities for implementing them.

Just staying alive and reasonably happy is purpose enough for anybody these days. The unconscious goal for millions is just this, staying alive and happy. Like the quip, "I eat to live and live to eat," they live for their own comfort and satisfaction. This is even true of many professing Christians who never do anything beyond taking care of their own needs. Self-interests become the ultimate strategy and happiness the highest good. But people never achieve real fulfillment until they get beyond their own needs to produce a return on God's investment in creating them.

Factors beyond our control keep most people from realizing their dreams in life. No matter how capable you are, you are limited in what you can do. You have a great capacity, however, for overcoming limitations. You are able to dream and create beyond the dimensions of your normal capabilities.

It is a denial of personal responsibility to say that I cannot achieve my purpose because of barriers set against me. A person can complain that he grew up poor and has little education and therefore cannot achieve a worthy purpose in life. But this is just an excuse. Many a person has overcome poverty, racial prejudice, educational limitations, and other barriers to be successful and productive and make a contribution to the welfare of humanity.

These misconceptions about purpose and achievement reflect the views of a large segment of contemporary American society. There are many, however, who have discovered the joy of living in harmony with the purpose of God. The next chapter will explore principles for such a life of purpose.

▼

F O U R T E E N

Finding your destiny

▼

"Dad, level with me," said young David Hartman. "Do you think I can ever be a doctor?"

The Hartman family was sitting at dinner in their Havertown, Pennsylvania, home. David was on his way to Gettysburg College the next day. Since age thirteen he had let the family know that he planned to be a doctor, a psychiatrist. His father, Fred, his sister, Barbara, and his mother all looked at each other with doubt on their faces.

After debating with himself that same old argument about David's abilities, Fred answered, "You'll never know unless you try, will you?" But in his mind he wondered what medical school would take a blind student.

Born with defective eyes, David became completely blind by eight years of age. The family had never pampered him, insisting that he learn to function as normally as possible. So David grew up seeing his blindness as a bother but not a tragedy.

His ambition to be a doctor drove him to leave Overbrook School for the Blind and finish at Havertown's public high school. There he had made good grades, won a place on the varsity wrestling team, and was elected student council vice-president his senior year.

David's faculty advisor at Gettysburg had serious doubts about his plans and tried to talk him into a less challenging career choice. But David would have none of it and convinced him with his passionate arguments. He did well in his classes, making a near-perfect 3.8 grade point average. As graduation neared in 1972 he applied to ten medical schools. By April, eight had turned him down. He was crushed when the ninth rejection notice came. Finally came a letter from Temple University School of Medicine in Philadelphia. He had been accepted.

Medical school for David was a different experience from that of sighted students. In introductory anatomy he had to use his hands to identify organs in a cadaver. The study of microscopic tissue structures was even more of a challenge—he had to depend on the descriptions from other students as to what they saw in the microscope. His textbooks were read on audio tape by Recordings for the Blind volunteers. In every case he dealt positively with the obstacles he faced.

Then on May 27, 1976, David Hartman received his M.D. degree. He completed six years of residency at Temple University Hospital and finally achieved his dream of becoming a psychiatrist and a specialist in rehabilitation medicine.[1]

David Hartman's story is remarkable. It demonstrates the indomitable drive in man for achievement. Made in the image of God, he is created with a sense of purpose. He knows that his life is meant to have meaning beyond mere existence. He dreams of achievements that will call for his best and more. When this desire for achievement is threatened, he experiences the emotional warning signals of *frustration* and *boredom*.

In this chapter we will examine the desire for achievement and our calling to the high purpose of God.

The Desire for Achievement

God is a God of purpose and made man with a sense of purpose. Before the foundation of the world God established His eternal purpose (Eph. 1:4; 3:11). He has decided that His purpose ultimately will be fulfilled. Isaiah states God's intention as he writes, "My purpose will stand, and I will do all that I please" (Isa. 46:10).

Along with an innate sense of purpose, man was also given a desire for achievement. This inherent desire for achievement involves several elements: *meaning, conquest, distinction,* and *expression.*

First, the desire for achievement includes the hope for *meaning.* We have a natural sense that our lives should have meaning beyond the moment in which we live and the space on which we stand. We somehow know that we are to do something with our time and energy. Achievement is an answer to the question, "Why am I here?" The desire for achievement is a longing for meaning, for a reason to get up in the morning, for my time and activity to have some significance beyond mere survival.

Achievement also means *conquest.* Human beings are conquerors. At their worst they cruelly overcome their fellow man. At their best, they boldly set out to subdue the earth. They conquer the wide oceans by building boats to sail them. They conquer the mountains of the earth by climbing them. They conquer the air by learning to fly.

Business executives have long recognized that it is not the money that motivates the real achievers. It is the game. It is the conquest, the challenge to surpass someone else or to beat one's own record. It is the invigorating smell of battle—to overcome the obstacles, to outperform the competition, to solve the complex problems. In everything from medical research to sports, we face the same challenge—to solve the problem, set a record, explore the unknown, do what's never been done.

Thirdly, achievement means *distinction.* We hope that the expenditure of our attention, energy, and creativity will give us a special place in history, will set us apart from all others. We name cities, mountains, even stars after ourselves. We build stone monuments to ourselves. We establish foundations to continue our good deeds after our death. We have a dream of immortality, and we hope that our children will honor our name and thus give us distinction after we are gone.

A fourth element in the desire for achievement is the drive for personal *expression*. We have an urge to express ourselves, to create, to capture images and ideas and communicate them to others in a striking way. From Navajo sandpainting to high-rise architecture, we express ourselves in creative ways. One of us writes a great novel, another carefully crafts a thank-you note. From music and dance to gardening and decorating, from renowned artists to ordinary people, the desire for personal expression urges us on to achievement.

Like any other of these basic desires, the desire for *achievement* calls man to get beyond himself. We like a sense of movement, that life is going somewhere, that there is something to look forward to, something to finish, something to accomplish. We like to think that what we are doing will leave something standing, affect some other person, provide a benefit for ourselves or others.

The Desire for Achievement

Inherent to our nature is a desire for *achievement*. Created in the image of God, we are made as purposeful beings. We search for significance for our lives. We strive to accomplish something meaningful with our time and energy. We want to confirm that the meaning of our lives goes beyond the moment in which we live and the place where we stand.

This inherent desire for achievement may become so suppressed, however, that we may be content to have no goals or aims. We may never think about it. Instead, we experience a nagging undercurrent of uncertainty as to what to do with our time and our talents. We may not even know that this desire was placed in our hearts by our Creator. We may think our self-indulgence and apathy are normal. This is what sin does to efface the image of God in us.

A Christian can relate responsibly to the area of purpose by understanding four biblical principles. They are the principle of *freedom*, the principle of *responsibility*, the principle of *fulfillment*, and the principle of *time*.

The Principle of Freedom

God created us intentionally and reveals a purpose for our lives. In Psalm 139:16 we find this statement, "All the days ordained for me were written in your book before one of them came to be." Even before we are born, God "writes down" a plan for our lives. This plan is so fully developed as to include all the days of our lives. This idea has long been a comfort to Christians who have sought to find God's will for their lives. It can also create a lot of tension if the interpretation of God's will is narrowed to a detailed plan from which the believer dare not depart.

Garry Friesen has examined traditional views of the will of God in his book, *Decision-Making and the Will of God*.[2] He states that the traditional view sets forth three aspects of the will of God: God's *sovereign* will, God's *moral* will, and God's *individual* will. As he studies passage after passage of Scripture, however, he comes to the conclusion that there is no biblical basis for the individual will of God.

Friesen writes that man is to operate within the scope of God's sovereign will because he has no other choice. He will be able to discern the sovereign will of God only as he looks back on events that have already taken place. He says that God challenges man to operate within His moral will. This requires obedience to the ethical commands and principles of Scripture. But God gives each person the freedom to decide for himself whether he will respond to God in any given situation or choose some other path.

This interpretation means that God's will is not an individual blueprint drawn for my life. It is rather a set of principles in the Scriptures that are there to guide me. Purpose in life means finding God's purpose. That purpose is laid out, not as a daily schedule of preordained activities, but as a pattern for thinking, attitudes, and behavior that is consistent with the moral standards that God has set forth in the Scriptures.

How would we interpret the words of Psalm 139 from this viewpoint? The psalmist is saying that in His sovereign will God knows every detail of my life and has already recorded all of the events that will take place in it. He is not saying that

God has planned every event of my life and that I must seek to act out that plan moment by moment. God has revealed a moral framework within which I am to live my life. Whether I do that is my choice, and God allows me the freedom not only to succeed, but to fail. He allows me the freedom not only to comply with His moral will, but to reject it.

This understanding of the will of God has several very positive features about it. In the first place, it takes the focus off us and our personal pilgrimages and places it on God and His sovereign purpose. Another feature of this approach is the emphasis on freedom. Obviously God has given us great freedom to choose whether to comply with His will or to reject it. A third implication is that God can make up for our errors and adjust to our foolishness. He is able to redeem the situation and transform it into something usable for His purposes.

Dealing with Purpose

▼ *The Principle of Freedom:* God purposely created you and intends a purpose for your life.

▼ *The Principle of Responsibility:* You are responsible for what you do about God's purpose for your life.

▼ *The Principle of Fulfillment:* Your life fulfillment comes only in the wholehearted pursuit of God's purpose.

▼ *The Principle of Time:* Responsibility for your purpose focuses primarily in what you do with your time.

Perhaps the most significant aspect of this interpretation of God's will is the emphasis on fellowship with God. Finding God's will is a matter of becoming involved with Him rather than being preoccupied with whether each activity and decision of mine is or is not His will. I am seeking to live in fellowship with the risen Christ, to respond to His call upon me, to allow Him to reshape my thinking and behavior in any way He wishes. In the process, He guides me in remarkable ways toward the right places and times for connecting with His activity. Though every step is a step of faith, His leadership is confirmed time and again.

The will of God provides a clear plan for my life, but it is not a completed script for me to read. As I discover the will of God in more detail in Scripture, I continue to adjust my life accordingly and to follow His direction.

I am always to live in fellowship with Him so that I may adjust my own attitudes and behavior to His purposes. I am not searching for God's will for my life. I am simply searching for God's will, through seeking to know Him and living obediently in fellowship with Him day by day.

The Principle of Responsibility

You are responsible for what you do about God's purpose for your life. As I have already said, each person is responsible for what he or she does in each area of life. This responsibility implies an accountability to God, to others, and to ourselves. God has given such freedom that what we do with our lives is our own responsibility.

If I accept responsibility for my own purpose in life, then I set aside excuses for not succeeding and believe that God has gifted me to live in a fruitful way within the scope of His will. He has made me a dreamer and holds me accountable for what I do with my dreams. I am responsible if my aims in life are self-centered. I am responsible if I refuse to take initiative and just let my life drift along as circumstances direct it.

The Principle of Fulfillment

Life fulfillment for a Christian comes only in the whole-hearted pursuit of God's purpose. Any number of things can be done that bring benefit to you and to your neighbors. You could devote your whole life to the production of food so that you can make a living and others can be nourished. Or you might devote your life to the construction of buildings, so that you derive an income and others might be sheltered. Or you might create music to earn a living and to delight others. All of these could be worthy purposes and surely make life more enjoyable and fulfilling for everyone concerned.

Any pursuit, however, which does not take into account the purpose of God, can be worthy of the devotion of an entire life. One human life is too valuable to be spent solely on temporal accomplishments, however grand they may be. Not only is life valuable in the span of the years we may live, it goes on beyond that for eternity. Only as we operate within the scope of the will of our Creator can we find a purpose worthy of the highest expression of His creation, man himself.

The Principle of Time

Responsibility for your purpose focuses primarily on what you do with your time. So many factors are involved in pursuing a worthy purpose with your life. There is one factor, however, that cannot be controlled. It is time. You cannot stop it, speed it up, suspend it, recover it, save it, or give it away. You will use each moment only in the present and only one time. What you do with it may dramatically affect the opportunities and circumstances future moments bring. But you cannot control time. You must learn to manage it.

Managing time means making the most of it in terms of your priorities and goals. Allen Lakein, in his book, *How to Get Control of Your Time and Your Life*, makes clear that the only way to take charge of your life is to take charge of your time. He insists that this requires intentional planning. "Planning is bringing the future into the present, so that you can do something about it now."[3] Every area of personal responsibility requires the management of time.

Lakein suggests that we begin to manage our time by identifying our lifetime goals. From our lifetime goals we derive short-term and immediate goals. The management of the very hours and moments of the day should relate to these goals. This gives us a day-by-day reference point for what we will do with our time. That reference point is not in the circumstances, the appetites of the moment, the suggestions of other people, or even those matters that seem urgent. The reference point for priorities in a given moment is our own life purpose and goals.

In the practical sense, time management requires daily attention to the use of the hours available to me. This means I will set goals and plan how to achieve them. I will organize my time by the use of various tools such as planning calendars and activities lists and daily schedules. I will tackle the more important tasks now and leave the less important ones for later. In all of this, my intention is to use the time available to me in a way that honors God's purpose for my life.

Time in the present moment can be *wasted*, used in a way that brings no particular return for the effort. Time is wasted when no thought is given to how it might be used, when no effort is made to use it for any fruitful result or when no particular benefit is derived from its use either personally or for others. The habit of wasting time is a clear symptom of a failure of responsibility in the area of purpose.

Time can also be *spent*. We can spend our time for some benefit derived from the activity of those moments. There is an exchange of value involved. Energy and effort are expended during a certain hour for the return they bring during that hour. Though there may be residual benefit at a later time, the primary focus of spending is a benefit for the present moment.

Much of our leisure activity is like this. We spend time relaxing, playing, or being entertained largely for the immediate benefit it brings. Leisure is very important to the pursuit of a worthy purpose. Work will be much more productive if rest, play, and entertainment are scheduled as "rewards" for work and diversions from it. "All work and no play" not only "makes Jack a dull boy," it may also burn him out.

Keys to Time Management

▼ Begin with a commitment to the purpose of God.

▼ Write out a statement of your life purpose and goals.

▼ Write out long-term, short-term, and immediate goals.

▼ Use a planning calendar.

▼ Plan a schedule for daily activities and stick to it.

▼ Keep an up-to-date "to do list" for task priorities.

▼ Rank tasks by importance and do first things first.

▼ Refuse to be driven by urgency and crisis.

▼ Plan sufficient leisure time for a break from work.

▼ Plan your use of time in intimate fellowship with God.

Time can also be *invested*. This means using present time for a future benefit. You can connect what you are doing now to results you want at a later time. This refers again to your life purpose. You will evaluate the use of time in any given hour or day as to whether it contributes to that overall life purpose. You may also evaluate your time with reference to secondary goals that are derived from that overarching purpose. Either way you are investing the present moment for a future return.

God is at work in the world to shape it and to conform it to His will. His will includes the best for every person on this planet. Chapter 15 will include practical guidelines for discovering God's purpose and becoming involved in it.

FIFTEEN

The path to achievement

▼

There was an Earl Nightingale speech I heard as a high school sophomore that changed my life. It was my introduction to serious thinking about success. I had never before been exposed to the idea that I could choose an attitude that would open the door to whatever I wanted to do in life. I didn't know what I wanted to do with my life. I didn't have a dream of success.

But with hearing that recorded speech I was hooked. The next day I began to look for books along the lines of Earl Nightingale's talk. I read titles like *Success Is You*, *The Magic of Believing*, and *You Are Greater Than You Know*.

Through the years, as I became more familiar with biblical ideas, I learned that some of the motivational books and tapes placed too much confidence in man and seemed to have little use for God. Even some of the writers who mentioned Him seemed to see God as a force to manipulate rather than the sovereign Creator. As I sorted it out over the years, I came to the conclusion that the desire for achievement is a God-given longing, but it must be approached in a God-directed way.

In his book, *The Seven Habits of Highly Effective People*, Stephen Covey distinguishes between a *personality* model for success and a *character* model.[1] The personality model emphasizes personality growth, communication skills, strategies for influencing others, and positive thinking. While beneficial, these are secondary traits. The character model, on the other hand, emphasizes such traits as integrity, goodness, honesty, and other principle-based qualities; in other words, success depends more on character than technique.

You are what you think. If you think achievement is a matter of appearances and material success, that is what you will get. If, on the other hand, you see achievement as based on character, as lining up with the purpose of God, then you will achieve something entirely different. This chapter offers some biblical principles for the path to achievement.

Working with God

At a practical level the question of purpose comes down to this: How do you work with God? The best way to answer that question may be to see how Jesus worked with the Father.

On a particular occasion Jesus, with some of His disciples, came to the pool of Bethesda. A large number of disabled people were gathered there. One man caught His attention, a cripple in shabby clothing who had obviously been long disabled and poor. Jesus' brief conversation with the man convinced him that God had indeed prepared him for this day and was ready to heal him. He commanded the man to get up and walk.

After the healing of the lame man at the pool of Bethesda, Jesus explained what had taken place. In doing so He described this working relationship with the heavenly Father.

God's Invitation to You

The first principle for finding your purpose in life is this: *God wants to involve you in His work.* Jesus said, "My Father is always at his work to this very day, and I, too, am working" (John 5:17). In healing the lame man, Jesus didn't act on His own. Instead he responded to what the Father was doing. Wherever God takes us, whatever our circumstances, the Father is at work.

Also clear in Jesus' statement is the relationship of His own work to the work of the Father. The Father takes the initiative and the Son responds. The Father *always* works; the Son *also* works. Jesus never acted independently of the Father. He was convinced that the Father was already and always at work, and that His own part was to respond to what the Father was doing.

In his book *Eternity in Their Hearts*, Don Richardson gives striking accounts of missionaries finding God already at work, even among the most primitive tribes.[2] Though the tribal name for God was strange in their ears, the missionaries in unreached countries could recognize that He had already been working to prepare the people for His messengers. The missionaries' role was not to get something started in that remote place; it was rather to be God's instruments for the *fulfillment* of what the Father had already been doing. Those missionaries who learned this truth found the people much more receptive.

Imagine getting to work with the greatest master craftsman in your field. How would you approach such an apprenticeship? Would you offer your advice? Would you try to take the initiative and tell the master how to do the work? No. If you were wise you would come as a disciple and a servant. You would eagerly respond to every instruction. You would watch intently for any indication of the master's wishes.

God is the greatest Master Craftsman with whom one could ever hope to work. The work of God is an adventure of growth. We develop character qualities we never knew we needed. We are stretched and challenged. We quickly find out that we are in over our heads. The work of God is fully beyond our abilities. But as we are drawn into His work, our faith is strengthened and we are never the same again.

Right now God is seeking to involve you in His purpose. Can you think of anything that would block the way? Are you available for becoming involved in the work of God?

Avoiding Dead-End Streets

Not only does God want to involve you in His work, *God wants to limit you to His work.* As Jesus continued His explanation, He said, "I tell you the truth, the Son can do nothing by himself; he can do only what he sees his Father doing, because whatever the Father does the Son also does" (John 5:19). What a startling admission for the Son of God. "The Son can do nothing by himself." If this severe limitation was necessary for the divine Son of God, how much more is it necessary for us. Jesus said, "I am the vine; you are the branches . . . . Apart from me you can do nothing" (John 15:5).

When I was a college student, I played for a time in the symphony orchestra of our town. My instrument was bass violin. The conductor insisted that we not only play the right music but that we play it at the right time and in the right way. He would hold his baton aloft to be sure he had our attention. Then came the first downbeat. And we made music, after a fashion.

In the same way, the servant of God must not assume that he is free to launch out on any work that seems like the business of God. The Father insists that we involve ourselves only in the work He is doing. We do not call on Him to respond to us. We respond to His initiative to do His work in His time.

How often those who really try to serve God are weary and want to give up. How often they wonder why serving God should be so hard and so fruitless. Could it be that they have run down a dead-end street? They have set out to get something started for God instead of waiting for God to involve them in His work. God will not be stampeded into supporting our projects, however noble they may seem to us. He wants to limit us to His work.

When you wait on the Lord and get quiet before Him, you may realize that God's first work in your life will always be within you. He begins with who you are before moving to what you are to do. Instead of seeking something to do for God, we first need to know who we are to be by His grace. As He does His work in us, we will be prepared for what He intends to do through us. It is very often out of our own experience with God that we learn how to be agents of His grace in the lives of others.

Watching for the Burning Bush

Besides involving you in His work and limiting you to His work, God wants to show you His work. Jesus said, "For the Father loves the Son and shows him all he does" (John 5:20). It is obvious that we cannot be consciously involved in the work of God if we cannot see it. But God is a God of revelation. We can be sure that He will show us what He is doing.

I like to call this the "burning bush principle." Just as Moses' attention was arrested by the burning bush, so can we see "burning-bush" signs of the work of the Father where we are. He will show us—in other people, events, and circumstances—those signposts the Holy Spirit gives us to point out "God at work."

Many a servant of God is too busy to stop and see the burning bushes. Days are packed with important tasks. Planning, goal setting, necessary errands—all make for an agenda not receptive to interruptions. And the missing ingredient in such a ministry is, unhappily, the holy ground where we see God at work and become involved in what He is doing.

With just a little thought, we can see what a great difference it makes if we approach a day intending to be on the lookout for what God is doing. We pay attention to the people in our path. We look deeply into their faces for some signal of God's work in their lives. We look for need, for hurt, for openness.

God wants us to see what He is doing. He wants to involve us in His work. As He sets a "burning bush" where we can see it, He is inviting us to draw near. The closer we get, the more we understand what God is doing. Finally He draws us onto holy ground and involves us in the miracle of partnership in His redemptive work.

Three Tests of Purpose

Finding and following the purpose of God is never an easy task. Not only will your self-centered nature resist such a path, you will face subtle and persuasive pressures designed to turn you aside from God's purpose. Jesus faced three tests in His temptation experience as it is recorded in Matthew 4. We will face the same tests, designed by the enemy to distract us and draw us away from God's purpose. If you recognize them for what they are, you will be better prepared to pass the tests.

The first test the enemy uses is the *survival test*. Satan will tempt you to give your attention and effort to providing for yourself instead of trusting God to provide for you. When Satan came to Jesus, He had been out in the wilderness for a long time, and He was tired and hungry. So Satan's first appeal was for Jesus to turn a stone into bread and satisfy His hunger.

But Jesus' answer was clear. He said man is not to live by bread alone, but by every word from the mouth of God. He was saying, "Bread is not My business. Obedience is what I am about here. Even if I starve to death in this wilderness, I will not lift a finger to provide for Myself what the Father has promised to give Me."

Here's the point. If the enemy can get you to spend all your energy and time providing for yourself, he knows you will be distracted from God's purpose for your life. So he has won. He has effectively neutralized what God might have done in and through your life. In your busy-ness you are failing to trust God to meet your needs and you are unavailable to Him as an agent of grace for the needs of others.

The second test in the account of Jesus' temptations is the *security test*. The devil suggests that Jesus throw Himself down from the pinnacle of the temple so that He can prove the angels will keep Him from harm. His appeal went like this, "Surely it is better to check out your security now, before you really get into hot water. When an unruly mob is about to throw you off a cliff, it will be too late to see if you are adequately protected."

Jesus answered, "You will not put the Lord your God to the test." You either trust the Father or you don't. God has promised to protect you, but you do not try a test run to see if He will keep His promises. All the risks in the Christian life are real. There are no practice sessions.

149

What kind of protection do you need if you are to follow God's purpose for your life? Do you need to protect your feelings? Will you protect your reputation? How about your own privacy or schedule? How about your life? Or will you try to protect yourself from the risks involved in following the will of God? If so, you have failed the security test and the enemy has already won.

The third test to divert you from God's will for your life is the *success test*. Satan took Jesus to a high mountain and showed Him all the kingdoms of the world. Then he said something like this, "You see all those kingdoms? They can be Yours. Just kneel down and worship me. I know You came to be a king. Look, I'll make You king of the world. Is it too much to ask You to do it my way, as long as You get what You want?"

Jesus' answer was that man is to worship only God and serve Him alone. Worship means to celebrate God's worth as the Supreme Being, the Most High God. This settles the matter of ultimate priorities. Serve means to devote our energies to His business. So we are to put God as number one in our lives and dedicate our efforts to His purpose. This makes us servants, even slaves. Are you willing to be a nobody to pursue the purpose of God?

To the extent that you devote yourself to success you will not be available as an agent of God. If you follow your ambitions, you cannot follow Jesus. Jesus said that whoever follows Him must deny him or herself and take up the cross. This means we say "no" to ourselves and accept the sacrificial way of Jesus.

Purpose and Priorities

I was sitting with other parents in a large monthly meeting of the Cub Scout troop of our area. The various dens were being recognized for distinction in one way or another. Awards for rank were being given to the boys who had earned them.

In the midst of this activity, my nine-year-old, Matthew, left his seat and came to me. "Dad," he said, as he drew close to me, "could we get me a Day-Timer?"

"A Day-Timer?" I responded with a mixture of curiosity and humor. The Day-Timer is an executive appointment calendar I had used for years. "Why do you need a Day-Timer?" "To keep up with my schedule," he said, the tears welling up in his eyes. "I have so many things to do, I forget."

My heart sank as I realized he was serious. Here was a nine-year-old already experiencing the stress of a too-busy schedule. I told him we would talk about it when we got home. The rest of the meeting was a blur to me. I had an ache inside I couldn't shake.

My mind was flooded with a list of all the things he had to do. There was school, with a number of after-school and evening events, church activities, a children's Bible club at the church of a neighbor, lots of homework to do, Little League, Cub Scouts, chores around the house, and on it went. Of course Matthew had wanted to be involved in each one of these activities as it had come along. But now he was obviously in over his head.

Parenting and Purpose

Matthew's frustration was a clear signal to me that he was experiencing a threat to his desire for achievement. He was not able to manage his time. But a youngster like Matthew isn't finally responsible for what he does with his time. It was really our responsibility as his parents. The warning signal, his frustration, sent us to the drawing board for a full review of the family schedule in light of the purpose of God.

It is my own conviction that nothing you do in your entire life will be more important than bringing up godly children. Just think, if you have four children and each of them has four children, in four generations there will be 256 family units. That can be a wonderful godly heritage. You will be the patriarch or matriarch of a tribe! The question remains whether the generations that flow from you will be a force for good, for God's purpose.

The primary issue is character. No matter what else you do with your children, train them in godly character. But first, you must be godly. Your children will be like you. You will never teach them to be what you are not. And they will have

151

a hard time making a difference in today's world without the strength and certainty of godly character.

If children grow up with parents who are committed to keeping them happy, entertained, and distracted from misbehaving, they will expect to be entertained. They do not see themselves as responsible for identifying and pursuing a worthwhile purpose. They look around for something to do to entertain themselves. When they do not find such activity, they blame their boredom on the failure of others to provide it.

One of the most important child training responsibilities of parents is to teach children how to work. Productive and meaningful work is a vital part of the development of Christian character. To train children to work, begin with tasks that are suitable to their level of maturity, participating with them in the activity until they understand how to do it, insisting that they complete what they start, and refusing to allow their natural resistance to work to derail the process.

Children need to learn that work is normal and positive rather than seeing work as an interruption of their leisure and therefore to be avoided if possible. Work is not to be something parents impose on children in order to keep them in line or keep them distracted. It is not a punishment for misbehavior. When parents are positive and happy about work, children will learn to be so as well.

Parents do well to teach their children how to manage their time. Again, this training must involve activities that are suitable to the maturity level of the particular child. But over the course of time, children can learn to think for themselves about what they are doing with their time and energy. They can identify responsibilities and pursue activities that will fulfill those responsibilities. They can learn to use their time well and reward themselves with leisure when their work is done.

What parents do while the children are home will make all the difference in the character and skills their children bring to the challenges of adult life. Children who are not taught to take responsibility for purpose will be seriously handicapped in the real world. Simply keeping children fed and clothed is a far cry from preparing them for life.

An Action Plan

We have seen that finding God's purpose for our lives can be guided by principles Jesus gave in explaining His ministry. We can know that He draws us into His work, that He limits us to His work, and that He shows us His work. We have also seen that our commitment to the purpose of God will make all the difference in the future for our children. But the enemy is ready to distract us from God's purpose by tempting us to provide for ourselves, protect ourselves, and promote ourselves.

Consider these insights for dealing with your responsibility in the area of purpose:

▼ Affirm that God is already at work in your world.

▼ Avoid the busy work that is only a counterfeit of ministry.

▼ Expect God to show you His work and involve you in it.

▼ Remain available for instant obedience to the Spirit.

▼ Recognize that character comes before accomplishment.

▼ Begin with your own family to follow the purpose of God.

▼ Trust God in the tests that distract you from His purpose.

Next we move to the emotional pain of guilt. We will address the question of personal integrity, our responsibility in the area of morality.

▼

SIXTEEN

Is this right or wrong for me?

▼

Judah Rosenthal is the main character in Woody Allen's film, *Crimes and Misdemeanors.* He is a respected community leader, a successful ophthalmologist, a loving husband and father. His happy and prosperous life is suddenly jolted when he intercepts a letter to his wife from his mistress. Panicked by her threat, he consults a rabbi for advice, even though he is not a religious man. The rabbi advises him to confess to God and to his wife. Perhaps they will understand. Judah cannot imagine such a solution to the problem. He cannot take the risk. The real world doesn't work that way.

When his mistress threatens blackmail, he looks for a way out. He thinks about the stories from his childhood of the God who sees all. He fears the wrath of God, but he fears more to have his pleasant and ordered life destroyed. He decides to take his chances with God knowing about his sin. But he dares not risk exposure to his wife.

Judah's brother, a mobster, hears his story and offers a solution. It is simple. Put out a contract on his mistress and have her killed. Judah struggles with his conscience over this escalation of evil. But when the woman keeps up the pressure, he finally decides to do away with her.

Upon hearing the report of her death, he is smitten again with his wrong. He goes to her apartment to make sure no evidence of their affair can be found. There her unseeing eyes mock and horrify him as she lies dead before him.

For weeks he paces the floor at night, horrified at his crime and dreading God's wrath. He teeters between confession and insanity. Then a burglar is blamed for the murder. Time passes, and his wife never discovers his affair. Finally, he even stops agonizing over his crime. Everything returns to the happy and prosperous life he was trying to protect.

Charles Colson sees the movie as a powerful commentary on today's society. He says that the woman was not the only murder victim. Judah Rosenthal also killed his own conscience. This killing followed a systematic progression, not unlike the direction of today's society.

First, Judah had to get rid of God. Since his own desires conflicted with the demands of God, he eliminated God. He did this by refusing to acknowledge God, by behaving as though He didn't exist. Second, he redefined the standard of justice. Right and wrong could not be seen as absolutes. His new standard was his own interests. Third, he got rid of his old-fashioned feelings of sin and guilt.[1]

Though the standard used by one's conscience varies from one person to another, it is obvious that each of us has a built-in moral monitor. As much as any other factor, our character will be revealed by our moral judgments and consistencies. There is something in us that desires moral consistency, even if only a minimal "honor among thieves."

This chapter will describe the emotional pain we suffer in this struggle for integrity. The symptoms of the guilt-ridden person will be identified. We will also examine the biblical view of conscience.

Understanding Guilt

Guilt is the more active emotional response to a threat to moral integrity. The more passive emotion is *shame*. When the conditions causing these emotions are unresolved, the long-term and more serious expression of this emotional cluster is *remorse*.

Guilt is a sense of sorrow, self-reproach, and regret, perhaps with some fear of punishment. It is a reflection on behavior that violates one's own sense of moral uprightness. We have already discussed *embarrassment*. It differs from guilt in that embarrassment focuses on the opinion of others and how I look in their eyes. Feelings of guilt, on the other hand, can be experienced when no one else is aware of my failures. Guilt focuses on my inner standards, what I expect of myself.

We are using the word *guilt* here to refer to an emotion. More properly, guilt means legal or moral culpability. It means a person is chargeable with an offense. Psychologists have traditionally made a distinction between guilt and the emotion of guilt by referring to the emotions as "guilt feelings." Too often they used this terminology to indicate that the emotion of guilt is not legitimate, something like superstition. It is to be overcome through analysis or some other therapy.

The more passive emotion in this cluster is *shame*. Whereas guilt is experienced as an occasional pang of conscience, shame is an ongoing sense of moral failure. Shame involves the feelings of humiliation, dishonor, and disgrace. While guilt is an immediate response to some moral failure, *shame* is an ongoing sense of moral disgrace.

Def•i•ni'tion: Guilt, Shame, Remorse

Guilt is the central emotion in a cluster of emotional pain related to morality. It is the feeling of sorrow and regret over wrong behavior.

Shame is the more passive emotion in this cluster. It is a feeling of humiliation, dishonor, and disgrace, more related to one's overall self-respect than to specific acts of wrong doing.

Remorse is the deeper problem of guilt that develops when normal signals of guilt and shame are not addressed responsibly. It is a deep and torturing sense of guilt.

The word *shame* is used by some psychologists to indicate personal embarrassment. In this sense it is related to self-worth. Whereas guilt focuses on my bad behavior, shame makes me feel that I am a bad person. We speak of being guilty of *something,* but we say, "I am ashamed of *myself.*" Shame emerges when the guilt accumulates to the point of reflecting on my character. What I do that makes me feel guilty eventually makes me ashamed of who I am.

When the cause for guilt and shame is not addressed over a period of time, the third level of emotion in this cluster emerges—*remorse.* The word remorse comes from two Latin forms. One is the word *mordere,* which means "to bite or gnaw." The other is the prefix *re,* which means "again." A smitten conscience bites and gnaws at one's sense of moral integrity.

Remorse is a deep and torturing sense of guilt. It is the keen pain or anguish that comes from an unresolved breakdown in integrity. Remorse involves a cycle of self-reproach in which a person continues to accuse himself over and over for some bad thing he has done. It is the strong and unrelenting voice of conscience.

Emotional pain related to morality can be complicated by emotional injury or disease. Injury refers to the wounds one still carries because of experiences of legalism or continuing criticism and accusation by others.

When a person grows up with an overabundance of trivial regulations, he may find himself unable to function in a healthy way until he comes to terms with his legalism. In the opposite extreme, a person may grow up without moral restrictions or with such brutality and cruelty that he becomes insensitive to hurtful behavior. In either extreme, the impact of these experiences leaves him with wounds in the moral area that aggravate the normal function of conscience.

Disease, in this context, refers to faulty thinking. Not only can a person's normal moral sense be confused by the injury of past experiences, it can also be affected by wrong thinking about morality. We are prone to misconceptions because of our corrupted nature. Unfortunately, the media fosters these misconceptions about morality. With this faulty base of assumptions, conscience cannot operate in its intended way.

Understanding Conscience

The word *conscience* in the New Testament is *suneidesis*. The word means "to know together with oneself" or "to bear witness for or against oneself." Conscience is that internal witness that condemns or approves our behavior, attitudes, speech, or any other expression of moral values. The Old Testament has no word for conscience. The moral reference point for Old Testament thinking is not within, but without. It is the written Law of God.

Taking the whole of the biblical worldview into account, we can learn several lessons concerning the conscience.

Conscience is natural to man, as a God-given capability. The Bible assumes that we have a moral sense. Even though the Law is the authority for morality, conscience is referred to in the Old Testament as "heart" or other bodily organs. David wrote about his own struggle with guilt, "When I kept silent, my bones wasted away through my groaning all day long. For day and night your hand was heavy upon me; my strength was sapped as in the heat of summer" (Ps. 32:3–4). Paul writes, "So I strive always to keep my conscience clear before God and man" (Acts 24:16).

Conscience is not infallible, but it should be obeyed. Paul refers to a "weak" conscience as he writes about the problem of eating meat offered to idols (1 Cor. 8:7, 10, 12). This is the conscience of a recently converted Christian who is not well grounded in his freedom in Christ. Though his conscience is not correct in its witness, Paul insists that the young Christian should not violate it. He further commits himself to do nothing to provoke the weaker brother's conscience. Paul also testified that he had lived in good conscience all his adult life, even though he had made the dramatic change from persecutor of the church to preacher of the gospel (Acts 23:1).

Conscience reflects background, culture, and experience. Though the sense of right and wrong is built into our nature, the content of that morality varies from culture to culture. The law in any culture reflects the traditions of generations. There is an amazing consistency of thought among more sophisticated cultures as to how people are to treat one another.

On the other hand, cannibalism, brutality, and treachery are normal in some cultures. In *Peace Child*, missionary Don Richardson tells of his surprise to discover that the Sawi people of Irian Jawa saw great virtue in befriending someone in order to put him off guard, kill him, and eat him.[2]

Conscience must be educated through an understanding of moral principles. If a person's conscience is not intentionally informed, it will follow the normal patterns of the surrounding culture. "Let your conscience be your guide" is good advice, but it assumes a well-trained conscience. The psalmist writes, "I have hidden your word in my heart that I might not sin against you" (Ps. 119:11). This reflects a deliberate effort to educate conscience as to the objective requirements of the Law of God.

Conscience can be resisted until it becomes ineffective. Not only can we be misled by a poorly educated conscience, we can reject its witness until we are hardened against it. The Bible speaks of an evil or defiled conscience, referring to the person who knows he is wrong but continues in his immorality (Heb. 10:22; Titus 1:15). It also speaks of a seared or cauterized conscience, one that is deadened or silenced by the rejection of its witness (1 Tim. 4:2).

Over all, conscience is a faithful moral voice within, warning us of our wrong behavior. It is moral suicide to consistently reject its witness.

Symptoms of Ongoing Guilt

Hobart Mowrer wrote that the greatest problem in counseling today is unresolved guilt.[3] The offices of counselors are filled with those who suffer the pangs of conscience. Consider some of the symptoms and strategies of such a person.

▼ He feels condemned over his past behavior.
▼ He argues with himself over rationalizations about his moral failure.
▼ He tends to be critical of others, even in some areas of his own guilt.
▼ He may gravitate toward others with similar moral values.

▼ He may challenge theological ideas that are the basis for moral requirements.

▼ He may ridicule those with strict moral and religious convictions.

▼ He is unable to be open in relationships, lest others find out about his misdeeds.

▼ He may suffer physical symptoms as a result of his emotional conflict.

▼ He feels himself a victim of his own selfish impulses and further condemns himself for giving in to them.

The sense of condemnation is the first symptom of a guilt-ridden person. A religious background with a high standard of morality can lead him to believe that God is condemning him. He may also feel he is being condemned by others, particularly by family or other close relations. This sense of disapproval from others can be real or only imagined. Either way it is a source of distress.

He may be trapped in a self-indulgent moral bondage to alcohol, pornography, elicit sex, gambling, shoplifting, or any number of other habitual sins. Society today tries to remove the responsibility for these moral failures and calls them "diseases," but the person who suffers them is no better off. In fact, he may be worse off because he can continue in the self-destructive behavior and blame it on forces other than his own personal choice.

As we mentioned earlier, it is the secrets you carry that shape your self-concept. If your secrets are shameful, you may avoid close relationships with those who would be shocked by those secrets. Friends who were formally close are kept at a distance. Stories are manufactured to give others a better picture of who you are, to avoid their learning the real story.

Just as we all tend to move toward those who have the same values and interests, the guilt-ridden person may finally associate with others who are throwing off the restraints of moral integrity. Those who let themselves give in to homosexual behavior may begin to associate with others of the same bondage. Gossips, pornography addicts, drunks, and thieves all seek one another's company. Not only are they able to find others of like mind, they may corrupt some who have not yet fallen into their bondage.

Conscience in the New Testament

The weak conscience: the conscience of one who is not fully informed concerning the truth as revealed in Scripture and in Jesus Christ (1 Cor. 8:7, 10, 12).

The evil or defiled conscience: the conscience of a corrupted person who is aware of his wrongdoing and is thus defiled (Heb. 10:22; Titus 1:15).

The seared conscience: the conscience of one who has repeatedly refused its warnings; a deadened and perhaps silenced conscience (1 Tim. 4:2).

The pure conscience: the clear conscience of one who seeks to live by God's moral standards, a conscience that gives honest testimony (2 Tim. 1:3).

The conscience void of offense: the conscience of one who relates his moral values to the worship of God and obedience to His Word (Acts 24:16).

The good, clear, honorable conscience: the conscience of one who lives honestly in all matters, following God at all times (Heb. 13:18; Acts 23:1; 1 Tim. 1:5, 19).

Unresolved guilt can lead to significant stress, and that stress can cause physical symptoms of various kinds. Sufferers often complain of anxiety attacks, stomach troubles, arthritis flare-ups, and a host of other problems. This is not to say that every physical ailment is caused by emotional stress. Physicians have learned, however, to look for causes behind the symptoms when no apparent physical cause can be detected. This is a difficult area to diagnose because people are not prepared to reveal their moral secrets.

Attempts at Rationalization

If we are suffering from guilt, we may attempt to justify our behavior by blaming circumstances and other people.

There is a delicate balance between blame and shame in the mind of man. When our sense of personal guilt tilts the balance, we will try to find someone or something to blame to relieve the pressure.

Our minds are skilled at finding rationalizations for our own moral failures. We can make the most creative and ingenious excuses. Children can offer explanations for their misdeeds that will amaze their parents. We are so good at this rationalization that we often believe our own propaganda.

When blaming others and circumstances around us is not effective for rationalizing our guilt, we will try to attack the standards that provoke the guilt. We argue that the problem is not in our behavior but in the rules that condemn our behavior. Though we may not get our consciences to cooperate fully, we can say that these rules don't apply to us. We don't accept them anymore; they are old-fashioned, puritanical, legalistic.

We will probably receive a good bit of reinforcement in this view from our society. The trend today is to throw off the restraints of moral values that have been accepted throughout the generations. Traditional morality is out of vogue. It is for the few stuffed shirts of the religious right or the traditionalists of the Roman Catholic Church. To be modern and progressive is to do away with moral standards so that anything goes.

The self-centered nature of man strives for independence and autonomy. Especially loathsome is the idea of having to answer to God. So humanity tries to get rid of God and the moral absolutes that come from the character of God. The person who gives himself up to moral degradation will inevitably challenge theological truth. He will allow his personal conduct to dictate his theological beliefs. But this is not a new phenomenon. You may often discover the roots of a person's theology by checking his or her biography.

People who have not come to terms with their own moral responsibility are irritated by others who have high moral standards. In order to justify their moral slackness, they may attack others' moral standards with ridicule. They speak of moralists as ignorant, primitive, out of date, and tradition bound. They present themselves as having superior understanding. They are enlightened, progressive, informed, and objective. Theirs is but another effort at getting rid of the authority of moral absolutes and those who advocate them.

The symptoms and rationalizations of a guilt-ridden person indicate the distress he or she is experiencing. What remedy can he find for his misdeeds? There seems to be no remedy for that person's guilt unless he or she is willing to accept God's forgiveness. But forgiveness calls for repentance and confession. This requires accepting full responsibility for one's own attitudes and actions. There can be no final solution without that acceptance of responsibility.

The next chapter will deal with principles to guide us in our desire for personal integrity. We must find that moral freedom is found in the narrow path of moral responsibility.

▼

SEVENTEEN

Freedom in the narrow path

▼

"Dear Uncle Sam," the letter began. "You are a great guy, although sometimes I think you are pretty dumb.

"Way back in the '40s I ripped you off for a few bucks while working in a war plant. I didn't mean to. When I'd knock you off for a few bucks, I'd say to myself, 'Tomorrow, I'll do some extra work and make up for that.' But it did not work out that way.

"My doggone conscience has been working on me. So, to shut it up, I'm sending you this money order for $400. I think it is a little more than I chiseled you for, but that is all right because I know you need the money." The letter was signed, "One of your conscience-stricken nephews."

Each year letters like this flow into government offices across the country. Some are handwritten, some typed. They contain checks, money orders, or cash, in amounts ranging from small change to thousands of dollars. Some 450 such letters eventually get to the desk of the keeper of the Conscience Fund in Washington.

The fund was started in 1811 when James Madison was president. A citizen anonymously sent in five dollars with a letter saying he had defrauded the government. Since then the Conscience Fund has received over six million dollars, currently running about $120,000 a year.

A divorced mother of two small children wrote that she owed $1,400 in taxes. "I was in terrible need of money that year," she wrote, "and I guess I thought I needed the money more than you did. I am sending two money orders totaling $800 with this letter. I promise I will send the remaining $600 very soon. I feel like a criminal or something. I realize a lot of people have cheated on their taxes, and some don't even need the money. I am sorry this has happened. I have never broken any kind of law before. I have not received any kind of notice on my taxes. I am only doing this for my own peace of mind and for my children."[1]

Some Americans today would think the writers of these letters need counseling. They must be mentally unbalanced to take such a thing so seriously. Others would see it as a sign of hope that the soul of the nation is not yet corrupted beyond recovery. Whatever your opinion about contributors to the Conscience Fund, one thing is clear. Man has an inherent sense of right and wrong.

The Desire for Integrity

God is holy. In creating man in His own image, He made him with the moral sense we call "conscience." He also placed in him a desire for *integrity*. Though corrupted by sin, nevertheless man has a longing for honor and virtue. Even the worst criminals often try to defend their virtue in the face of terrible crimes. "I'm not really so bad," they say. "I didn't really mean to do it."

In the first place, the desire for integrity means a longing for *consistency*. Most people have a pretty good idea of right and wrong. In their minds they may fully intend to do the right thing. But the self-centeredness of human nature presents them with another agenda. They have appetites that are not in harmony with their own professed values. Consistency would mean always behaving according to those values.

Integrity is the integration of moral commitments and behavior.

The Desire for Integrity

God is righteous and holy. He made man as moral, with a desire for personal integrity. Integrity means the integration of moral convictions and moral behavior. It involves a desire for consistency, virtue, and respect. When the desire for integrity is threatened, the warning comes in the form of *guilt, shame,* and *remorse.*

The desire for integrity also means a desire for *virtue.* This means purity, decency, and uprightness. Bill Bennett's *Book of Virtues* provides a collection of stories, poems, and essays about qualities like self-discipline, compassion, responsibility, honesty, and loyalty. In his introduction to the book, Bennett writes, "These stories speak to morality and virtues not as something to be possessed, but as the central part of human nature, not as something to have but as something to be, the most important thing to be."[2] That is what virtue means. It is something to be.

The desire for integrity also means a hope for *respect.* Integrity is not only a matter of inner virtue, it has to do with reputation as well. No one likes to be disliked and scorned. Every person would like to be known for something, honored for some quality or achievement. The desire for integrity is a hunger for that honor. It is the longing for a reputation that causes others to know who you are and to speak of you with admiration.

The normal desire for integrity seems to be smothered in many of today's youth. Our society does not champion virtue. They do not receive training in morality. Instead they get courses on how to use condoms. They look in vain for role models who exemplify genuine character and integrity. Their heroes are often foulmouthed rappers, arrogant athletes, or immoral actors.

Instead of societal pressure to be morally upright, the pressure is to be "bad" or "cool." Young gang members are respected if they are brutal, if they are willing to take a life.

There is no shame for immorality, indecency, and dishonesty. The campaign of the last thirty years to rid the nation of its traditional values seems to have worked. Instead of encouraging the desire for integrity, today's culture gives full reign to self-indulgent and destructive appetites.

We can know, however, that the desire for integrity is part of our nature. If children are presented with the right training and examples, they will respond. They will accept the truth. For older youth and adults already set in their way, the revolution of Christian conversion can break up those old patterns and open the way for a new life.

The Measure of Morality

An ongoing debate today concerns "values." Instead of the "rules" of another generation, today everyone wants to talk about "values." Whereas *rules* means commands to be obeyed, *values* means preferred or esteemed qualities, attitudes, and behaviors. The debate is over what the values are to be. Should they be the old-fashioned "family values" of traditional America? Or should we promote the new values of the present day?

The old values were ideas like responsibility, truthfulness, hard work, honesty, loyalty, kindness, helpfulness, faith, moderation, patriotism, and frugality. For generations these qualities have defined what it means to be an American. Like a Norman Rockwell painting, our vision of America has pictured ordinary, salt-of-the-earth neighbors who were consistent, dependable, friendly and, well, *neighborly*. Even though everyone did not live up to these values all the time, everyone generally agreed that they were best.

The traditional values were rooted in religion. The Judeo-Christian tradition provided a cultural foundation for character and behavior. There was a reference point, a source of truth, an ultimate authority, and that was God Himself. Protestant Christianity, particularly Puritanism, left a strong emphasis on responsibility to the community. One's behavior and attitude could not be seen as an independent matter. The very social fabric was threatened when the children of the community did not comply with accepted values.

So the traditional values centered on responsibility. Each person is responsible for his own actions. If he does well, he will be respected and will prosper. If he behaves badly, he will receive the just rewards of his actions. He is not only responsible for himself, he is responsible to his family and his community. He must answer to them because his actions reflect on them. Of course, rebels in every generation have embarrassed their relatives and neighbors. But they were the exception that proved the value of the rules.

The new morality, which became a serious social movement in the sixties, proposed a different set of values. The new call was for freedom instead of responsibility. This freedom was to overturn all the old rules and taboos. The basic assumptions behind this movement were not new ideas. Academics and scientists had already created a philosophy that rejected God. Along with this denial of God came a rejection of Creationism and religious authority, particularly in the area of ethics. These views surged onto the American scene in the sixties to infect a whole generation of young people.

Morality in Conflict

Traditional Morality	The New Morality
Responsibility	Freedom
Truthfulness	Situation ethics
Hard work	Anti-materialism
Obedience	Autonomy
Loyalty	Free love
Moderation	Self-indulgence
Patriotism	Pacifism
Frugality	Back to nature
Accountability	Tolerance
Faith	Secularism

The new values, rooted in freedom, were more a reaction to the old values than a carefully thought proposal of new ones. The new freedom was freedom from rules, restrictions, disapproval, and social pressures. Instead of the work ethic, young people loaded in Volkswagen vans and wandered the country. Instead of loyalty and commitment, they practiced "free love" with anyone available. Instead of frugality and prosperity, they promoted back-to-nature simplicity and communal living. Instead of self-discipline came self-indulgence through hallucinogens and other drugs, promiscuous sex, and the abandonment of traditional social graces.

Even though reactionary, the "new morality" of the sixties brought a new set of values that dominates contemporary thinking today. The new values are self-esteem, tolerance, acceptance, compassion, equal outcomes, the brotherhood of man, social welfare government, secularism, peace, and equality. These values call for politically correct speech, the acceptance of homosexual behavior as normal, and abortion to be accepted as a woman's right. Marriage is considered outdated, honesty is viewed as optional, and individual expression is unassailable.

Whereas the traditional values were rooted in religious law, the new ones are based on personal autonomy and independence. Instead of God as the ultimate source of authority for right and wrong, the new values call for the individual to decide right and wrong for himself, based on his own self-interests. The result of this shift in values has been a devastating moral decline. As the results come in, even those who have promoted the new morality have become alarmed at the damage. Crime, marriage failures, illegitimate births, brutality, child abuse, slothfulness, and selfishness are rampant.

The Fork in the Road

Whether we realize it or not, each of us ultimately takes one of two roads when it comes to moral values. These two paths illustrate the development of moral values in the real world. Let's consider the principles for distinguishing these two paths as they are revealed in Psalm 1. This psalm contrasts the moral life of the godly and the ungodly. One makes God the source of moral authority; the other has no place for God in his life. From the biblical viewpoint these are the only two choices.

First, the psalmist gives the ungodly man's approach to moral values. This is presented as what the blessed man *does not do*. "Blessed is the man who does not walk in the counsel of the wicked or stand in the way of sinners or sit in the seat of mockers."

Though this is speaking of the godly man, the one who is blessed, it is really referring to the patterns that can be observed in the ungodly man as his moral values are developed.

Notice the figurative terms *walk*, *stand*, and *sit*. They refer to one's lifestyle, loyalties, and beliefs. Your "walk" means your manner of living, your daily habits of behavior. Your "stand" means the position you take on certain issues, your opinion about them, your convictions. "Sitting" has to do with your settled outlook. We talk about the "seat" of government and refer to a judge's position as "the bench." So your "seat" means the philosophy you espouse, the authority you accept.

Though the "blessed" man rejects this approach, look at where the ungodly man goes for his values. First, he "walks" (patterns his lifestyle) after the "wicked," those guilty ones who are against God. He simply mimics what he sees in those around him. This is peer pressure at its most basic level. Man naturally rejects God and His law, so the ungodly person will fall into this pattern unless he is trained in a different one.

The second aspect of the moral values rejected by the godly is "standing" in the way of "sinners." This means the ungodly "takes his stand" in the "manner" or "habit" of those who reject God's moral law. Notice the progression of his moral development. First he lives like those around him, without reference to any standards. Then he becomes loyal to that pattern, as his own habit, so he takes his stand there and defends it. This sounds very much like a "gay pride" march.

The third picture is when the ungodly man comes to a judgment about his moral values. He rationalizes them philosophically. He "sits," "dwells," "remains," in the "seat" or "assembly" of the "mockers," "boasters," or "scorners." These are those who have settled on this ungodly lifestyle and have justified it with arguments and rationalizations. Their outlook is arrogant, disrespectful, self-centered. This is where the ungodly man ends up. He has started with living like those around him, becomes loyal to that pattern, and finally justifies it as normal.

The godly man, by contrast, is described in verse 2, "But his delight is in the law of the LORD, and on his law he meditates day and night." Instead of following the lifestyle of the godless, he has an objective reference for morality in the written Word of God. He can withstand the peer pressure of the world around him because he has a moral compass, not only to guide himself, but to evaluate their ethics. The Word of God shapes his lifestyle, his loyalties, and his philosophy.

The same three terms, *walk*, *stand*, and *sit*, are found in Paul's letter to the Ephesians. There, however, they are presented in a different order. In Ephesians 2:6 Paul writes that "God raised us up with Christ and *seated* us with him . . ." (my italics). In 4:1 he urges his readers to "live a life [*walk*] worthy of the calling you have received." In 6:13 we read, "Therefore put on the full armor of God, so that when the day of evil comes, you may be able to *stand* your ground . . ." (my italics). This order is sit, walk, stand.

The significance of the order in these passages is remarkable. Instead of beginning with his walk, or lifestyle, the godly man begins with sitting, his position as a new creation in Christ. He starts with the Word of God, which shows him God's law and grace and tells him who he is. Before he confronts the question of values, he receives the authoritative Word from God. Secondly, he walks, ordering his lifestyle according to God's law instead of the behavior of his peers. Finally, he stands in the moral and spiritual conflict with the confidence of his convictions, ready to do battle for the truth.

There is much more in Psalm 1 to consider, but space will not permit dealing with it all in detail. Notice, though, the contrast in the destiny of the two types of people. The godly are like fruitful trees, while the ungodly are like the useless chaff blown away by the wind (vv. 3–4). Whereas the Lord watches over the way of the godly, the wicked will be separated in judgment and have no place among the people of God (vv. 5–6).

Can you see your own moral development in these verses? Can you see the approach needed in rearing children? The biblical plan is to begin as a learner, sitting to learn the Word of God. This is followed by a walk that puts the wisdom of God into practice. Finally, the godly person is prepared to stand for what is right and true. The godly person has learned God's truth and has proved it in his or her own experience. The godly are strengthened within against the temptation and rationalization that would lead them astray.

The Meaning of Character

The Christian life is not merely a better *quality* of life; it is a different *kind* of life. Whereas quality emphasizes the superiority of the Christian life, kind focuses on the essential nature of that life. The change from the life without Christ to the life with Christ is a change at the core of your being. It is a shift from being centered in self to being centered in Christ. This different kind of life involves distinctively Christian character.

In the debate today about values, the matter of character has often been overlooked. "Values" are a set of ideas you accept as superior and valid according to your own best judgment. Character, on the other hand, is who you are. Christian character is forged by a set of nonnegotiable, God-given truths, to which the Christian must submit. Character is hammered out in the laboratory of experience.

What does the word *character*, really mean? The word is derived from the Greek word *charassein*, which means "to engrave." So "character" originally came from the idea of making a mark and so came to mean the particular "marks" or qualities of a thing or a person. Character is what distinguishes you, the qualities that define your attitude and behavior. In common usage "character" has come to mean the positive qualities that make a person commendable. It means something like "virtue" or "integrity."

Dealing responsibly with the message in our emotions will require a commitment to Christian character. Character is a complex idea, involving reputation, conviction, principle, and self-image.

Character can mean *reputation*. The Bible says, "A good name is more desirable than great riches" (Prov. 22:1). This verse, though, does not call us to the task of creating an image for ourselves. It means that what others see in us will give us a "name" among them. If they see personal integrity they will think of our name in positive terms. Knowing what to expect from us, they will tend to trust us and anticipate how we are likely to behave in a given situation.

Character requires *conviction*. The tests life throws at us strike at the pivotal point of character, conviction. Conviction refers to that set of internalized values a person determines to follow. Character may well be defined in terms of the nonnegotiables in your life. Are there those convictions and beliefs you will not even consider compromising? Or will you take each situation in terms of its own merits and try to determine the advantage of one line of action over another?

Character calls for *principle*. Conviction must have some content, some meaning. This meaning is what we are calling principle. A principle is a fundamental truth or law upon which behavior may be based. Principles are guidelines for making decisions and acting. To say someone is "a principled person" means he or she lives according to certain authoritative truths or laws.

Character involves *self-image*. Rather than applying deeply held convictions or absolute principles, we most often behave in a way we think will reflect who we are. This self-concept is built up over the years by what others tell us about ourselves, by experiences, and by our own choices as to the kind of people we intend to be. You may have said yourself, when faced with some temptation, "I'm just not that kind of person." This sense of moral identity is especially important in the Christian, who is a "new creation" in Christ (2 Cor. 5:17).

There is a core character built into our nature through the image of God in us. That character is defined in the revelation of God in Scripture. As we interact with our world, the emotional signals tell us where adjustments need to be made. As you read the message in your emotions, you will be alerted to how you are dealing with life. You will be able to respond in such a way as to keep your attitudes and behavior within the bounds of Christian character.

▼
—

E I G H T E E N

The power of integrity

▼

Riley and Tracy were two of the finest young people in the church. Everyone had watched their courtship with interest and delight. The date for the wedding was set. It was to be a beautiful church wedding with pretty girls and handsome young men, Christian wedding songs, and a masterpiece of a cake to be baked by the groom's sister. The whole church family looked forward to it.

Then one Sunday Riley asked the pastor to meet with him and Tracy that afternoon. He said that it was important, but his drawn expression said "urgent." When they met, Riley told the pastor that Tracy was pregnant. He made no excuses, took all the responsibility, saying he should have had better control of his passions. After they discussed it a while, the pastor asked Riley, "What do you think God wants you to do about this?"

"I've already thought about that," he said as he looked at Tracy, "and we've talked it over. We think the only thing to do is bring it to the whole church. I want them to learn this from me and not hear it from rumors. If they all come to the wedding and know what we've done, our testimony will be worthless. We wanted it to be a witness to our families. We wanted to let everyone know what we stand for. Now that's all ruined. But if we don't confess it ourselves, it will only be worse. We will be hypocrites."

The pastor told them they were doing the right thing. That night in the evening worship service, the pastor told the congregation that Riley wanted to speak to them. Then he sat down with the people to listen. The young man went to the pulpit and repeated what he had said that afternoon, taking full responsibility for everything. He did not want Tracy to say anything. She just sat there in the pew, listening with a mixture of embarrassment and admiration.

When he finished, the pastor stood again, "You have heard what Riley has confessed tonight. Now, what do you have to say to him? It is important that we respond." With that he stood quietly looking over the earnest faces of the people. After a brief pause an older woman, in a real sense the matriarch of the church, stood and turned to speak to Riley where he sat with Tracy.

"Riley, I've known you since you were born. I've watched you grow up in this church. I knew your daddy, one of the finest men I've ever known. I have been proud of you and happy for you and Tracy. You've made a mistake. But you've had the courage to stand up and take full responsibility for it. I'm sorry for what has happened. But I've never been more proud of you than I am tonight. God has forgiven you, and I forgive you."

As she sat down several were wiping tears from their eyes. Then one after another stood, from the oldest to the teens, each saying something of the same thing. After everyone who wanted to had spoken, the pastor led in a prayer for Riley and Tracy, thanking God for their courage and His forgiveness, and thanking Him for the fellowship and love among His people. As he closed the prayer, the people gathered around the young couple and wept and rejoiced with them.

What happened that night was the church at its best. No one condoned the self-indulgence of the young couple. Neither did anyone condemn them. Their confession opened the way for forgiveness and reconciliation. This was God's answer to the problem of guilt.

More than twenty years ago, in his book *Whatever Became of Sin,* psychiatrist Karl Menninger went against the grain by raising the question of responsibility for sinful behavior.[1] Most psychotherapy then, and now, tries to help people discover *why* they act wrongly rather than have them face their sins and accept responsibility for them. Moral misdeeds are often labeled as "illness," insulating the guilty person from responsibility.

The problem of sin ultimately brings us to God. He is the not only the One who is finally offended, He is the only One who can offer a final solution.

Living in the Light

Dealing with sin is the key to responding to the cluster of emotions in the area of morality. *Guilt, shame,* and *remorse* are all signals of a threat to personal integrity. In all likelihood that threat is caused by some action on our part that brings a conflict between our convictions and our behavior. Remember, *integrity* is basically the integration of belief and behavior, a consistency between our moral values and our moral decisions.

A key passage on sin contains some of the most important principles in the Bible for a healthy, wholesome life of moral integrity. In 1 John 1:5–2:2, the apostle advocates "walking in the light," living a life of openness, honesty, and responsibility before God and man. This passage offers a biblical strategy for moral integrity.

The first principle is this: *Moral integrity is based on the character of God.* Verse 5 reads, "This is the message we have heard from him and declare to you: God is light; in him there is no darkness at all." The character of God is "light" and whatever contrasts with that character is "darkness."

The common view today is that there is no absolute standard of right and wrong. Each person is to determine for himself what his moral values are. This means each person is his own authority. It means that what is wrong for one person can be acceptable for another. It also means that the old laws, rules, and taboos can be overthrown in favor of the freedom to do whatever one wishes.

The biblical view stands against this philosophy at every point. There is the "light" of God's character and His law, and all other moral guidance is darkness. The basis for the law of God is the character of God. God told Moses, "Speak to the entire assembly of Israel and say to them: 'Be holy because I, the LORD your God, am holy'" (Lev. 19:2). What God commands is based on who He is. His laws are not just arbitrary rules designed to keep man from having any fun. They reflect God's holiness and protect man.

We know what is right and wrong through the revelation of God in the Bible. But the pinnacle of God's revelation of Himself is in Jesus of Nazareth. In His life, His character, and His teachings we have all we need to face any moral challenge. Jesus used the metaphor of light and darkness to refer to Himself when He said, "I am the light of the world. Whoever follows me will never walk in darkness, but will have the light of life" (John 8:12).

A second principle for moral integrity is that *fellowship with God requires living by God's truth.* "If we claim to have fellowship with him yet walk in the darkness, we lie and do not live by the truth" (1 John 1:6). We may ask immediately why anyone would claim to be associated with God if he did not want to comply with His instructions. This verse makes clear that the claim of association with God, while not living in the light of His moral character is living a lie.

Principles for Moral Integrity

▼ Moral integrity is based on the character of God.

▼ Fellowship with God requires living by God's truth.

▼ Living by the light of God's truth provides a basis for Christian fellowship.

▼ Purification for sin comes through the atoning sacrifice of Jesus.

▼ Forgiveness and cleansing of sins requires truthful confession.

▼ When we confess our sins, Jesus Himself comes to our defense.

King Saul tried to do this very thing (1 Sam. 15). He had disregarded God's instructions and been dismissed by God from his reign. Even though he insisted that he *had* obeyed, he knew it was merely a rationalization to keep up appearances. Finally, he appealed to Samuel, God's spokesman, to walk up to the place of worship with him so that the elders of the people would not know that God was displeased with him. It was more important to him to appear to have God's favor than actually to have God's favor.

It is amazing today to see churches in which the common factor around which the people gather is that they all practice homosexuality. Professed Christians refuse to accept the authority of biblical morality while insisting they are in fellowship with Him. Like Saul, they like to *appear* devout, without having to go to the trouble of obeying God. But genuine fellowship with God requires living by God's truth.

A third principle for moral integrity is found in 1 John 1:7. *Living by the light of God's truth provides a basis for Christian fellowship.* The verse reads, "But if we walk in the light, as he is in the light, we have fellowship with one another." Here is a oneness and communion among people that is not possible on any other basis. Christians who live in the light of God's truth have a bond that makes them one. They understand each other. They know what to expect from each other.

Personal autonomy and independence cannot provide a basis for Christian fellowship. If each person is his own authority and each can do as he pleases, there can be no intimacy. When each is submitted to the same authority, however, they can meet on common ground. They share the same values, the same convictions, the same commitment. They are both surrendered to the same Lord and determined to please Him.

This trusting, open fellowship is one of the most joyous and fulfilling benefits of life in Christ. But it cannot be experienced apart from walking in the light. Unless we live in openness, honesty, and responsibility with one another, there will inevitably be shallow relationships, mistrust, and uncertainty. This intimate and trusting fellowship is vital to dealing with guilt.

A fourth principle for moral integrity is this: *Purification for sin comes through the atoning sacrifice of Jesus.* The text continues, "and the blood of Jesus, his Son, purifies us from all sin" (1 John 1:7b). Here is the promise for purification, cleansing from all sin. This includes all sin, every possible sin we might commit. There are no sins so foul or heinous that they cannot be cleansed.

The basis for this cleansing of sin is clear. It is the "blood of Jesus." We might think that God forgives sin simply because He decides to be generous. "I'll let you off this time," He says, "but don't let Me catch you doing that again." But this idea would require setting aside the law of God. That is not possible. Jesus said, "I tell you the truth, until heaven and earth disappear, not the smallest letter, not the least stroke of a pen, will by any means disappear from the Law . . ." (Matt. 5:18).

God cannot wink at or overlook sin. That would be a denial of His integrity. Unlike the American justice system, where the guilty are set free on technicalities or excuses, those guilty of sin before the court of heaven will have their just punishment administered. The "blood of Jesus" means that He received the judgment of death for you and me. His blood covers our sins.

As we live in the light of openness, honesty, and responsibility, we can experience the cleansing of sin made possible by the death of Jesus on our behalf. Walking in the light not only removes barriers that hinder our fellowship with one another, it also removes the barrier—our sin—to our fellowship with God.

The next principle is the pivotal one. *Forgiveness and cleansing of sins requires truthful confession.* John writes it this way, "If we confess our sins, he is faithful and just and will forgive us our sins and purify us from all unrighteousness" (1 John 1:9). On either side of this statement is a warning about denying sin. Trying to say we have no sins is to deceive ourselves, to reject the truth, to make God out to be a liar, and to exclude the Word of God from our thinking. The only way to deal honestly with sin is to confess it.

The Greek word for "confession" means to say the same thing as another. So confession of sin means to agree with

God about it and to express that agreement. There is only one viewpoint about sin that holds any authority. It is God's view as presented in Scripture. To confess your sin is simply to call it what God calls it—no excuses, no rationalizations, no shading of the meaning, no search for causes in your background. It is the full acceptance of responsibility for your moral misdeeds.

The sixth principle for moral integrity is a great encouragement to us. *When we confess our sins, Jesus Himself comes to our defense.* The next verses make this principle clear, "But if anybody does sin, we have one who speaks to the Father in our defense—Jesus Christ, the Righteous One" (1 John 2:1). The word used here means that the risen Christ serves as our attorney before the court of judgment, pleading our case on the basis of His own death for our sins. He not only took our execution, He is our lawyer in court.

If such a defense were made in a human court, how would it go? "Your honor, my client has pleaded guilty. We understand that the mandatory sentence for his crimes is death. But I would like to call to the attention of the court that this sentence has already been carried out. My client cannot be charged for these crimes because his debt has already been fully paid." In a sense, Jesus pleads that very point of law, based on His own execution in our behalf.

So when you confess, you are not hoping for leniency. You know that justice will be done to the full extent of the law. But you also know that the execution of Jesus of Nazareth was in your behalf. Paul wrote, "For what I received I passed on to you as of first importance: that Christ died for our sins according to the Scriptures, . . ." (1 Cor. 15:3). This is part of what it means to have Christ as your Savior.

So the Bible offers a set of principles for moral integrity different from what you will hear in the contemporary world. Based on these marvelous truths, any of us can have our guilt removed. The key to our part is confession.

The Miracle of Confession

How do you go about confessing your moral misdeeds and experiencing release from guilt? Let me again suggest that you take pen and paper and write out your thoughts. First write out in graphic detail how you feel about your sins, your failures, your meanness, your selfishness. Include in the story not only your behavior but also your attitude. Attitude is the wellspring of behavior. Until you see the sin in your attitude, you have not dealt with the central problem.

You are going to the chamber of secrets to clean house. You will look behind and beneath, leaving no place unexplored. You may find yourself uncovering old scenes and stories you thought you had forgotten. Sometimes we think we can "let bygones be bygones" and eventually get past old failures. But the record is still there. Nothing has been done to clear the offense. There in your chamber of secrets is everything that has not been brought out through confession.

Not only does the rotten and shameful stuff in your chamber of secrets affect your self-esteem, it can also cause mental and emotional trouble. Psychiatrist Hobart Mowrer stated that "you are your secrets."[2] He saw "hidden guilt as being the central problem in all psychopathology."[3] The neurotic person is basically one who has not accepted the responsibility for his misdeeds and suffers the reaction of his psyche to the garbage in his chamber of secrets.

Remember, the message in your shame and guilt is that your personal integrity is threatened. That threat can only mean you have failed to behave according to your values. Your conscience is writhing in pain because of the conflict of belief and behavior. If you ignore this message, it will come out in some other way, with symptoms you may not immediately connect with your guilt. You must pay attention to the message in your emotions. Otherwise you can become physically and mentally sick.

After you have written the story of your moral failures, now you are to move to part two of your confession. The first part could well be "What I Have Done and How I Feel About It." Part two is "What God Says About My Sin." Now you write a clear and objective assessment of your experience from the perspective of the principles for moral integrity. Take each one and apply it to yourself. Personalize it by writing something like this, "Whatever my past actions, and however I have tried to explain them, moral integrity for me must be based on the character of God." Now go on to elaborate on that truth as it applies specifically to your experience.

This part of your exercise is actually a statement of faith. It is an affirmation of the firm truth that sets all your uncertainty and rationalizations aside. This exercise is also a conversation with God. You are openly and honestly telling Him your story. You are allowing Him to expose long-hidden sins that you might not mention. You are aligning yourself with His truth as it speaks to your experience. All of this is confession.

As you write part two of your exercise, you will begin to sense the tremendous relief and peace of coming clean. You are accepting the forgiveness and cleansing that only God can give. Your emotions may overflow during this exercise, with the pain of facing yourself and the peace of a clean slate. As you complete the exercise you may know that there is more to do. You must come clean with others as well.

Moral integrity calls for responsibility. If your moral failures have affected others, you will want to be open and forthright with them about these failures. This is also confession. Mowrer stated flatly that "until one has 'worked through' and resolved his guilt in the face of all mankind, he is not fully healed and whole."[4]

You will remove the natural fear of being found out by others by clearing these nasty memories out of your chamber of secrets. This doesn't require telling everyone about your sins. It is obvious that everyone is not at all interested in your story. For your own peace of mind, however, you should carry your openness to the point that you don't care who knows your story. You are open and honest about your misdeeds and secretive about your kindnesses.

There is another important benefit of this openness. When you are in the kind of fellowship with others that involves trust and accountability, you will find your own willpower greatly strengthened. A secretive, private person has little reason to restrain his appetites. If you are not in community with others who would be affected by your behavior, it is much easier to let yourself go. Trusting fellowship with others opens your life to their inspection and broadens the scope and implications of your responsibility.

As you walk in the light of an open, honest, responsible lifestyle, you will find a great freedom. You are free to be yourself, warts and all, with others. You are free to maintain your moral integrity because of the greater strength of will that comes with being in community. You are free from the shame and guilt that eventually leads to remorse, even mental illness. "Therefore confess your sins to each other and pray for each other so that you may be healed" (James 5:16).

An Action Plan

Here is a summary of insights from this section to guide you as you respond to the message in your guilt, shame, and remorse.

▼ Listen to the voice of conscience.

▼ Refuse to rationalize your moral misdeeds.

▼ Reject the "new morality" in favor of biblical standards.

▼ Determine to grow in the virtues of Christian character.

▼ Live in the light of openness, honesty, and responsibility before God and man.

The next section will deal with the emotional pain clustered around worry. What does worry tell us? How can we respond to its message and stop allowing worry to plague us? How can we gain the security we desire?

▼

NINETEEN

How can I keep it all?

▼

Are you worried? If you aren't you probably should be. Just think of all the things there are to worry about. Recent news will give us a partial list.

First, take medical problems. A major investigation is looking into patient deaths due to errors on the part of doctors and nurses. Several cases have been cited in which chemotherapy dosages were four times what was required. Just a mistake. Then there is the ebola virus outbreak in Africa, with local politicians pointing out that only a plane ride by an infected person will bring it here. There is also a virulent new staph infection that eats away at your flesh. Watch out for that!

If medical problems don't worry you, then what about crime? Your chances are one in ten of being mugged. You could be shot on the freeway. You could be the victim of drug-crazed and deranged teenagers who kill just for the fun of it.

How about pests? A new warning has come about the killer bees. Then there is the deer tick that carries Lyme disease. And the fire ants are on their way to your area.

If these aren't enough, you could worry about your finances. Who knows what effect the latest action of the Federal Reserve is going to have on your retirement plans. You could lose your job. How can the Australians possibly be serious when they say so glibly, "No worries."

You are probably thinking now that none of this is funny. It is all too real and all too possible. These are the very things that make us all worry. But we don't stop there. We have our own private worries as well.

The old Anglo-Saxon word from which we get our word *worry* was *wyrgan*. It meant "to strangle." "Worry," as a transitive verb, literally means "to bite and shake with the teeth as a dog with a shoe." So the meaning was about annoying or bothering something or someone, making another troubled or uneasy. I can remember my father using "worry" in this way when I was a child, "Son, don't worry with that. Just leave it alone." It is from these original ideas that we derive our customary meaning, "to be anxious or troubled."

But let's go back to the dog and the shoe. Here is the picture of a puppy with your old house shoe. He gets a good grip on it with his teeth and shakes it from side to side with the aim of killing it. Then he lies down, the shoe still in his mouth, to rest a bit. You try to retrieve your shoe. He rolls those big brown eyes at you and growls as you tug it. This is great fun. We'll play tug-of-war. You shake your finger at him and admonish him in no uncertain terms to release the shoe. But he just gets a better grip and growls. If this process goes on for very long, the shoe will be slobbered on and shredded.

So how is this a picture of worry? It shows us that worry is connected with possession. We worry about our things, our loved ones, our health, our future, and so on. We mentally cling to these treasures with a stranglehold. If a turn of events threatens to take a cherished possession away, we growl and clench our teeth, refusing to give it up. In the process we are in the "fight" stance from the "fight or flight" instinct.

Does this sound familiar? I can remember sitting up late one night to wait for our daughter to get home. I was trying to read, but my eyes were drawn back to the clock every half minute. She should have been there an hour ago. That ambulance siren I heard a while back kept ringing in my mind. It was not that I didn't trust Anna; it was the dangerous, unpredictable world out there I didn't trust. Emotionally I was clinging to her, holding her to myself, standing defiantly to dare any circumstance or event to take her from me. She was my baby and I would not give her up. That was worry.

This chapter will explore the emotional pain associated with worry. Then the symptoms of the chronic worrier will be sketched, as will misconceptions about worry and security.

Understanding Worry

Worry is the emotional pain at the center of the distress we experience in the area of possessions. While worry is the more active and aggressive expression of this cluster, the more passive is *insecurity*. If the causes behind these emotions are not addressed, the unresolved conflict will become *fear*. These painful emotions signal a threat to your desire for *security*.

Worry is the feeling of tension and uneasiness you experience when something or someone you value is in danger. The danger does not have to be real. You can worry about imaginary problems or a threat that might possibly come. Worry has your body in a defensive, fighting mode. You feel tense, a sinking sensation is in your stomach, and your mind is locked onto the possession you fear losing. A bout with worry may keep you from sleep, affect your appetite, and bring on other physical ailments.

Def•i•ni'tion: Worry, Insecurity, Fear

Worry is the central emotion in a cluster of emotional pain associated with the responsibility for possessions. As the more active expression of these emotions, worry is the tension and distress over the anticipated loss of some valued possession.

The more passive emotion is *insecurity*, a general feeling of danger or vulnerability. If the causes behind these emotions are not resolved, the more serious expression of this cluster is *fear*, a sense of personal danger on all sides.

The emotions in this cluster signal a perceived threat to your desire for *security*.

Sometimes we like to make a distinction between "worrying" and "being concerned." Is there really any difference, or are we simply trying to give our worry a little nobility? To be concerned means to be influenced, moved, or affected by some condition. It indicates serious interest, with a personal stake in the matter. Worry, on the other hand, means you are troubled, apprehensive, and uneasy. So we can see that these ideas do overlap. You move from concern to worry, however, when you feel threatened with a personal loss.

Any time you are worried, ask the question, "What exactly is it I am fearful of losing in this situation?" You do not really worry about matters that do not threaten a personal loss to you. Worry is the distress over losing something you value. The greater and more personal the value, the more intense the worry is likely to be when it is threatened. In one sense, worry is grieving over the loss of something or someone before it is lost.

While worry is the more active expression of this emotional cluster, the more passive is *insecurity*. This means a sense of danger, exposure, or jeopardy. But instead of being focused in the specific loss of something valued, it is more diffuse, more personal. The emotion of insecurity has you feeling vulnerable, unprotected, unsafe. Whereas *worry* is focused on some feared loss, insecurity is a general sense of personal threat from all sides.

In today's circumstances, there are thousands of persons who feel insecure, especially the elderly and those who live alone. It is easy to see how they have good reason to feel insecure. They are often unprotected, left to their own devices for any kind of security. The threats are real. Many an elderly person watches the evening news about some grisly murder and lies in bed imagining that every unusual sound is the murderer trying to break in.

If the causes of chronic worry and insecurity are not addressed, the result is the unresolved expression of these emotions, *fear*. Fear is such a general term and used in so many different contexts. But here we mean a deeper sense of insecurity in which the person feels personally in danger. Those experiencing fear have a sense of foreboding, apprehension, or terror. It is a horror that grips them to the point that it is the primary factor in shaping their activity.

A phobia is an irrational fear with some rational basis, over which the person has little or no control. The fear of flying, for instance, is somewhat warranted. Planes do crash from time to time. You could die from flying. But even if you go over the statistical chances of surviving a flight, the person with this phobia is not impressed. Therapists today are attempting to alleviate this fear by incremental exposure to the experience of air travel until the person can stand it.

Emotional *injuries* of past experiences may cause a person to be a worrier. Traumatic experiences of personal danger or tragedy can leave scars that color every situation with foreboding. Coming to terms with such experiences can be a long process. The *disease* of faulty thinking can also lead to worry and insecurity.

From the viewpoint of faith, there is a clear answer to worry and insecurity in the Bible. Though it may seem radical to some, it addresses the issue head-on and leads to a new outlook.

The Chronic Worrier

Worry is the emotional signal of a threat to your desire for *security*. The idea of security is broader than safety from physical harm. It includes emotional and relational security as well. In one sense chronic worriers are plagued with possessiveness. They are very much aware of any seeming threat to anything they think of as theirs. It can be their health, a friendship, their jobs, their family members, financial stability, a particular goal they hope to reach—anything they think is rightfully theirs.

All of these "possessions" are important to worriers' security. They do not worry, however, about those things that are not theirs. I have heard people express concern about events far away on the other side of the world. This may be a humanitarian interest, but it is not worry unless there is some threat of personal loss.

Here are some of the common symptoms of chronic worriers.

▼ They are usually disturbed about some threat to their security, however unlikely and trivial.

▼ They will often try to involve others in their sense of impending danger by talking about their worries.

▼ They may suffer physical symptoms like stomach disorders and insomnia.

▼ They see the source of their worry as "out there" in the circumstances rather than "in here" in their thinking.

▼ They cannot seem to shake off the replaying of the imagined danger in their mind.

▼ They tend to rationalize their worries by trying to give plausible arguments for them.

▼ They seem happy only when all they hold dear is safe at hand to enjoy.

▼ They may develop facial expressions that reveal the ongoing habit of worry.

▼ They try to manipulate people and situations to secure and protect their possessions.

▼ They give an inordinate amount of time and attention to caring for and securing their possessions.

▼ They may be demanding and possessive with the things and people they consider to be theirs.

Taken all together, these symptoms may not apply to you or anyone you know. But if only two or three of them apply, they point to a chronic worrier.

Misconceptions about Possessions

In today's society there are a number of misconceptions about possessions, security, and worry. This is the faulty thinking that often sets us up for worry and makes it seem consistent with the facts.

The first misconception is that *the quality of life can be measured in terms of possessions*. There is obviously some truth in this idea. It is easy to see that my quality of life is dependent on good health. So if my health is a "possession," then the statement is true. This is also the case for relationships with loved ones. Of course the comfort and convenience of a nice home also makes for a better quality of life. Having plenty of money for what I need and want affects my quality of life.

The question here is simple: Does what I have define who I am? You may object that this is a question of identity rather than quality of life. When we say quality of life, we are using a term that is often set against sanctity of life. Those who advocate the *quality* test rather than the *sanctity* test have argued that a deformed or retarded child should be aborted because his or her quality of life will be so poor. They have argued for assisted suicide in the case of terminal illnesses because the quality of life is gone.

What if you lost everything you possess? Would life be over? Is there not something more to life than the things you think of as yours? Is there not character and personal integrity? History is full of accounts of those who have lost everything—family, material possessions, position, reputation—but found life still precious. How do people survive in the horrible conditions of concentration camps? Is life not holy, worth more than anything external to it?

Perhaps the best wisdom is to see life itself as a holy gift from God. From the biblical viewpoint a person can still find joy when everything is lost but God, the Giver of life. Habakkuk, a godly man who lived in a terrible time, wrote,

> Though the fig tree does not bud
>   and there are no grapes on the vines,
> though the olive crop fails
>   and the fields produce no food,
> though there are no sheep in the pen
>   and no cattle in the stalls,
> yet I will rejoice in the LORD,
>   I will be joyful in God my Savior.
>   Habakkuk 3:17–18

Though this makes no sense to the world, the believer knows that even if he loses everything, he or she still has God.

Getting this perspective allows us to see the relative value of the things we cherish. It helps keep first things first.

Another misconception about possessions is this: *A person is owner of his possessions and can do with them as he pleases.* As we have already noted, autonomy and independence are important themes in contemporary thinking.

The individual is seen as his own final authority. His "hard-earned wealth" is his to do with as he pleases. He should spend it on himself and his family. He deserves it. He earned it. He gave a fair exchange of sweat and hours and creativity for it. He has every right to control its use.

Most of us respond to such thinking with a resounding "Amen!" It is part of our heritage as Americans. We reject the idea of oppressive government or employers or any other agency confiscating our resources or forcing us to spend them in ways we oppose. But for believers there is another dimension to this question. What about God? Does He have no say in what we do with our resources? Is it not an integral aspect of the Christian life to be under the authority of Christ?

There is an underlying selfishness in the view that I can do as I please with what is mine. Is the only purpose of God's blessings for me to satisfy my own appetites? Am I responsible for anyone else? Am I to ignore the needs of others around me? Beyond material possessions, am I to see my family, my health, and my future as being all for my own benefit?

Misconceptions about Possessions

▼ The quality of life can be measured in terms of possessions.

▼ A person is owner of his possessions and can do with them as he pleases.

▼ A person can adequately protect his wealth if he handles it carefully.

Paul addresses this issue directly, "What do you have that you did not receive? And if you did receive it, why do you boast as though you did not?" (1 Cor. 4:7). Everything we have is a gift and blessing from God. The Bible rejects the idea that we are our own final authority. We are to acknowledge the authority of God in the use of everything we have. "You may say to yourself, 'My power and the strength of my hands have produced this wealth for me.' But remember the LORD your God, for it is he who gives you the ability to produce wealth" (Deut. 8:17–18).

A third misconception about possessions by contemporary society is that *a person can adequately protect his wealth if he handles it carefully*. When a person is the final source and authority for his own possessions, he has two responsibilities. First, he must produce all the wealth he will ever have. Second, he must also protect his wealth from the various threats to it. There is no protection beyond what he can do on his own.

Protecting one's wealth is a major challenge. We know there are those who would steal from us, unseen economic forces that would render our wealth worthless, and other unnamed threats we cannot control. How can we possibly defend ourselves against all these threats? When the Wall Street crash came that ushered in the Great Depression, there were a number of financiers in New York and elsewhere who took their own lives. Their fortunes were gone. Their jobs were gone. Their lives were over.

The Bible makes clear that we are to handle carefully everything we have. There is no room for sloppy business procedures or wastefulness. But behind it all is the clear understanding that God is our Protector. Even our "possessions" like health and loved ones are in His hands. Even though we will take every reasonable precaution, we cannot guarantee the security of anything we cherish. We come into this world without a thing and leave the same way.

Life in this world is, at best, uncertain. Built into nature is an element of chaos that keeps us aware of our finiteness. Just think of all the ways your cherished possessions can be threatened. Just imagine how quickly tragedy can strike. Can you handle it? Can you cover all the possibilities? Where do you go for protection against such threats? There is only One who can handle it. Trust Him.

▼

TWENTY

Under new management

▼

Howard Hughes had done it all. He had inherited a flour-
ishing business that made him an instant millionaire. He had
moved to Hollywood to make movies, winning an Academy
Award in 1928 for *Two Arabian Knights*, which he produced at
age twenty. He told Noah Dietrich, his business manager, that
he was determined to become the world's most famous movie
producer, the top aviator, and the world's richest man.[1]

He seemed to succeed on all accounts. With almost unlimited funds from his business, he produced a series of films,
some of them classics. As a pilot, he set cross-country and
around-the-world speed records. He dated a number of beautiful Hollywood actresses. Through Hughes Aircraft he developed new planes like the Flying Boat and the FX-11 jet
fighter. He ran TransWorld airlines.

But behind all this apparent success was a shy, antisocial
man so afraid of disease that he took extraordinary precau-
tions against germs. He would gargle often and avoid people
with colds. On one occasion he burned all his clothes when
he heard that a woman he had dated had been exposed to a
venereal disease. At times he made the people who worked

with him carry out elaborate hand washing rituals and wear white cotton gloves when handling documents he would later touch.

Hughes died April 5, 1976, on board a private jet bound for Houston from Acapulco. The last years of his life he became a complete recluse, addicted to codeine, living in darkened rooms, in contact only with the employees who kept him alive. For all his genius, vast resources, and opportunities, Howard Hughes's life was a tragedy by any measure.

No doubt some who saw Hughes on television in his prime or read of his exploits had envied his wealth and fame. In the Paul Simon song *Richard Corey*, the singer describes the man's affluent life and repeats, "I wish I was Richard Corey." We may envy those who appear to have everything, even want to be that person. Sometimes the truth is out, however, when, like Richard Corey, the person with everything goes home to "put a bullet through his head." The last ten years of his life, Howard Hughes found relief from his torture only in heavy doses of codeine.

Of course it isn't the wealth in itself that is the problem. There are thousands of wealthy people whose lives are fulfilled and fruitful. The problem is in the perception that having everything we want would make us happy. In our natural desire for security, we often think it is to be found in material wealth. But the security we seek is much more complex than that.

This chapter will deal with the desire for security and explore biblical principles for fulfilling this desire.

The Desire for Security

God is Creator and Owner of all that is. In creating us in His own image, He made us *possessive*. He placed man in the beautiful garden of Earth and charged him to manage it for Him. With possessiveness came a desire for *security*, an instinct for protecting what was his to manage. That desire was to be centered in his faith in God, the source of his security. But with the coming of sin, man was separated from this trusting relationship with God. Now his security seemed to be in his own hands.

Today the security business is one of the fastest growing areas in the American economy. Products ranging from bulletproof vests to deadbolts are hot items today. Various forms of pepper gas and handheld alarms are sold at convenience stores. Handguns are being purchased by people who never thought they would own a gun. Some states are passing new laws that allow citizens to carry concealed handguns for protection. Private police forces are growing so fast as to outnumber public police. Americans have become accustomed to seeing armed guards in malls, hotels, almost every place of business.

Business executives are warned to protect themselves against kidnapping. They are often provided with elaborate electronic surveillance equipment, trained guards, powerful weapons, and bulletproof limousines. Celebrities and public officials are seldom seen without bodyguards. Homes are fitted with security systems that can detect the slightest movement of an intruder on the grounds or in the house. It is normal procedure now to pass through metal detectors and have your hand luggage x-rayed before boarding a plane.

Along with all these security measures, there is a growing sense of insecurity. There is a suspicion that no matter what we do to protect ourselves, it won't be enough. In some neighborhoods, children are in danger every day from the stray bullets of gun battles. Parents are fearful to let them play unsupervised in the city parks. The desire for security goes far beyond protective measures against criminals. In involves several basic elements: food, shelter, protection, strength, and the future.

The desire for security begins with the basic need for *food*. A well-stocked food pantry gives a sense of security. From the earliest generations of man, he has sought to gather, grow, and store food for himself and his family. I can remember the sense of security we had as a family to know that we could get by on what we produced off our land, with little dependence on outsiders. Today we must depend on food suppliers at every level. Nevertheless, security still means enough food to eat.

Our natural desire for security also extends to *shelter*. At its basic level, the desire for shelter simply involves getting in out of the cold and rain. Animals instinctively look for shelter from the elements, a place to be warm and dry, to bear young, to rest. For man this desire for shelter is much more complex. He wants comfort, convenience, his books and recordings around him, plenty of room for privacy. Each of us has childhood memories of hearing the wind whistle at the corners of the house and the sound of rain on the roof, while we snuggled warmly in our beds. That is security.

The Desire for Security

God is Owner of all that is, so He made us in His own image as *possessive*. With this He also gave us a desire for *security*. He intended to be our Source for every kind of security. A threat to our desire for security is signaled by the emotional pain of *worry, insecurity,* and *fear*. Responsible behavior in the area of possessions will require understanding and applying the principles of stewardship.

A third basic aspect of the desire for security is, of course, *protection*. As we have noted above, the word *security* is now associated almost exclusively with protection. From man's beginnings, he has had to protect himself and his family from predators, robbers, and marauding enemies. In today's sophisticated, high-tech society, we still feel the need to protect ourselves from those who would rob and kill.

Security calls for *strength*. In many ways, man's ability to provide security for himself and his family is dependent on his personal strength. Early on man provided food by the sweat of his brow and fought off enemies with his own hands. Now, however, there is still an underlying fear of being weak and, therefore, vulnerable. This fear comes home to us most often in our concern for our health. We dread the idea of being helpless and dependent, our bodies wasting away so that we cannot take care of ourselves. As much as anything else, we are insecure about our health.

The desire for security also has a *future* aspect to it. To be safe and well-fed today does not leave us without worries. We inevitably think of tomorrow. We wonder whether we have enough resources to take care of tomorrow's needs. We try to anticipate the threats we and our families might face. We buy insurance to guarantee health coverage. We set aside money for that "rainy day" we all expect. We try to make plans for taking care of our families after we are gone. The desire for security always includes a secure tomorrow.

Responsibility for Possessions

The desire for security comes from our responsibility for possessions. In creating us, God gave us everything we need for a full life. He placed within our reach the resources and materials for feeding, housing, protecting ourselves and our families, staying healthy and strong, and making arrangements for the future. With all this provided, God holds us responsible for how we manage the rich abundance of the planet.

Just as the desire for security goes beyond protection, the responsibility for possessions goes beyond material goods. God expects us to handle whatever we have in a responsible way—our time, our money, our energy, our family, our health, our creativity. With our natural desire for security, we tend to cling to what we possess as the guarantee of that security. No matter how much we have, however, we may find, like Howard Hughes, that we still feel threatened and insecure.

God's intention was never to have us own the resources of the Earth. There is a distinct difference between *possession* and *ownership*. Possession means "control," "occupancy," or "use." On the other hand, ownership means the "title," "right," or "claim" on a thing. Concerning ownership, the Bible says, "The earth is the LORD's, and everything in it, the world, and all who live in it; for he founded it upon the seas and established it upon the waters" (Ps. 24:1). God says to us, "What is this I hear about you? Give an account of your management" (Luke 16:2).

The traditional biblical word for management is "stewardship." In the management of God's creation, our role is always that of *steward*. The word means "agent," "caretaker," "administrator," or "custodian." It always pictures a person

197

into whose hands a trust has been committed. The steward is not the owner, even though he does have possession of what has been entrusted to him. He will handle his trust according to the owner's instructions and expect to answer for his management.

When my wife's father died, his will named Sharon executrix of his estate. This meant it was placed into her hands to manage according to his instructions. This is a clear example of what stewardship means. As her husband, the responsibility fell to me as well. Though the estate was not worth a lot of money, the job of managing it was a lot of trouble. Since the will was a legal document, and we had agreed to take care of things after his death, we had full control over everything he left.

God has placed His vast resources into our hands, to manage according to His instructions. Because I have a title to three cars, that makes me the official owner, according to the state of North Carolina. I am also joint owner of a house, with the savings and loan, and listed accordingly in Wake County. I think of all this stuff as mine. I expect to have control of it. I am responsible to maintain it. I get the benefit of using it. But, in the biblical view, everything I have is God's. I am not *owner* but *steward*.

In our natural drive for security, however, we generally think of our possessions as our own and as our primary source of security. We work to gather all we can and to keep all we get so that we can be safe from hunger, storms, robbers, and every other threat. As Jesus introduced the parable of the rich fool, He said, "Watch out! Be on your guard against all kinds of greed; a man's life does not consist in the abundance of his possessions" (Luke 12:15). The principle is simple: our lives are not in our possessions.

A woman was being interviewed after a fire in California in which her home was lost. With a cry of despair she told the television reporter, "Everything we had accumulated in thirty years is gone. We have to start over. Our whole life is gone!" I am not sure she really meant to put it that way. But it came out that everything worthwhile in her life was lost in the fire. Her possessions were her life. She cannot imagine not being surrounded anymore by her familiar and comforting things.

We can understand her sense of loss. Any of us would be distressed over such a loss. But as attached as we might become to our possessions, our life cannot be in our things. On a CBS report of another similar fire loss in California, a man replied, "It was just a house. We can get another house. We thank God that no one was harmed." His comment may strike us as a bit too indifferent, but he has the right idea. He can get another house, but he can't recover a lost family member.

The Job Description

Imagine checking the job listings in the newspaper and finding this ad:

> Family-owned company seeks agents for international distribution of assets. Position carries complete benefits package with unusual opportunities for advancement. Housing and all expenses provided. No experience necessary. Contact *Kingdom Enterprises.*

This sounds like a very good opportunity. It really seems too good to be true. You probably believe, as I do, that when something sounds too good to be true, it probably is.

But God offers us just a position as His agents on Earth. As we represent His interests, He provides all the needed resources. This is stewardship.

One of the best pictures of stewardship is the experience of Joseph recorded in the book of Genesis. You remember that Joseph was a favorite son of Jacob. His brothers did not appreciate that favoritism nor Joseph's dreams in which they all bowed down to him. So they sold him into slavery and he was carried along to Egypt. There he went to work for a man whose wife tried to seduce him. When he refused her she lied and accused him of attacking her.

So Joseph wound up in prison. But even there he was put in charge of the other prisoners. He correctly interpreted the dreams of two of Pharaoh's servants: one was executed while the other was restored to his job. Later, when Pharaoh had a series of disturbing dreams, the servant remembered Joseph and they sent for him. He listened to the dreams retold and interpreted them as God's warning of seven years of abundance followed by seven years of drought.

So Joseph advised Pharaoh with a plan for preparing for the lean years to come. Pharaoh put him in charge as his second in command in all of Egypt. He was to see that enough food was stored in the good years to last through the lean years. So Joseph went from the prison to the palace. He was rich and powerful like no other in Egypt. This is a picture of stewardship. But notice that it is not so much a performance as it is a position.

In the first place *stewardship means freedom from bondage.* Joseph had been in jail; he was in debt to society, with nothing of his own and no freedom to move. That, of course, sounds like the financial situation of many people today. They are in debt. The have no room to move. They see nothing but a gloomy future ahead of them. It reminds me of that scene in one of the *Indiana Jones* movies where the walls are closing in on the heroes and threatening to crush them.

Jesus said, "No one can serve two masters. . . . You cannot serve both God and Money" (Matt. 6:24). For many of us, Money does not serve us, we serve Money. Whatever Money requires, we must do. If Money says work longer hours and neglect our families, we must do it. If Money requires the sacrifice of our integrity, we go along. But most prisoners want out of this prison. They don't want to be in bondage to debt, worry, greed, or selfishness. Stewardship is the way out.

Stewardship also means servanthood. Joseph was essentially a manager, an administrator, serving Pharaoh. He was to carry out his duties in keeping with Pharaoh's wishes. Jesus told a parable about stewardship, beginning with these words, "Again, it will be like a man going on a journey, who called his servants and entrusted his property to them"

(Matt. 25:14). Like those servants, our Master has gone away. We must operate according to His policies without Him looking over our shoulders. But we know He will return one day to ask for a report. That is stewardship.

Imagine a restaurant manager who decides she doesn't like the standard operating procedure of the company. Maybe she's a McDonald's manager, and she decides she would like to sell Whoppers like Burger King. So she decides to go her own way. What do you think will happen when her regional manager checks on her? Right. She will either do it the company way or move on to other employment. The company policy manual for Kingdom Enterprises is the Bible. We have plenty of freedom within the scope of those policies.

Stewardship also means abundant possessions. In the story of Joseph, it is obvious that he had great wealth. To be Pharaoh's chief administrator meant having everything he could want. All of Egypt was his. He lived in a palace, wore the finest of clothing, and had chariots and military escorts everywhere he went. This was quite a change from the jail. But nothing he had was really his. It was all Pharaoh's. He had use of it. He could control it. But he didn't have title to it.

Imagine a street scene as Joseph came by. His escort of military officers would part the crowd, shouting, "Make way. Bow down." The people would step back and bow their heads in respect. So two ordinary Egyptians sneak a look as Joseph passes. One shakes his head and says to the other, "Poor guy."

"What do you mean, 'Poor guy'? That's Joseph, Pharaoh's chief administrator. He's the richest and most powerful man in all Egypt, except for Pharaoh himself."

"Yeah, sure. I see the chariots. I see the escort. I see the fancy clothes. I even know where he lives. But none of that stuff is his. It all belongs to Pharaoh. He has nothing."

"So what? It doesn't seem to bother him. Who cares if it's all Pharaoh's. He's still got it, even if it isn't really his."

"But just think of not having a stitch to your name. At least I own the clothes I wear. I own my tools. I own my plot of ground and my house."

"What? Those rags you're wearing? Who would want them? And your old broken tools and that dump you have built on that little pile of sand you call a farm. Who would want any of it? What if you do own it?"

Let me break into this imaginary conversation now. Can you see the point? If you are a servant of the King, you have everything the King gives you. He places in your hands all you need to carry out your duties. Why should you insist on *ownership* when *stewardship* is such a better deal?

Keep in mind that if you are the owner, you must supply all the wealth and see that it is protected from loss. If God is the Owner, He will supply everything and protect it from loss. Your role is to manage what He puts in your charge and to manage it according to His policies. The supply is unlimited because everything comes from His treasury.

The next chapter will deal with how to enter into the position of stewardship. The guiding principles for this job are astounding. You need never be concerned about security again. You need never worry again.

▼

TWENTY-ONE

The secret to security

▼

It was a long drive, especially at this time of night. I had finished a meeting in Houston and left late that evening for home in Arlington. For a while I had listened to Bill Mack on the radio from Fort Worth. Then I had followed the truckers on the CB as they chatted about the location of "Smoky" and where to eat. Finally I turned off the radios and just sat thinking. It was a clear starry night, no sound but the tires and the wind, nothing to see but the stretch of interstate just ahead as my headlights pushed the darkness aside.

My thoughts turned toward my family. In that swift stillness I seemed to get beyond the pressures of work and schedule. Almost like a dream, the important things came forward in my mind to demand attention. I imagined them asleep in that familiar house on Whiteway Drive—Sharon, still too young to be mother of four, Michael and Mark approaching those troublesome teen years, Matthew almost two, and Anna just a baby.

Suddenly it was clear. My priorities were set in order. Here was my treasure, my joy, my precious trust from the very hand of God. I thought about my responsibility. How could I possibly give them what they needed in love, wisdom, and understanding, not to mention food, clothing, and protection. This was beyond me. How easy it would be, even in the safety of our home, for some insidious disease to slip in and attack one of them. How easy for the evil in this world to take them from me.

I found myself praying, tears dampening my face, "Oh God, I can't do this; it is beyond me. They need so much from me. Each one, in a unique way, looks to me for so much. I feel like an empty shell standing before their searching eyes."

The answer came as clearly as I have ever heard it. "Give them to Me. I will love them. I will meet their needs. I will provide for them, materially and spiritually. I will protect them. I will do everything you cannot begin to do."

It was that simple. "Give them to Me." I was not the key to meeting their needs. I was merely an agent of His supply. Years ago I had given my future to God as I answered His call to ministry. But I had never, in the same final way, given my family to God. Sharon and I had talked about it. But now it was just as real as an official transfer of ownership placed before me to sign.

What answer could I give? Not only was He calling me to surrender my family to Him, He was calling me to be to them what only He could make me. It was as though I took everything precious to me and placed it in His hands. It was done. They were His now. Of course, they had always been His, but now it was a vital matter of trust, a basic understanding in my relationship with Him.

The Message of Worry

From the transaction that took place on Interstate 45 that night long ago came a new understanding of my role as husband and father. Though I had never realized it, I had been acting as owner and sole provider. Now it was clear that I was but a custodian, a steward of God. He would take care of all the precious treasure He placed in my life.

The worry and insecurity I had experienced about my family was a clear message in my emotions. I was threatened in the area of possessions, particularly in my ability to take care of them. The answer was so simple. Paul stated it plainly, "Do not be anxious about anything, but in everything, by prayer and petition, with thanksgiving, present your requests to God" (Phil. 4:6). There it is: Instead of worrying, present your requests to God.

Worrying, then, is a signal that something has not been given to God. When worry comes, it is warning that I am clinging to something that is precious to me, fearful of losing it. Like a child clinging to the toys he just received at the birthday party, I want to cry and scream in my frustrated efforts to keep it all. But if I really entrust my treasure to the hands of God, I have no need to worry. Everything is safe there.

Is it your health you worry about? Give it to God. In a quiet time of "prayer and petition, with thanksgiving," just place your life and health into His hands. Is it finances? Give it to Him. Is it your family? He will take them. Is it your own future and ministry? Present it all to Him. Then accept your role as steward of His treasure. Concentrate on learning how to manage His things in His way. This may call for some significant changes. Now, however, you are clear about your role. You are not owner; you are steward.

Worry signals a fear of losing something. If you give it to God you have already "lost" it. You must give it up, even though you may still enjoy it by His grace. But whatever happens to it from that point on is up to Him. Though you will take care of it as best you can, you know that even your best is not good enough. Now your stewardship is on His terms. You are His agent for provision and protection you could never give on your own.

Do not stop with the "giving up" part of your role as God's steward. Move on to the positive, active work as an agent of God's generosity. Remember, in God's economic system you cannot give without receiving. "Give, and it will be given to you. A good measure, pressed down, shaken together and running over, will be poured into your lap. For with the measure you use, it will be measured to you" (Luke 6:38). Worry reminds you that you need to give something to God. But keep on giving.

The Material Key to Spiritual Riches

There is a connection between your handling of money and your ability with spiritual matters. You may want to have a dynamic relationship with God in which your prayers are being answered and you daily experience His direction and provision. You would like to have such a Christian experience that proves day by day that God is alive and present. There are many biblical principles for living this kind of life. Unless you honor this one, however, all your other expressions of faith and devotion may be fruitless.

Here is the principle: *God will trust you with spiritual power and riches on the basis of your handling of material resources.* You may think of money as mundane and insignificant as compared to the great spiritual matters. Some Christians are even indifferent about money. They see it as beneath them, unworthy of their attention, unspiritual. But this is wrong thinking. Jesus makes clear that you will only be trusted with spiritual resources as you properly handle dirty, old, worldly, unspiritual money: "Whoever can be trusted with very little can also be trusted with much, and whoever is dishonest with very little will also be dishonest with much. So if you have not been trustworthy in handling worldly wealth, who will trust you with true riches? And if you have not been trustworthy with someone else's property, who will give you property of your own?" (Luke 16:10–12).

Do not think that you are above money. You will never get beyond it. God delights to use this basic medium of economic exchange to demonstrate His faithfulness. The person who proves himself trustworthy with money can then be trusted with more significant matters. Do not risk operating without spiritual power, having your prayers go unanswered, leaving your family and ministry vulnerable to attack, just because you can't bring yourself to trust God with money.

Let me suggest a plan for putting your role as steward to the test. Follow these principles for a test period of six months or a year and see what God does. Keep a log of what you are doing so you can document what happens. Involve your family in the experiment so that everyone mature enough to understand can participate. If you are already living by these principles, use these suggestions as a checklist to remind you of your strategy.

An Employment Agreement

First, *enter into a stewardship covenant with God,* based on what the Bible teaches about stewardship. This covenant will begin with the transfer of ownership to God. I suggest you take a piece of paper and write out a statement acknowledging God's ownership of everything in your possession. It is His already, but by faith you are going to officially transfer ownership to him, leaving no question about it from now on. Maybe you could write something like this:

Stewardship Covenant

(Place and Date)

   I, _____, as a follower of Jesus Christ, having surrendered my life to Him as Savior and Lord, do hereby acknowledge the full and unrestricted ownership by God of everything I possess. In the presence of the witnesses named below, I relinquish all claim upon the possessions identified in this document, also to include any other undesignated possessions that presently exist or may be received in the future.

   I also, freely and without duress, do hereby enter into the service of God as steward. In this position I will faithfully, to the best of my ability by His grace, manage all the possessions He places in my hands according to His policies as contained in the Bible. I understand that it is His intention to provide everything needed, in normal and extraordinary ways, for the fulfilling of my duties as His agent.

Signed: _____

Witnesses: _____

   _____

   Pursuant to this covenant, the known present possessions are as follows:

At this point, list everything you possess: life, health, family, job, future, car, house, clothing, time, affections, and so on. Make as creative and exhaustive a list as possible. Have each family member make a personal list. Young children can understand much of what you are doing. It will be a great experience for them to enter into such a relationship with God at an early age. You may want to use simpler wording for them. After everyone has completed his list, talk about it together and sign as witnesses for one another. Then commit the decision to God in prayer.

Notice that this covenant is not a giving plan to support the church budget. Stewardship goes far beyond tithing or giving to the building fund. God has much more in mind for you.

Allocation of Resources

The second principle is: *Expect God to direct your use of possessions for His purposes.* There are needs around you God wants to meet, using you as His agent. Before the covenant, on your own, you could not afford to consider seriously many of these needs. In fact, you were not even aware of them. Now that God can trust you to do what He wants done, He will call needs to your attention and even tell you how you are to meet them. Since His resources are unlimited, He may surprise you by drawing rather heavily on your present possessions, even using what you thought you needed for yourself.

To the extent that you obey His instructions, He will supply all that you need for His "projects" and more for yourself besides. Paul puts it this way, "And God is able to make all grace abound to you, so that in all things at all times, having all that you need, you will abound in every good work" (2 Cor. 9:8). Notice in this verse how many times the word *all* or *every* is used. This is an indication of God's ability and His intentions.

This giving of yourself and your material resources is like planting a seed of faith. That seed may be all you have, but when you plant it in obedience, it will produce a good return. Again, Paul puts it clearly, "Remember this: Whoever sows sparingly will also reap sparingly, and whoever sows generously will also reap generously. Each man should give what he has decided in his heart to give, not reluctantly or under compulsion, for God loves a cheerful giver" (2 Cor. 9:6–7).

You may want to give what you need the most in order to have more. Are you short of money? Give as directed so more will be supplied. Are you pressed for time? Give time where it is needed by someone else and you will have more time. Are you lonely? Give companionship and love and you will receive an abundant return. It is what you give up by giving away that will bear fruit. Jesus said that unless a seed is given up through planting, it remains alone, but if it is planted and dies, it bears much fruit (John 12:24). So what you give is a complete loss to you and a seed planted for great return.

Here's a warning. If you enter into stewardship, you will have more than you ever did before, more than you need. Can you accept that? "Now he who supplies seed to the sower and bread for food will also supply and increase your store of seed and will enlarge the harvest of your righteousness. You will be made rich in every way so that you can be generous on every occasion, . . ." (2 Cor. 9:10–11). Your wealth will be increased as you are faithful so that God can do more through you than before.

God will have you give to ministries that are doing His work. Be alert for those. He will have you help those in need. Expect to have them cross your path. He may show you a need so great that you cannot even imagine meeting it. But if He intends to meet that need, He may well do it through you. In many cases He will stretch your faith, drawing present resources down to a dangerously low supply. But He knows what He is doing. In His economy, what you receive depends on the measure of your giving.

The Chamber of Secrets

Here we are, back at the chamber of secrets. It is here that we find the third principle I am suggesting: *Keep your activities secret so that the honor may go to God.* In the passage quoted several times above, Paul mentions the outcome of the generous giving he is asking of the Corinthian Christians. Their generosity, he says, "will result in thanksgiving to God" (2 Cor. 9:11). If God is to get the honor, however, His steward must remain in the background. This brings us back to Jesus' teaching about doing our good deeds only for the eyes of God.

Even though it is not always possible to keep your giving and ministry secret, you are to make every effort to do so. The purpose, remember, is to avoid doing it for the recognition and approval of others. It is none of their business. This is a matter between you and your Lord. You do what He requires because that is your job as steward. The work is His work and He can make it known if He so chooses. All you want is His approval.

One of the most delightful experiences I have had in giving will illustrate in a vivid way how God works. Since it happened twenty years ago, its value for me and for the others involved has been long since used up. They have spent the money, and I have spent the joy of obeying God by giving it. There is nothing left of it in the chamber of secrets but a fragrance, the sweet memory of a wonderful experience with God.

The neighbors who lived next door to us in Arlington were visited by their daughter and son-in-law, recently appointed Wycliffe missionaries to somewhere in Central America. Sharon and I had only once talked briefly with them. We learned from our neighbors that they were planning to leave any day, with their four-year-old daughter, on the long drive through Texas and Mexico to their assignment. We were impressed with their courage and dedication. We could understand the misgivings of our neighbors; it was a long and dangerous trip.

Late one evening I was reading in the living room when a clear word came to me out of the blue. I was told to give one hundred dollars to the missionary couple. I put my book down to ponder this a minute. It was ridiculous. I hardly knew these people. I had no idea of any need on their part. Besides that, I didn't have a hundred dollars and had no way to get it this time of night. So I went back to my reading.

The thought was insistent. There could be no question about it. After putting it off for five or ten minutes, I decided

I had to do something about it. I took all the money from my wallet. Not nearly enough. So I began to search the house. Sharon was taking a bath. I called to her through the door, "Do you have any money stashed in the house?" She couldn't imagine what I needed it for, but she told me where I could find a few more dollars. To my amazement, after a fairly quick search, I actually found a hundred dollars, quite a lot of money in those days for our household.

So I wrote a note to the couple and told them that God had instructed me to give them the money. I encouraged them in their mission and quoted several promises of God about meeting all our needs and protecting us from harm. I told them that we would pray for them. I put the note and the money in an envelope, sealed it, and went next door. By this time it was about 11:00 P.M. Our neighbor came to the door and told me that her children were already in bed, but that she would give them the envelope. I went home not sure what was going on but sure I had done the right thing.

The next morning, the young missionaries loaded up their Volkswagen van and left. Our neighbor told us that they had been very uncertain for several days, unable to decide to go ahead and leave. She said that last night they were greatly encouraged that God would take care of them so they decided to leave immediately. She said that they had been praying for some sign from God of His care and provision. She did not know what was in our envelope, but she said it meant a lot to them.

I was thrilled beyond measure to hear this report. Without any knowledge of their prayers and the desperate crisis of faith they were going through, God used us to assure them of His care. The frightening part is that I actually argued with Him about it. Two or three months later we received a letter from the young woman. She told us they were settled at the mission and had begun their work. She said the trip was hard but uneventful. And she said that they might not have gone without the very direct and tangible assurance from God that He would be with them and meet all their needs.

Keep It Simple

The final suggestion is this: *Be satisfied to live simply.* As simple as it sounds, this is a very complex issue. For one thing, *simple* means different things to different people. There are Christians in every economic category who have become faithful stewards. There are some who are wealthy beyond what they will ever need. Others live hand to mouth. But if they are faithful stewards, they *all* experience the joy of having possessions in perspective.

Simplicity means living simply. It means living within the scope of your normal income level. Learn to say no to yourself about buying things you do not need. Simplicity means making your home a center of hospitality and ministry. But be sure to distinguish between "entertaining" (fancy and impressive) and "hospitality" (making others feel welcome). It means keeping priorities in order—people above things. Recognize that stewardship is basically a matter of trust. It means trusting God to meet all your needs, so that you are free to be His agent in meeting the needs of others.

An Action Plan

As you respond to the message in worry and insecurity, here is a summary of insights on stewardship.

▼ Accept God's ownership of all that you have.

▼ By faith enter into a covenant with God as His steward.

▼ Be alert to God's direction as to the use of resources.

▼ Pursue your stewardship as secret service to God.

▼ Make necessary changes to live simply.

Our next chapter moves to the common distress of discontent. What causes us to be discontent? How can we find the peace we all seek?

▼

TWENTY-TWO

Where can I settle down?

▼

Michael Crichton's novel *Jurassic Park* is about a dinosaur theme park. But this is not Disneyland. Here there are real dinosaurs, recreated from DNA taken from ancient insects trapped in amber. The idea is to create a drive-through zoo of animals from millions of years ago. What an attraction!

As the story develops, the eccentric mastermind behind Jurassic Park keeps assuring everyone that everything is on schedule. He is sure it will all go as planned, even though a few "bugs" yet remain in some of the systems. Every security precaution has been taken. Every detail has been planned into the giant computer that monitors and operates the entire park.

But everything doesn't work as expected. That's what makes the story really interesting. A few problems arise, like the vicious raptors breaking out and stalking the people. A greedy thief shuts down the security system. Then the flesh-eating, ferocious Tyrannosaurus Rex gets free and prowls for dinner. In the end nearly everything seems to break down, bringing on a gripping struggle for survival for the heroes of the story.

Actually this failure of the well-laid plans was predicted by one of a group of scientists flown in to tour the park. He is Ian Malcolm, a mathematician and expert in "chaos theory." He contended that any system so complex as Jurassic Park will inevitably experience a fatal breakdown of order. It is the way such systems work in this world. No matter how we might plan for order, the element of chaos is always lurking in the shadows.

Chaos theory contends that the behavior of complex systems cannot be predicted by normal cause-and-effect thinking. Too many variable factors are involved. There is an element of chaos in all of creation, but there is an underlying order in the confusion and unpredictably. The common example is the weather. The factors involved in weather developments are so numerous and so unpredictable that forecasting more than two or three days in advance is only a guess.

Much of our own experience demonstrates the chaos factor in life. The oft quoted Murphy's Law captures the idea, "If anything can go wrong it will." Something is always coming loose, breaking down, or falling apart and ruining our plans. Though we tend to see these outbreaks of chaos as abnormal, they are really a part of the way this world is designed. There is a randomness at the roots of the created order that keeps us guessing and busy.

Ironically, God created us with a deep desire for peace, order, and certainty. Ever since Adam and Eve were evicted from the Garden of Eden, humans have been searching for that paradise. We long for peace, rest, assurance, a dependable and predictable environment. We are looking for the home we lost in the fall of Adam. No matter where we live or what shape our situation takes, we are still not fully content.

This chapter will deal with the cluster of emotional pain centered in *discontent*. These feelings are signals in the area of *situation*, warning of a threat to your desire for *peace*. The chapter to follow will explore what we mean by "situation" and a strategy for dealing with trouble. Then we will offer a specific prescription for dealing with discontent. First let's define the emotions in this cluster.

Living with Discontent

There are few negative emotions more common than discontent. From time to time everyone seems to express some dissatisfaction with the way things are going. In some workplaces griping and complaining comprise most of the conversation. It can be the same at school, at home, anywhere people get together. The practice is so common that companies have institutionalized it with complaint departments and grievance officers.

The more active expression of this cluster of distress is *discontent*. It is a feeling of dissatisfaction with present conditions, the desire for something more or different. Discontent usually focuses on those specific factors you don't like.

You may be discontented with your job because of the working conditions, the lack of challenge, or the attitude of your supervisor. You may be discontented at home because of repairs needed on the house, noisy neighbors, or a strained marriage relationship.

Discontent is the feeling of sadness, irritation, and disappointment that signals a threat to the peace in your life. The basis for discontent is the picture you have in mind of the way things ought to be. You know what it would take to make your situation pleasant and enjoyable. Any point where conditions do not measure up becomes a focus of attention. It draws your eye and your ire because it spoils your ideal.

Def•i•ni'tion: Discontent, Restlessness, Uneasiness

The emotional pain associated with one's situation is identified as *discontent, restlessness,* and *uneasiness*. It signals a threat to personal peace.

Discontent, a sense of irritation and disappointment, is the more active manifestation of this distress, focusing on the undesirable factors in the situation.

Restlessness is the passive form, a more general and unfocused sense of discomfort and uncertainty.

Uneasiness is the sense of fear and hopelessness when conditions are unresolved and no change is anticipated.

Restlessness means you feel a need for change, even though you may not know what change would satisfy you. Restlessness is a feeling of uncertainty, discomfort, and irritability. You sense that matters are unresolved, that you are not settled, that something needs to be done to supply whatever is lacking in your present situation.

When I am on vacation visiting relatives, I begin to feel restless after about two days. I am antsy and distracted because I don't want to be there much longer. My dad used to say that after three days fish and company begin to stink.

Restlessness is a sense of displacement, that you are not where you should be or want to be. Restlessness can also relate to time, when some event is expected but has not yet occurred. You are waiting for the delivery of your new recliner, but it hasn't come. You are not discontented, just restless.

The third term in this cluster is *uneasiness*. This is the expression of this emotional cluster that becomes ongoing when the cause of the distress is unresolved. Uneasiness means to be disturbed by anxiety or apprehension, to be unsettled. It is an undercurrent of unrest, gloom, and some sense of hopelessness. Life seems to have little in it to make you happy, and you are afraid it isn't going to get any better.

I experienced this distress one time when my job had become a dead end. I tried to find a way to inject new possibilities into it, but to no avail. At first I experienced *discontent*, in which I focused on all the negative factors in the job. Then came *restlessness*, when I felt I needed to make a change but couldn't identify what it was. Finally, I became *uneasy*, not sure I would be able to find peace there or anywhere else. Each of these expressions of emotional pain was a clear warning that my own peace was threatened.

The Restless Person

The element of chaos is in conflict with order in this world, and we are caught in the tug-of-war between the two. We want to settle down and find peace, to find rest and serenity, to be at home. But the chaos built into creation breaks out to unsettle everything again. In such conditions, we can understand why we feel so restless.

Let's look at some of the symptoms of the restless person and some questionable strategies he employs to find relief.

▼ He believes his restlessness comes from outward conditions rather than inner attitudes.

▼ He is nervous, edgy, irritable.

▼ He is listless and lacking in energy.

▼ He complains about his situation to whomever will listen.

▼ He tends to have a negative outlook.

▼ He is not a happy person.

▼ He seems to be enemies with the circumstances around him.

▼ He may let things go and be untidy in his space at home and at work.

The restless person is getting a constant signal that he is threatened in his desire for personal peace. To deal with this threat, his natural impulse is fight or flight. From these natural tendencies, he will try a number of strategies for resolving his situation.

One strategy is to attack others. The restless person may maintain a state of war with family members and fellow workers. He is unhappy and wants everyone to know it, with the unconscious hope that someone will fix his troubles.

Another strategy of attack may involve the impulsive launching of a project to change the situation. On a whim, he may come to the conclusion that he would be happy if the wall between the living room and dining room were removed. So he may suddenly tear down the wall. Family members come home to see things in a mess. But once he finishes the project, he will find that the change does not bring him happiness.

Impulsive shopping is another common symptom of restlessness. This is such a serious problem that medical researchers are trying various drugs now to quell the compulsion to shop. The compulsive shopper buys what he does not need with money he may not have to satisfy a need he cannot explain. The result is a house full of purchases and a mountain of debt.

The person suffering from chronic restlessness tries to find relief in major changes. She may suddenly quit her present job, convinced that there is bound to be another job somewhere in which she can be content. The search to find work she likes may actually be a search to find herself. This movement from job to job leaves her family with uncertainty and insecurity.

Other impulsive changes may involve moving to another house, even another city. The restless person searches for the job, the housing, and even the church where he can feel at home at last. In the moving process he seems to be happy as he anticipates the peace the change will bring. All too often, however, he soon discovers that the new situation is not what he thought it would be.

He may seek a change of ideas. The restless person may not only move from church to church, he may delve into various cults and philosophies in hopes of finding answers. The New Age movement attracts many who are looking for inner peace and serenity.

People from all over the West Coast flocked to Antelope, Oregon, in the mid-eighties. They went there to be near the Bhagwan Shree Rajneesh, a Hindu guru from India who had purchased a ranch there and built an elaborate compound. Some sold their homes, their cars, and even their clothes and gave all their money to the Bhagwan. They gathered in thousands, donned red clothing, and chanted and danced to worship their guru. When the Bhagwan's chief assistant was arrested and the Bhagwan was deported, his followers dispersed without finding what they were looking for.

The restlessness of man goes deeper than the changes he can make in his circumstances. He is Adam, searching for the Garden of Eden, that paradise where all is well and he can be at peace.

Misconceptions about Peace

Contemporary thinking follows predictable patterns about the desire for personal peace and the restlessness we experience. This thinking naturally arises from the self-centered handicap of our nature. The result is a set of remedies that contain an element of truth and may look promising but ultimately will not solve the problem. Let's take a look at some of these misleading remedies.

Peace of mind is a medical problem best addressed with therapy and drugs. The number of persons on mood-altering drugs runs in the millions. For some, antidepressants have become as normal a part of life as taking vitamins. They are prescribed most of the time, not because the physician can identify the cause for distress, but because he cannot. Though some of these patients are suffering from chemical imbalances or other largely physical problems, most are under stress because of the pressures of life.

In many cases these drugs can help deal with the symptoms while a person in therapy comes to terms with his or her stress. Very often, however, there is no effort to find the cause. The "feel better" solution is a permanent one. Since the patient has relief from the emotional distress that naturally accompanies problems, he may not actually deal with the problems themselves.

In many of these cases the basic outlook of the person is the real source of his trouble. It is his *interpretation* of his life situation that brings on the stress, not the situation itself. This is where counseling is needed. In many cases it involves coming to terms with the past, where injuries from childhood experiences have left festering wounds.

A primary factor in personal peace is the environment in which one must live and work. This statement does have an element of truth. The conditions we must face day after day do often determine our own peace and well-being. But the story cannot end here. There is a peace that transcends one's immediate situation. The problem is not primarily "out there" in our circumstances. It is "in here" in the interpretation we place on them.

We are often impressed at the sense of peace experienced by someone who has just fallen prey to some tragedy. A tragic accident has taken the father of three preschoolers. What will the mother do? After the initial shock we are amazed at her serenity. She talks about her faith in God's care and focuses her attention on the needs of her children. Why does one person respond this way and another go into a lengthy depression? Though many factors can be involved, the answer is often in the difference in interpretation, particularly from the viewpoint of faith.

Misleading Remedies in the Search for Peace

▼ Peace of mind is a medical problem best addressed with therapy and drugs.

▼ A primary factor in personal peace is the environment in which one must live and work.

▼ The lack of personal peace is caused by social ills.

▼ Personal peace is found by discovering oneself.

▼ Personal peace comes with a simplified lifestyle.

When conditions at work or at home are distressing, wise people will do whatever they can to make changes. There are often situations, however, when changes are beyond your reach. What then? The only change you can make will be a change in the way you see the situation. Even in a Nazi prison camp, Corrie Ten Boom saw reasons to praise God and thank Him for His blessings. Her situation was horrible beyond description, but she saw it through the eyes of faith.

The lack of personal peace is caused by social ills. This idea is but an enlargement on the previous one. Instead of thinking of the particular immediate situation, we are here called upon to look at the whole of society. Again, the problem is "out there" rather than "in here." Poverty is cited as a cause of crime, moral breakdown, and other such social ills, even though the times of greatest poverty in this nation did not produce these results.

The social ills that seem to be taking this country to ruin are tragic indeed. No one wants to see these conditions continue to worsen, and everything possible should be done to stem the tide of moral and social decay. But these social ills are not the cause of most personal stress.

I remember making a pastoral call to encourage a woman who was recovering from surgery. As I started to leave, I asked if she had some personal concern I might pray with her about. I knew her husband was an alcoholic. After some hesitation, she answered tentatively, "Well, I am always concerned about world peace." It may be easier to talk about some sweeping problem than to face the very personal troubles we live with.

Personal peace is found by discovering oneself. This is a very popular view today, particularly in what is called the "New Age" movement. This ill-defined mixture of eastern religion and other old cultic views is focused in a personal mystical experience of self-discovery. Instead of seeking to find God, you are urged to see that the divine is in you. You are urged to chant or dance or meditate in order to reach into the inner chambers of your own psyche to find the answers you need.

Other approaches to self-discovery follow the lines of personality typing, temperament analysis, and other pop psychologies. Self-help books promise to help you discover the real you while finding answers to personal peace and success. Psychiatrists and other counselors see millions of counselees every week to help them understand themselves and root out their "hang-ups."

While some of these efforts at self-discovery may help, they are limited at best. Understanding yourself is very important for dealing with faulty thinking. Knowing the strengths and weaknesses of your personality and temperament can also be of help. We will never understand ourselves, however, until we begin to understand God. The key to knowing ourselves is knowing the God who made us in His own image.

Personal peace comes with a simplified lifestyle. I must confess that I have a real affinity for this idea. I like the thought of living simply, close to the natural order of things, eating right, exercising well, and avoiding the clutter and greed of materialism. There are benefits here for all of us. But this cannot be the final answer to personal peace.

People will naturally try to find peace without coming to terms with the Prince of Peace. That deeply ingrained streak of independence keeps us probing for answers anywhere, as long as they don't involve surrendering to the authority of

God. But only in finding peace with God through Jesus Christ will we find that inner peace our Creator wants us to have.

The message in your discontent is clear. You are threatened in your desire for peace. Your situation is marked by trouble that keeps you unsettled and uncertain. The natural chaos in this world intrudes in your life from all sides.

To understand that message more fully, we will next look at what a "situation" is and a biblical strategy for responding to trouble.

▼

TWENTY-THREE

A place to call home

▼

It was a shock. Something they never expected. As they entered the family room from the garage, she suddenly stopped. There was glass on the carpet from a shattered patio door. They stood motionless as the reality dawned on them. Someone had broken in while they were gone. A check through the rest of the house proved the worst. Everything was pulled out of drawers and closets and scattered around the rooms.

They called the police and tried to determine what had been taken—stereo equipment, television, VCR, clothes, jewelry, silverware, microwave, a guitar—anything that could be sold quickly. After the police left, without giving much encouragement, the couple began to clean up the mess. The wife sat down and cried as her husband tried to comfort her. Someone had broken into their own private refuge and taken their things. They felt angry, vulnerable, and violated.

In one sense your home is symbolic of your life situation as a whole. Just as your home can be entered and ravaged by a burglar, so can your situation be attacked by trouble. Every aspect of your life is open to attack. When you are threatened, you will get the signals of the attack through the emotions we have already described—discontent, restlessness, and uneasiness.

The threat is to your own desire for peace. You long to have your life marked by the serenity and certainty of real peace. This desire is built into your nature as a human. Because God is the Creator who brought order out of chaos, light in the darkness, and filled the emptiness, He has made you with the desire to shape your own situation for peace and order.

Before we look further at the meaning of this peace, let's define more clearly what is meant by *situation*.

Understanding Your Situation

The total environment of your personal world is your "situation." The word comes from the Latin root *situ*, meaning "site" or "place." It is your "place" in the scheme of Creation. Everything you think, all you say, whatever you do, must take place within the bounds of your situation. At the same time your responses are all affected by that situation. The various elements of your situation continually bring pressure on you to respond.

Here we are using the word in two ways. Your *life situation* is made up of a constant flow of *immediate situations*. At any given moment your situation is the immediate environment of your activity. Not only must you deal with that immediate situation, you must keep the broader life situation in mind. Your situation involves all the contexts of your normal traffic pattern. It takes you into various relationships and responsibilities that are totally separated from the other situations.

As part of a seminar, I have conducted informal surveys to discover how unique each person is in his life situation. Husbands and wives were asked how familiar they were with the various circumstances and relationships of their spouse. Most of them thought they knew pretty much about it. But when I asked the women whether they knew their husband's barber, they just laughed. That was unknown territory. So was the wife's hairdresser to the men.

We proved pretty quickly that each person has a unique situation, a traffic pattern like no other, a personal world all his or her own. As well as we think we know each other, it is impossible for us really to know. Each of us experiences life in a unique way. This is a part of the wonder of God's creation.

Defining precisely what we mean by a "situation" is difficult. Since one situation flows into the next, it is difficult to draw the boundaries. Our subjectivity also makes the definition difficult. We can include in our definition or exclude from it any factors we choose. Being unique as we each are, any description of a shared situation will have variations based on the interests and alertness of each person involved.

Alvin Toffler wrote that though the boundaries between situations may be hard to draw, each situation has a certain completeness about it. He named six identifiable components that make up every situation: *things*, the physical setting of natural or man-made objects; *place,* a location or arena within which the action occurs; *people*, the cast of characters involved; *social location*, the place in the network of society; *thought,* the context of ideas or information; and *duration*, the span of time over which the situation occurs.[1]

The faster pace of modern life shortens the duration of your situations. You have less time to respond to the circumstances around you. This sometimes hectic pace can create stresses our grandparents did not experience. Modern life has also stretched the boundaries of your situations far beyond earlier generations. I can communicate almost instantly by telephone, fax, or e-mail and thus extend the reach of my situation around the world.

For the Christian, however, no matter how complex his situation or how fast the pace, he knows that the key factor is always God Himself. Wherever we are and whatever we face, we can claim the promise of God's presence, "Never will I leave you; never will I forsake you" (Heb. 13:5). Jesus assured the disciples, "I am with you always" (Matt. 28:20, NKJV). Whatever the other factors in your situation, the overwhelming reality at every given moment is the presence of God.

Even with God present, however, trouble can intrude at any moment. As we deal with the message in your emotions at this point, we are primarily concerned with those factors in your situation that seem to threaten your peace. It is trouble, not blessing, that seems to be the intruder. Let's consider that intruder and how to respond to it.

The Intruder

We have noted how easy it would be to come home and find your home damaged by burglars. Trouble of any kind is like a burglar who breaks into your life and steals your joy. Trouble can come quickly like an accident or injury. It can come slowly like a debilitating disease. It can be as minor as a flat tire or as devastating as an earthquake. You may try to avoid this *Intruder*, but no matter what you do he still comes, usually when you least expect it.

Built into our way of thinking is the idea that we have a right to be happy. There is no great mystery in this. We all prefer to live our lives without problems, heartache, tragedy, and disaster. We like the path of delight, where everything works as it should, where we are never disappointed, and where no sudden painful blows interrupt our tranquillity. It is normal to human thinking to want a life without trouble.

Since we assume that the norm should be happiness and success, we think of trouble as an *Intruder*, an unwelcome interloper who has no right to be in our lives. If life was intended to be trouble-free, then the problems we face must be aberrations, malfunctions, or glitches. So when trouble strikes we don't like it a bit. It is not supposed to happen. We complain, we gripe, we become depressed, we try to find someone to blame. It is so unfair, so unreasonable. Why do things like this have to happen to me?

It is an easy step from this *preference* for peace to the idea that I have a *right* to peace. When trouble comes the common question is "Why me?" The human mind is programmed to think that someone somewhere owes me a life relatively free of pain and sorrow. With that as my birthright, I resent the trouble that disturbs my peace and hinders my progress. I can become bitter and spiteful, wanting to strike out and get even for the unfair treatment life has given me.

One young man had experienced a series of reverses in his pursuit of his career. Discouraged and frustrated, he could not imagine what was wrong. Life itself seemed to be set against him. As we talked, he moved between bitterness and resignation.

"I told Andrea the other day," he explained, "that sometimes I feel there's a plot against me. It's like when we were kids in high school and someone would tape a sign to your back that said KICK ME. I feel like someone must have hung a sign on me inviting the whole world to kick old Gary."

As you try to make sense of it, this perplexity with trouble can lead you to skepticism about the meaning of life and the forces that control it. You may find yourself demanding that God justify His actions in allowing the pain and suffering you have experienced. You may take up the cause of all mankind and challenge the justice and love of God for allowing such cruelty to continue. You may either doubt God's power to do anything about it or doubt His love for doing nothing if He is able. You may even conclude that He does not exist, that all of life is an accident with no purpose.

This resentment of the Intruder can deepen into a philosophy of life preoccupied with the pain and suffering of the world. Such an outlook is dominated by a despair that colors the joys and blessings of life with the dull gray paint of resentment and bitterness. All of man's highest aspirations are seen as futile. His dreams are but a cruel joke dangled in his mind by an unseen force that has designed life for misery and disappointment.

Listen to the words of one such skeptic, from a letter written by Bertrand Russell, July 19, 1903:

What else is there to make life tolerable? We stand on the shore of an ocean, crying to the night and the emptiness; sometimes a voice answers out of the darkness. But it is the voice of one drowning; and in a moment the silence returns. The world seems to me quite dreadful; the unhappiness of most people is very great, and I often wonder how they all endure it. To know people well is to know their tragedy: it is usually the central thing about which their lives are built. And I suppose if they did not live most of the time in the things of the moment, they would not be able to go on.[2]

But what about it? Is this a reasonable outlook? Is there a better way to interpret life? Can we paint a positive and hopeful picture that includes not only the delights but the distresses of life?

Perhaps it's time we take a new look at trouble. Instead of an Intruder who breaks into your life, how about a different characterization? Maybe trouble is really a wise old *Tutor* who is almost a part of the family. She has been with you all your life, so you know her well. Even though she is very unattractive, you would miss her if she were gone. You admit you flinch and shrink back when you see her coming. But she has taught you so much. Hard though her lessons are, she has changed your life.

The letter of James was written to Jewish believers scattered in cities to which they had fled from the persecution in Jerusalem. But then they experienced more persecution and poverty. How were they to deal with it? Let's examine the passage in James 1:2–4 and note three principles that form a basis for a creative response to life's troubles. Your challenge and mine is not to gain a life free of trouble but to develop a positive strategy for dealing with trouble.

A Positive Interpretation

The first principle for a creative response to trouble is to interpret every situation in positive, hopeful, expectant terms. Look at James 1:2, "Consider it pure joy, my brothers, whenever you face trials of many kinds." The Greek word for "consider it" is an accounting term for making a ledger entry. It means "put it down for joy." So James is instructing his readers to interpret their trials in terms of joy.

No doubt this seems like nonsense to our natural thinking patterns. We see no reason for joy in trials. A deeper look, however, will reveal that this interpretation is based on the assumption that the key factor in your situation is God Himself. The writer declares that the testing of your faith produces perseverance and results in maturity. Your interpretation can take on an entirely different tone when your trouble is seen in that light.

Some of us may think we have had about every kind of trouble possible to a person. But think again. Notice the reference to "trials of many kinds" (James 1:2). It suggests an almost unlimited variety of troubles out there you might experience.

I am amazed and impressed today with the wonderfully creative possibilities for trouble. Remember that the killer bees are coming! And I am losing my hair. The toilet is leaking. Those blood tests have to be done again. The newspeople are warning us about fires, floods, tornadoes, and earthquakes. There are thieves and muggers out there waiting to attack. The possibilities are endless!

The wording is picturesque also when James writes, "whenever you face trials of many kinds." The traditional interpretation is "fall into various trials." You are pictured walking along the path unawares when suddenly you fall into a pit dug in the path and covered with leaves. This is a vivid portrayal of how we experience most of our troubles. We fall into them before we realize it. They take us by surprise. Everything seems to be going well when suddenly there you are in a hole, bruised and dirty, looking for a way out.

It is your interpretation of the trouble that largely determines how you will deal with it. Christopher Peterson, professor of psychology at the University of Michigan at Ann Arbor, studied the process of change brought on by a personal crisis. He learned that your interpretation of the crisis makes all the difference. He says that "it's the pessimist who's the lousy coper, the one blinded by a negative attitude to viable solutions." On the other hand, "the optimist is happier, healthier and a better problem-solver. He says, 'I'm going to handle this thing.'"[3]

That optimism is all the more effective when it is rooted in faith, knowing God is ultimately the key factor in your situation. With this faith you can interpret every situation in positive, hopeful, expectant terms.

Signs of Purpose

Here is the second principle, taken from verse 3: *Analyze where God is at work in the situation for His purpose and your good*. James continues with his reason for considering it pure joy to encounter trials, "because you know that the testing of your faith develops perseverance." Immediately we notice that you can respond with joy in the face of your troubles because you know something. It is this inside information that allows you to interpret the situation in a positive way.

A person who has inside information is always ahead in knowing what to make of a given situation: the landscape man who tells me my droopy rhododendrons are not sick and will be all right; the neighbor who was unconcerned when a huge dog came charging at us as we stood talking in the street (it was his dog); the medical doctor who was not at all alarmed by the lump on my back. What do these experiences have in common? The person with inside information is able to accurately interpret the situation.

Christians have inside information about the troubles of life. They know that this trial is only a test of their faith. The world is not out of control. There is still meaning in whatever happens. The words of Romans 8:28 have not been canceled, "And we know that in all things God works for the good of those who love him, who have been called according to his purpose." So the Christian looks carefully at the situation to watch for indications of purpose, to see the hand of God at work.

Every trial is a test. I think of the test in every trial when I hear a radio test of the emergency broadcast system. "For the next sixty seconds this station will conduct a test of the emergency broadcast system. This is a test. This is only a test." Every time trouble lays a trap for you, listen for those words. Watch for their confirmation in the situation. "This is a test. This is only a test."

What is being tested? Is it your patience? Is it your stamina? Is it some other Christian virtue? James writes that it is a test "of your faith." A test of faith is simply a test of whether you will trust God in this trouble. Whether in a minor irritation or in a major tragedy, the question is still the same, "Will you trust God?"

He is the God of no loose ends. Nothing escapes His notice. He is not surprised by the trouble that has befallen you. He intends these troubles to be a part of the normal pattern for human life. He has aims in mind for your character, for advancing His purposes, for working everything together for good. It gives God particular glory to bring good out of evil. In fact, that is a sure way to recognize His hand at work. Look at the cross. Out of the greatest evil came the greatest good.

A Divine Agent

Here is our third guiding principle: *Act carefully as an agent of God for the fulfillment of His purpose.* Your response to trouble moves now to action. "Perseverance must finish its work so that you may be mature and complete, not lacking anything" (James 1:4). Here we see that something is going on in the midst of your trial. You can come out of it more mature and complete. You can profit from the experience. God is at work.

"Perseverance" means steadfastness, stability, constancy. This is the outcome of the testing of your faith. You respond in faith and you are given the steadfastness to come through the trial with grace. Whatever the storms of circumstance that blow around you, you stand firm and constant. But this new stability is not just for this occasion. It is to "finish its work" and create a lasting strength in you for the future. You are becoming more mature, more complete, more whole as a Christian.

What is needed to counter the troubles of life? Strength of character. What is God doing in the midst of your trials? He may be doing more, but at the least He is strengthening your character. Just as muscles naturally grow stronger when regularly placed under stress, so character can grow when we experience personal stress. Without the troubles that tax our strength of character, we would never develop the character God intends.

If the test of your trouble is to have its full benefit, however, you must act as God's agent and not in your own self-interests. Notice the point in your own life where the pressure comes. Is that the area that needs strengthening? Determine not to avoid the test or try to pretend it is not there. Rather yield yourself and the entire situation to God with the confidence that He is at work and has drawn you into that work with Him.

Sometimes the action needed in response to your trouble is not what you might ordinarily do. It is not "you." It doesn't fit your temperament. It goes outside your comfort zone. When courage is needed for this kind of risky action, you are probably on the right track. God is drawing you out of the safe haven of comfortable responses. Maybe He is developing character you never knew you needed.

Now that we have considered a strategy for responding to trouble, we will move on to the very practical application of these principles. As you read the message in your emotions about your situation, you can respond in such a way as to turn every problem into a faith possibility.

▼

TWENTY-FOUR

The struggle for peace

▼

It was ten years to the day since we had arrived in Portland. Now we were leaving. Our decade in the Northwest had convinced us that it was one of the most beautiful places on earth. Words could not capture the majesty of Mount Hood with a sunset gilding its snowy peak, the rugged Oregon coast with the thundering surf during a winter storm, the lush forests, the awe-inspiring Columbia Gorge. We had come to stay, convinced we would spend the rest of our lives here.

After seven years there, we had begun to realize we couldn't stay. A sense of call had grown until we knew we would have to return to the South, probably to teach. At first I was grieved, feeling we were leaving paradise for parts unknown.

Finally the direction became clear and the call was to teach at Southeastern Seminary in Wake Forest, North Carolina. We began the three-thousand-mile journey with anticipation for what lay ahead and tearful good-byes for what we would leave behind. The five-day trip crossed the continent, providing long days on the interstate and plenty of time to think about the past and the future.

The cross-country drive was therapeutic, a geographical representation of the emotional and social changes the family was making. Somewhere in Missouri or Tennessee we began to see red clay in the fields, oaks and pine trees, and rolling hills. A sense of peace began to stir in me. I called Sharon on the CB. "I can't really explain why," I said, "but I have the distinct feeling of coming home."

The peace of that moment is still fresh in my memory. To say it felt like coming home is to say how positive I felt. Home means roots. It means belonging. It means the familiar surroundings of a thousand memories—the faces of kinfolk, the secret haunts of childhood, the sounds of conversation and rocking chairs and a creaking screen door. Home means love and acceptance. Someone has said that "home is where they have to take you in whether they want to or not."

In the heart of every person is a special longing for home. For some it is a real place. For others it is still a dream. Instead of growing up at "home," in the rich sense of that word, some grew up with shouts and curses, fighting, uncertainty and fear, unplanned moves to stay with relatives, words like "divorce" and "weekend visits."

Every one of us tries to transform our situation into "home." But home is not so much a place as a state of mind—a peace of heart, a serenity, a sense of place that goes beyond geography. Home is a rest from wandering, a place to plant and build, a belonging and contentment.

When we talk about situation and the contentment and peace we desire, we call up thoughts of home. God made us with this sense of place and home—this desire for peace. He gave Adam and Eve a home with everything they needed, even His presence. With that paradise lost, how do we respond to the emotional message of *discontent, restlessness,* and *uneasiness*? This chapter will suggest keys to contentment and peace and spell out a specific prescription for discontent and restlessness.

At Home with God

Augustine said, "Our souls are restless until they find their rest in Thee." David wrote in Psalm 16:1–2, 5–6:

Keep me safe, O God,
>for in you I take refuge.
I said to the LORD, "You are my Lord;
>apart from you I have no good thing." . . .
LORD, you have assigned me my portion and my cup;
>you have made my lot secure.
The boundary lines have fallen for me in pleasant places;
>surely I have a delightful inheritance.

Ever since they were driven from the garden because of sin, the children of Adam and Eve have wandered in search of home. They have looked for the Garden of God. But they have not found it as a "place" on this earth. However pleasant the tangible place of residence here, we are not yet home until we rest in relationship with God. "For here we do not have an enduring city, but we are looking for the city that is to come" (Heb. 13:14).

In this sense, home is the return of the soul to God. But it is not only when we die that we come home. We can come to God now through Jesus Christ. We can forsake the independence that drove Adam from the garden. We can come home to God like the prodigal son. We can leave the pigpen of our self-will and receive the loving acceptance of the Father who has waited and watched for us all this time.

Even for those who have put their faith in Christ, there is a need to come home. We can be so distracted by the cares and interests of life that we are drawn away from the home of our personal relationship with God. Like a family at dinner with personal conflicts, we can be in the faith but out of fellowship with God. We can experience the silence of strife, the coldness and distance of disharmony, the unrest of conflict.

A beginning point for contentment is your own personal relationship with God. Jesus told His disciples, "Remain in me, and I will remain in you. No branch can bear fruit by itself; it must remain in the vine. Neither can you bear fruit unless you remain in me" (John 15:4). The word *remain* here means "abide," "dwell," or "continue." It sounds as though Jesus is saying, "I am your home; live here. As you make Me your home, I will live in you. We will be inseparable and My life and grace will be yours. I will do My work through you."

235

Real contentment for a Christian is not possible without giving attention to this "abiding." This home relationship with Christ is our centering point. It is where we go when we have ceased wandering. It is the place of rest and belonging, of complete fulfillment. Paul urges us to take all our anxieties and translate them into requests, through prayer and petition. The result? "And the peace of God, which transcends all understanding, will guard your hearts and your minds in Christ Jesus" (Phil. 4:7).

What You See Is What Gets You

When Matthew was about four, our whole family went out for lunch at Thanksgiving. Denny's had a special meal of turkey and dressing, cranberry sauce, and all the traditional fixings. After the plates were brought, Matthew looked his over in anticipation, then he stiffened on his booster seat. "I don't want peas," he announced. He liked everything else on his plate, but he was going through a "peas are yucky" phase.

It is normal for us to be discriminating, to identify what we like. We prefer certain foods over others, certain clothes, certain music, certain styles in decorating and furnishing. And there are things we do not like. In our constant restlessness for ordering our situations, we tend to focus on what we don't like, what we want to change.

As a speech teacher, part of my job is to identify what needs to be changed. I tell the students that I am like a dentist, probing and poking for cavities. Did you ever go to a dentist who complimented you on your beautiful teeth? I haven't. My experience is that they would much prefer to dig around with that sharp little instrument to see if they can stick it in a hole and get a rise out of me.

This cavity search can become a lifestyle. If you are not careful you are always focused on what displeases you, what needs to be changed, and what is missing. Instead of being drawn to the positive factors in your situation, you are drawn to the negative ones. It is what you see that gets you, with delight or dissatisfaction.

Everyone sees his or her situation in a selective way. The environment around you at any time is too complex and de-

236

tailed for you to take it all in. Two different people in the same room will note different things. After visiting with neighbors, Sharon might ask me if I noticed the pattern on the curtains. I couldn't swear they even had curtains—I was looking at their stereo system. Your attention is drawn to what interests you.

What you see may tell more about you than it does about the scene before you. It can reveal your attitude, your mood, your priorities, and your values. When Charlie Brown sees the cloud shapes as "a horsy and a ducky" instead of the art masterpieces his friends see, you learn something about Charlie.

One beautiful Sunday morning as the pastor was greeting his departing flock, the sourpuss of the church came along. The pastor wondered what she would complain about today. "Isn't it a beautiful day, Mrs. Thorn?" he asked. "Well, I dunno," she replied, scanning the clear blue sky. "I'm sure it's raining somewhere."

Discriminating Tastes

The preference for one thing over another is a very important factor. In the Garden, God told the first couple which trees they might eat of and the one they could not. The dietary laws of the ancient Hebrews distinguished clearly between clean and unclean foods. Days were distinguished from one another. Tribes were distinguished. There was a clear pattern of the holy and the unholy, the clean and the unclean, the acceptable and the unacceptable.

The Bible makes clear throughout what behavior is acceptable and what is not. If anything is clear about the Christian, it is his distinctiveness in society. He or she is to be holy as his God is holy. "Holy" means separated for dedicated uses. In today's confused society, the Christian needs the keen eye of a master craftsman, able to detect the tiniest flaw in any new idea or practice or fad that comes along.

But the power of discrimination can turn selfish. Instead of discerning what is acceptable to God, you can test everything by whether it pleases you. This is the trap of discontent. Your mind dwells on factors in your situation that are irritating, incomplete, and displeasing. A certain mannerism or habit in a family member, the yapping dog next door, an old sagging chair, the lack of recognition at work.

I am, basically, an old grump at heart. My mind can get a train of thought going in the complaint direction as soon as I wake up in the morning. By the time I've had my shower, I am a walking encyclopedia of gripes. If I pursue this thinking the rest of the day, I will edge out the expression of the Holy Spirit in my attitude. I will make myself miserable, along with everyone who has to deal with me. There is only one answer. Stop! Make the attitude adjustment. Confess the selfishness in my heart and get back into fellowship with Jesus.

We are back to the need for discipline. The handicap of the selfish nature will inevitably surface unless we intervene to override our natural reactions. But beyond the daily need to walk in the Spirit, we can do something about our misplaced discrimination on a long-term basis.

The Miracle of Gratitude

Thanksgiving is always a special time to me. It usually means a gathering of the whole clan at our house—our four children and eight grandchildren, plus a few guests. The event involves the traditional meal—turkey, dressing, ham, salads, pies, and everything else. One tradition we have enjoyed is gathering before the meal to sing some songs and give testimonies about what we are thankful for from the past year.

On some occasions it is a very moving time, with tears and hugs of gratitude for others in the family. Sometimes we learn something about one of the family members that we hadn't realized, a look into a very personal walk with Christ. Some of it seems rather mundane, expressing gratitude for family, home, material provision. But the theme that runs through it all is that God is the source of every good thing. He is the ultimate Provider who deserves our thanks.

Though we have Thanksgiving on the calendar, how much real thanksgiving do you think takes place? It seems to me that gratitude is not natural to us. Maybe that is why the Bible repeatedly admonishes us to "Give thanks to the Lord!" I believe, though, that gratitude is the key to contentment and peace. From a prison Paul wrote, "I thank my God every time I remember you" (Phil. 1:3). This letter is marked by joy and love. Toward the end of it he wrote, "I have learned to be content whatever the circumstances. I know what it is to be in need, and I know what it is to have plenty. I have learned the secret of being content in any and every situation, whether well fed or hungry, whether living in plenty or in want" (Phil. 4:11–12).

What is this "secret of being content"? It is obviously not connected with the circumstances. That is our first mistake. We think, "I would just be content if . . ." Paul was not a Stoic, one who claimed to be indifferent to pain or pleasure. He much preferred to have plenty rather than to be in want. He preferred to be free to travel and pursue his ministry rather than being in prison. His "secret" was obviously something beyond his circumstances.

He reveals the secret in the very next sentence, "I can do everything through him who gives me strength" (Phil. 4:13). In this statement he claimed the power to put up with any situation, however disagreeable. He had the amazing ability to transform any place into a "home" of sorts. The secret was the presence of Christ. It was through His strength that Paul could do whatever was required.

If you find your "home" in the person of Jesus Christ, it doesn't matter where you are or what you face. He will give you peace. He will strengthen you for the living of that hour or those months. The history of Christianity is full of accounts of believers who experienced horrible conditions and yet found their strength in Christ: "Some faced jeers and flogging, while still others were chained and put in prison. They were stoned; they were sawed in two; they were put to death by the sword. They went about in sheepskins and goatskins, destitute, persecuted and mistreated—the world was not worthy of them. They wandered in deserts and mountains, and in caves and holes in the ground" (Heb. 11:36–38).

None of us wants to experience anything so horrible as this. We are just human enough to want safety, comfort, and plenty to eat. But does the relative blessing of our situation deny the secret to contentment? No. The secret is still Jesus Christ. How much more should we find peace when we have so little to disturb our peace. He is present. That is the greatest blessing of all and the primary factor in any situation.

A Prescription for Discontent

Discontent is a matter of perspective. No matter how unpleasant your situation, you can interpret it in very different ways. If you wish to be content in Christ, determine to interpret your situation in a way that allows you to be satisfied with Him. Then take action to shape your situation in whatever ways you can for the good of all those involved.

Begin with a writing exercise. As suggested in previous chapters, part one of the exercise is to write in descriptive detail, "My Situation and How I Feel About It." The purpose of this is to describe your situation and your feelings about it as fully as you can. Do not second-guess yourself or chide yourself for feeling the way you do. Just write it down. Allowing your emotion this full expression will spend some of its churning energy.

Then write part two of the exercise, "But the Truth Is." Now you are to put the whole story in perspective from the viewpoint of biblical principles and your relationship with Christ. In a sense you are responding to yourself. In this conversation with yourself, you allow your discontented self to speak unhindered until your piece has been said. Now your believing, reasoning self will respond with an interpretation of the situation and the feelings from a more objective viewpoint.

You will find that the writing of the exercise will help you to get out of your emotional hole. Instead of sitting in the middle of your unhappy situation, you get up and walk around it to get a different view. During part two, go ahead and write down ideas for how to change the situation. God made you creative. He intends you to bring a spark of spiritual genius to your troubles. He wants to guide your thinking toward solutions and changes you may never have considered.

Write down everything you could actually do to improve your situation. Make a list of at least ten, preferably more, specific changes you can make to influence the situation for the better. Ask God to inspire your thoughts for some really creative ideas. Then choose the most likely items for the list and put a plan together.

Also put down ideas for how to get your thinking on a more positive track. Since discontent reflects a negative interpretation, think how you might take a more positive one. A simple action to take in this regard is to memorize the following passage and determine to live by it:

> Rejoice in the Lord always. I will say it again: Rejoice! Let your gentleness be evident to all. The Lord is near. Do not be anxious about anything, but in everything, by prayer and petition, with thanksgiving, present your requests to God. And the peace of God, which transcends all understanding, will guard your hearts and your minds in Christ Jesus.
>
> Finally, brothers, whatever is true, whatever is noble, whatever is right, whatever is pure, whatever is lovely, whatever is admirable—if anything is excellent or praiseworthy—think about such things.

Philippians 4:4–8

As you write out part two of the exercise, include in it a list of everything you are grateful for. Like that old hymn says, "Count your blessings, name them one by one, and it will surprise you what the Lord has done." Instead of focusing on the negative factors, give thanks to God for His good gifts to you—your family and friends, your health, your material possessions, your freedom, your salvation, His presence. Make the list very specific. This is an important part of intentionally turning your thinking from negative to positive.

Remember the chamber of secrets? This is where you keep your good deeds in memory, stored up only for you and God to enjoy. Determine that part of your plan will be secret, selfless service. Plan some specific actions for the benefit of others in your situation. Keep these acts of love and service as secret as you can. Make it your aim to be a servant for the betterment of others, rather than remaining preoccupied with your own complaints.

Remember, the secret to contentment is the real and personal presence of Jesus Christ in your situation. Talk to Him about it. Trust Him with it. Present your requests to Him. Follow the example of His attitude.

An Action Plan

Here is a summary of ideas for dealing with your discontent.

▼ Be honest with yourself about your discontent, restlessness, or uneasiness.

▼ Acknowledge the presence of Jesus Christ as the primary factor in your situation.

▼ Try to interpret your situation in positive, hopeful, expectant terms.

▼ Analyze where God is at work in your situation for His purpose and your good.

▼ Determine to act as an agent of God for the fulfillment of His purpose in your situation.

▼ Do the writing exercise when you are discontented.

▼ Practice thanking God for His blessings "one by one" whether you feel like it or not.

▼

CONCLUSION

Sorting out mixed emotions

▼

I met Katherine on a plane into Dallas. I am not sure how we got into our discussion of her husband, Lloyd, but her distress was a strong motivation for her to talk about it. She had only been married to Lloyd for two years but long enough to know he was in serious trouble in his attitude toward life.

Lloyd had been very successful in his business, but he decided to turn it over to others and retire. He and his first wife, Theresa, were planning to travel abroad. They went to Europe and wandered its beautiful, old cities. They had everything they wanted—money, time, and each other. Lloyd was grateful to God for his blessings.

Then Theresa became ill with cancer. Their travels were abruptly halted as their whole life became devoted to her recovery. They turned to God in prayer. Lloyd asked people at church to pray. He asked friends to pray. He asked family members to pray. He asked for healing and believed it would be given. After a few short months, however, Theresa died. Lloyd was devastated. He reacted to her death with bitterness. How could God take her away from him? How was that loving and good? He said he would never pray again, except to ask for forgiveness just before he died.

Within less than two years, Lloyd married again. But he was not the same man. Katherine had not realized how bitter he was. Now she was reaping the results in his often angry and hostile attitude toward her. Lloyd was also drinking as he never had before.

He did not go back to work after Theresa's death. He did little but watch television and play an occasional game of golf. Some concerned friends and old business associates invited him to play golf with them in an effort to get him out. But Lloyd's bitterness spilled over into hostility toward them as well. He never initiated a golf game but complained that no one cared about him when they didn't call.

What would you tell Lloyd? Can you trace his distress to the areas of responsibility indicated by his emotions? What could he do to come out of his trouble? As we conclude this study, let's use Lloyd's experience to review some important insights about the message in your emotions and to see the complexity of mixed emotional signals.

Trouble upon Trouble

Lloyd's story makes it clear that the emotional pain we suffer often comes in several forms at once. As I have counseled with troubled people through the years, I have noticed that they seldom indicate only one area of emotional pain. In this study we have identified seven clusters of emotional distress so that each one could be defined and distinguished from the others. But it is never as tidy as that in actual experience. Usually there is one area of trouble that spills over into one or two more.

Even though Lloyd suffered more than one kind of emotional pain, the primary trouble was with *bitterness*. He was very angry with God at the death of his wife. He had everything planned for their retirement. He had everything under *control*. But the cancer took Theresa. Lloyd had prayed as never before in his life. He had tried to believe she would be healed, asking others to pray for her healing as well. This must not happen: she must not die. But she did, and there was no one to blame but God.

Bitterness, as you know, is the emotional signal of unresolved *anger* and *resentment*. It is an indication of the failure of responsibility in the area of *authority*. Lloyd had never really come to terms with authority. All his life he was used to being in charge. Even his relationship with God was not so much a humble surrender as a business partnership. Now Lloyd demanded that God answer for this terrible and senseless act. Hadn't they all prayed for healing? When God was silent, he vowed never to speak to Him again. Like a pouting child, he would make God suffer for His mistake.

Problems in *authority* had spilled over into *relationships*. His hostility and anger toward God affected his relationships with everyone he knew. He was sullen, resentful, lonely, even isolated. He blamed others for his *loneliness*, complaining that no one cared about him. God didn't care; why should anyone else? The one person who tried the hardest to love him suffered most. He seemed at times to pour all his bitterness out on Katherine, leaving her in tears, feeling helpless and frustrated.

Another area of responsibility affected by his bitterness was *purpose*. Lloyd's attitude seemed to be that God had ruined his life and now he had no reason to live. He could have gone back to his business, but he refused. He would show God. He would just sit and scowl. He would let Him know in no uncertain terms that He had failed him miserably. Why go back to work? What did it matter? He was *frustrated* at having his retirement plans spoiled. He was *bored* at having nothing meaningful to do. If he couldn't have what he wanted in life, it had no meaning for him.

The diagnosis of Lloyd's areas of irresponsibility is clear because of the message in his emotions. If you were his friend, however, and you hoped to help him, you would want to sympathize with him in his pain. It is easy to think trouble like this can be dealt with on a rational basis. That is partially true. Unless a person understands how his own mind is working and what his emotions are telling him, no amount of sympathy will remove his trouble. At the same time, you are not likely to be heard unless you demonstrate compassion.

Remember, if you were Lloyd and had experienced what he did, you would probably feel the way he did about it.

Injury and Disease

As we have indicated, the *injury* of past experiences and the *disease* of faulty thinking can be underlying causes of our trouble. Lloyd's loss of his wife left him emotionally wounded. Since he did not know how to deal effectively with his loss, the wound became infected with bitterness toward God. You may be thinking that he is not the first one to lose his wife. Others have come through such an experience without bitterness. Lloyd was highly susceptible to this injury, however, because he already suffered the disease of faulty thinking in the area of authority.

Because he had grown up with the idea that he should have his way, he could not handle such a devastating reversal. How could this happen? He had prayed. Isn't that what God requires for getting your way? Lloyd was not following this line of thought consciously, but he was in the habit of dealing with life on those terms. It was the only way he knew, and it had worked fairly well up to now. Nevertheless, it was faulty thinking. Our desire for control cannot finally be satisfied by having our demands met. Responsibility for authority calls for coming to terms with the authority of a sovereign God.

So his faulty thinking in the area of authority left him wide open to the injury of losing his wife. Wounds will heal unless they become infected. *Bitterness* is an infection that will keep the wound fresh with pain and inflammation until it affects other areas as well.

Lloyd's *frustration* and *boredom* were only secondary troubles caused by his bitterness. The same was true of his *alienation* and *loneliness*. His failure of responsibility in the area of *authority* had caused him to be irresponsible in *purpose* and *relationships*.

Faulty thinking may seem to work for a while. There are millions who do not understand what God intends for the seven areas of responsibility. Though their lives are not nearly what God wants for them, they seem to get by fine with their self-centered, self-serving approach. But life on this earth is such that this approach will not work in the long run. Something will expose the selfishness for what it is. Some experience that may be common to man will leave a deep wound the person cannot overcome.

In the midst of serious emotional distress, a person is not able to think clearly about his trouble. The alarm of his emotions may drown out the whisper of wisdom. In his natural protectiveness for ego, he will not be receptive to a line of thought that demonstrates he is wrong and must change. He thinks this problem is not his fault. The fault is "out there," not "in here." If you try to deal with the trouble only rationally, he may not hear you. The emotions may leave no room for a rational understanding of his distress.

Complex Combinations

Not only does a person's trouble spill over into more than one area, sometimes our feelings are a combination of emotions. It is easy to trace the emotional signals to an area of responsibility if the emotion is distinct. If you are angry or lonely, you can quickly see the connection between how you feel and the issue of companionship or control. You know you are dealing with the area of authority or relationships.

But what if you are away from your family and begin to feel *self-pity*, *loneliness*, and *boredom* all at the same time? You will probably call it being *homesick*. It is a complex mixture of emotions. Even so, you can sort them out if you think about it and try to put labels on the various aspects of your feelings. Then it makes sense to feel this way because you miss your family, feel sorry for yourself for being separated from them, and are bored because what you are doing is not nearly as important as being with them.

You will often find your emotions are a mixture. We do not live our lives in neat compartments. Every area of responsibility and interaction shades over into the others. There are feelings that seem to fall into the cracks between two areas. *Resentment*, for instance, seems to include not only an element of anger, but also some alienation as well. *Frustration* relates to your desire for achievement, a matter of purpose.

But it can also reflect your desire for peace, in the situation area.

A very complex emotion is *jealousy*. Most of us have experienced this "green-eyed monster" at one time or another. It is a monster indeed. Not only do you find *anger* in jealousy, you also find *worry* because of what you may lose, *self-pity* at possible rejection, and *alienation* from your loved one. You may also feel some *guilt* because you suspect you haven't given your sweetheart enough attention. As with more simple emotional signals, trace each facet of jealousy back to the area of responsibility and determine your response.

The diagram in chapter 1 showed the seven clusters of emotional pain, with depression and anxiety in the center. Each cluster contains three expressions of its emotional pain. One is more active, the second is more passive, and the third is the chronic distress that results when the cause of the trouble is unresolved. Beyond these is depression, a diffused, generalized despair that may not be clearly associated with one of the seven clusters.

Active	Passive	Unresolved	Diffused
Embarrass-ment	Self-Doubt	Self-Hatred	Depression
Anger	Resentment	Bitterness	Depression
Alienation	Loneliness	Isolation	Depression
Frustration	Boredom	Apathy	Depression
Guilt	Shame	Remorse	Depression
Worry	Insecurity	Fear	Depression
Discontent	Restlessness	Uneasiness	Depression

Depression can range from a mild feeling of "the blues" to a deep and paralyzing despair. When you are depressed, you feel tired, discouraged, and defeated. Depression is that sense of despair that says, "This is hopeless. Things are just not working out. It is not going to get any better. There is no way out. I am not up to dealing with it. Nothing I do will make any difference." Though depression can be caused by a threat to only one area, it often reflects an accumulation of trouble from several areas.

Serious and debilitating depression probably indicates both *injury* and *disease*. It is one stage beyond being merely unresolved to an emotional signal that may indicate you are running away from responsibility. You may have had an experience that leaves you so injured that you are not up to facing your responsibility. Or, though you would like to deal with the problem, you just do not know how. In the "fight or flight" reaction to threat, depression just says, "Give up. The fight is over. You lose."

How Should You Feel?

I am concerned when I hear someone say, "I know I shouldn't feel this way. That's what everyone tells me." Emotions are as natural as breathing. They are an integral element in our interaction with the world around us. God created us this way. He intended us to experience emotion, and we wouldn't want it any other way. The sometimes unpredictable flow of emotion is problem enough for us. But when we feel we are wrong in having such emotions, our distress is compounded.

Remember, emotions reflect an interpretation of what is going on in your life. Your internal security guard, whom we have called the *Monitor*, sends out emotional signals interpreting how events and circumstances appear to affect you. That interpretation is based on your own assumptions, the "programming" of your mental computer. So it is not what takes place in your life that causes the emotions, it is your interpretation of those events.

If you smell something burning in the kitchen, what do you do? You check the pots on the stove and try to determine which one has too much heat under it. Your primary concern is not the odor, though that might become a serious problem if ignored. Your main concern is with the food in the pot that is getting too much heat. Emotions are the fragrance of what is cooking in the pot of your thinking. You want to get behind the odor to the area taking the heat.

Instead of questioning whether you should feel as you do, accept your emotions for what they are, a coded message from your inner thoughts. The emotions are not the problem. The problem is the apparent threat to your well-being. The Monitor is sending you a message so you can deal with that threat. Trace the feelings to the thoughts behind them first. Then analyze those thoughts. Do they make sense of events and circumstances around you? Do they reflect a reasonable outlook? Are they contaminated by the injury of past experiences or the disease of faulty thinking?

When you analyze the threat behind distressing emotions, you may often conclude that the emotions are entirely justified. You *should* feel the way you do. It is natural to feel this way. Once you see the meaning in your emotional signals, you can decide how to respond. You have read the message in your emotions and can act accordingly. Do not fret about whether you should feel the way you do. Give attention rather to whether you should *think* the way you do and *behave* the way you do. Remember, you cannot feel your way into a new way of acting, but you can act your way into a new way of feeling.

Telling the Story

The first step toward resolving the trouble signaled by emotional pain is to describe the emotions. It will not be possible to read the message in your emotions until you clearly identify what the emotions are. If you are counseling with a friend, ask him the necessary questions to get him to describe how he feels. This is also the first step of a writing exercise to get to the root of the problem.

Part 1 of telling your story is "What Has Happened and How I Feel About It." Describe as vividly as you can what your experience has been and how you feel, telling the story in all its pain, humor, and tragedy. Don't worry about trying to tell it as you think you should. You may naturally be thinking, *I really shouldn't feel this way about it. What is wrong with me? I am embarrassed that I feel so strongly. I have always been able to control my emotions.* Any line of thinking in that direction will tend to squelch your freedom to describe how you feel.

You must be honest about it. If you really feel sometimes that you hate your husband, admit that to yourself as you write. If these emotions have full expression in this way, they will run out of steam enough for you to begin to think clearly and objectively about the problem. On the other hand, if you rant and rave, tell people off, or just withdraw into yourself, you will only make it worse. In doing the writing exercise, you're communicating with yourself and with God. And both of those hearers are sympathetic.

If you are helping a friend sort out her feelings, encourage her to do the writing exercise even if she has already told you her story. Be sympathetic without condoning hurtful behavior. Keep the discussion on feelings for part 1.

Part 2 of telling your story is to write a section entitled "But Here Is the Truth." This part offers an interpretation of part 1, based on principles from the Bible. While the "How I Feel" section described feelings of embarrassment and self-doubt, part 2 might reveal, "No one else realizes how embarrassed I feel. The truth of the matter is that I am made in God's image and precious to Him. I refuse to measure my value on the basis of the opinions of others. I am willing to be a nobody for Christ and let everybody laugh at me. I am only a servant."

This interpretation puts the clamoring emotions in perspective. You can also write out in part 2 what response you will make to the message in your emotions. Indicate exactly what you will do to deal with the problem. By the time you get through this second part of your story, your emotions usually will have calmed. You will see everything in a different perspective.

You will only get relief if you refute faulty thinking with the truth. This means you must want the truth more than you want to protect your fragile ego. It also means you must educate yourself in the truth of God's Word about how to live responsibly.

A Final Word

The chart on pages 34 and 35 summarizes the major ideas in this study. You can see there the seven areas of responsibility, with the distinctive way each area relates to the various issues addressed here: our creation in God's image, the inherent desire in each area, the corruption of the self-centered nature and its faulty thinking, the emotional pain experienced in that area, the contrast of the natural and biblical strategies, and the basic faith application for dealing responsibly in the area.

Remember, the key is responsibility. You must deal with reality as it truthfully is, not a faulty version that is more satisfactory to you. Insist on discipline for yourself, saying no to those impulses and reactions that come from the sinful nature. Your interpretations of your experience are what your emotions are signaling, not the experience in itself. Override the interpretive process wherever you must to correct misconceptions. Take action to correct the failure of responsibility. Just thinking about it is not enough. Reclaim the servant role as your approach to life.

There is a message in your emotions. As painful as these distressing feelings may be, they can serve you well by alerting you to a failure of responsibility on your part. When you are threatened in your inherent desires, the alarm will be given. Pay close attention. Identify the emotion. Trace it to the area of responsibility it reflects. Correct your interpretation and take action to respond. Let your emotions serve as they were intended to in God's design.

▼

Notes

▼

Chapter 1
1. Peter Marsh, ed., *Eye to Eye: How People Interact* (Topsfield, Mass.: Salem House, 1988), 80.

Chapter 2
1. O. Hobart Mowrer, *The New Group Therapy* (New York: D. Van Nostrand,1964), 68.

Chapter 7
1. Carol Tavris, *Anger: The Misunderstood Emotion* (New York: Simon & Schuster, 1982).
2. Ibid.
3. Ibid.

Chapter 9
1. John S. Savage, *The Apathetic and Bored Church Member* (Pittsford, N.Y.: Lead Consultants, 1976).

Chapter 10
1. Philip Yancy, "Love Made the Difference," *Christian Herald*, November 1978.

2. Craig W. Ellison, "The Roots of Loneliness," *Christianity Today*, 10 March 1978:12.

3. Ibid.

Chapter 11

1. M. Scott Peck, *The Road Less Traveled* (New York: Simon and Schuster, 1978), 84–89.

Chapter 12

1. James F. Marsh, "My Irascible Aunt Alice," *Guideposts*, June 1995.

Chapter 13

1. Gwynne Dyer, "Life: Long Ago and Far Away," *The Times-Colonist*, Victoria, B.C., 31 August 1982.

2. Ibid.

3. Ibid.

Chapter 14

1. Allen Rankin, "David Hartman's Impossible Dream" *Reader's Digest*, April 1977, 78–82.

2. Garry Friesen, *Decision-Making and the Will of God,* (Portland, Oreg.: Multnomah, 1980).

3. Alan Lakein, *How to Get Control of Your Time and Your Life* (New York: David McKay, 1973), 25.

Chapter 15

1. Stephen R. Covey, *The Seven Habits of Highly Effective People* (New York: Simon & Schuster, 1989), 21ff.

2. Don Richardson, *Eternity in Their Hearts* (Ventura, Calif.: Regal, 1981).

Chapter 16

1. Charles Colson, "What Woody Allen Taught Me about Sin," *Christianity Today*, 11 February 1991, 96.

2. Don Richardson, *Peace Child* (Ventura, Calif.: Regal, 1974).

3. O. Hobart Mowrer, *The New Group Therapy* (Princeton: D. Van Nostrand, 1964).

Chapter 17

1. Thomas J. Brazaitis, "U.S. Hears from Conscience-Stricken," *The Oregonian*, 20 August 1981.

2. William J. Bennett, *The Book of Virtues* (New York: Simon & Schuster, 1994), 14.

Chapter 18

1. Karl Menninger, *Whatever Became of Sin?* (New York: Hawthorn Books, 1973).

2. Mowrer, *The New Group Therapy*, 65ff.

3. Ibid., 135.

4. Ibid., 86.

Chapter 20

1. Raymond D. Fowler, "Howard Hughes: A Psychological Autopsy," *Psychology Today*, May 1986, 22–33.

Chapter 23

1. Alvin Toffler, *Future Shock* (New York: Bantam, 1971), 33.

2. Bertrand Russell, *The Autobiography of Bertrand Russell*, vol. I, (Boston: Brown, Little, 1967), 287.

3. William Thomas Buckley, "How to Cope with Crisis," *Reader's Digest*, July 1990, 93.

▼